CAREER EXAMINATION SE

THIS IS YOUR **PASSBOOK**® FOR ...

BUSINESS SYSTEMS ANALYST III, IV

NATIONAL LEARNING CORPORATION®
passbooks.com

PASSBOOK® SERIES

THE *PASSBOOK® SERIES* has been created to prepare applicants and candidates for the ultimate academic battlefield – the examination room.

At some time in our lives, each and every one of us may be required to take an examination – for validation, matriculation, admission, qualification, registration, certification, or licensure.

Based on the assumption that every applicant or candidate has met the basic formal educational standards, has taken the required number of courses, and read the necessary texts, the *PASSBOOK® SERIES* furnishes the one special preparation which may assure passing with confidence, instead of failing with insecurity. Examination questions – together with answers – are furnished as the basic vehicle for study so that the mysteries of the examination and its compounding difficulties may be eliminated or diminished by a sure method.

This book is meant to help you pass your examination provided that you qualify and are serious in your objective.

The entire field is reviewed through the huge store of content information which is succinctly presented through a provocative and challenging approach – the question-and-answer method.

A climate of success is established by furnishing the correct answers at the end of each test.

You soon learn to recognize types of questions, forms of questions, and patterns of questioning. You may even begin to anticipate expected outcomes.

You perceive that many questions are repeated or adapted so that you can gain acute insights, which may enable you to score many sure points.

You learn how to confront new questions, or types of questions, and to attack them confidently and work out the correct answers.

You note objectives and emphases, and recognize pitfalls and dangers, so that you may make positive educational adjustments.

Moreover, you are kept fully informed in relation to new concepts, methods, practices, and directions in the field.

You discover that you arre actually taking the examination all the time: you are preparing for the examination by "taking" an examination, not by reading extraneous and/or supererogatory textbooks.

In short, this PASSBOOK®, used directedly, should be an important factor in helping you to pass your test.

BUSINESS SYSTEMS ANALYST III, IV

DUTIES

As a Business Systems Analyst III, you would supervise lower level Business Systems Analysts, and develop system requirements for future or to be state of large business analysis projects or series of smaller projects. You would supervise more difficult business analysis projects requiring supervision of staff with specialized skills and management of business analysis projects involving use of a broad range of tools and techniques across the major business analysis knowledge areas.

As a Business Systems Analyst IV, you would supervise lower level Business Systems Analysts, and manage all phases of business systems analysis for large business analysis projects, or a series of smaller projects. You would direct business systems analysis activities; write agency business analysis standards and process documents; analyze and revise flow charts, process models and technical specifications describing as is or to be business processes; and determine the impact on agency business systems.

SCOPE OF THE EXAMINATION

The written test will cover knowledge, skills and/or abilities in such areas as:

1. **Understanding and interpreting written material** - These questions test how well you comprehend written material. You will be provided with brief reading selections and will be asked questions about the selections. All the information required to answer the questions will be presented in the selections; you will not be required to have any special knowledge relating to the subject areas of the selections.

2. **Administrative supervision** - These questions test for knowledge of the principles and practices involved in directing the activities of a large subordinate staff, including subordinate supervisors. Questions relate to the personal interactions between an upper level supervisor and his/her subordinate supervisors in the accomplishment of objectives. These questions cover such areas as assigning work to and coordinating the activities of several units, establishing and guiding staff development programs, evaluating the performance of subordinate supervisors, and maintaining relationships with other organizational sections.

3. **Understanding and applying administrative principles** - These questions test for knowledge of how to effectively manage and direct an organization or an organizational segment. These questions cover such areas as developing objectives, formulating policies, making decisions, forecasting and planning, developing personnel, organizing and coordinating work, communicating information, providing leadership, and delegating authority and responsibility.

4. **Preparing reports and official documents** - These questions test for the ability to prepare reports and other official documents for use within and among governmental agencies, in legal or regulatory settings, or for dissemination to the

public. Some questions test for a knowledge of correct grammar, usage, punctuation, and sentence structure. Others test for the ability to present information clearly and accurately, to use the proper tone, and to organize paragraphs logically and comprehensibly.

5. **Evaluating conclusions based on factual information** - These questions test your ability to evaluate and draw conclusions from factual information presented. Each question consists of a set of factual statements and a conclusion. You will be asked to determine whether the conclusion can be proven to be true by the facts, proven to be false by the facts, or if the facts are inadequate to prove the conclusion.

6. **Working and interacting with others** - These questions test for knowledge of how to effectively approach work and maintain professional relationships with others in the workplace. Each question presents a situation and a number of possible approaches for handling it. Question topics may include working with supervisors and coworkers, interacting with members of the public, handling conflict, and managing workplace demands and priorities. The questions are not specific to any job title or place of work.

7. **Analyzing and evaluating information** - These questions test for the ability to analyze, interpret, and draw reasonable conclusions from information presented in text, data, images or symbols. This may involve identifying a significant problem or issue; focusing on relevant data and text; identifying trends, relationships, and significant features; assessing relevant alternatives; suggesting or evaluating possible conclusions; and applying logical principles to information provided.

HOW TO TAKE A TEST

I. YOU MUST PASS AN EXAMINATION

A. *WHAT EVERY CANDIDATE SHOULD KNOW*

Examination applicants often ask us for help in preparing for the written test. What can I study in advance? What kinds of questions will be asked? How will the test be given? How will the papers be graded?

As an applicant for a civil service examination, you may be wondering about some of these things. Our purpose here is to suggest effective methods of advance study and to describe civil service examinations.

Your chances for success on this examination can be increased if you know how to prepare. Those "pre-examination jitters" can be reduced if you know what to expect. You can even experience an adventure in good citizenship if you know why civil service exams are given.

B. *WHY ARE CIVIL SERVICE EXAMINATIONS GIVEN?*

Civil service examinations are important to you in two ways. As a citizen, you want public jobs filled by employees who know how to do their work. As a job seeker, you want a fair chance to compete for that job on an equal footing with other candidates. The best-known means of accomplishing this two-fold goal is the competitive examination.

Exams are widely publicized throughout the nation. They may be administered for jobs in federal, state, city, municipal, town or village governments or agencies.

Any citizen may apply, with some limitations, such as the age or residence of applicants. Your experience and education may be reviewed to see whether you meet the requirements for the particular examination. When these requirements exist, they are reasonable and applied consistently to all applicants. Thus, a competitive examination may cause you some uneasiness now, but it is your privilege and safeguard.

C. *HOW ARE CIVIL SERVICE EXAMS DEVELOPED?*

Examinations are carefully written by trained technicians who are specialists in the field known as "psychological measurement," in consultation with recognized authorities in the field of work that the test will cover. These experts recommend the subject matter areas or skills to be tested; only those knowledges or skills important to your success on the job are included. The most reliable books and source materials available are used as references. Together, the experts and technicians judge the difficulty level of the questions.

Test technicians know how to phrase questions so that the problem is clearly stated. Their ethics do not permit "trick" or "catch" questions. Questions may have been tried out on sample groups, or subjected to statistical analysis, to determine their usefulness.

Written tests are often used in combination with performance tests, ratings of training and experience, and oral interviews. All of these measures combine to form the best-known means of finding the right person for the right job.

II. HOW TO PASS THE WRITTEN TEST

A. NATURE OF THE EXAMINATION

To prepare intelligently for civil service examinations, you should know how they differ from school examinations you have taken. In school you were assigned certain definite pages to read or subjects to cover. The examination questions were quite detailed and usually emphasized memory. Civil service exams, on the other hand, try to discover your present ability to perform the duties of a position, plus your potentiality to learn these duties. In other words, a civil service exam attempts to predict how successful you will be. Questions cover such a broad area that they cannot be as minute and detailed as school exam questions.

In the public service similar kinds of work, or positions, are grouped together in one "class." This process is known as *position-classification*. All the positions in a class are paid according to the salary range for that class. One class title covers all of these positions, and they are all tested by the same examination.

B. FOUR BASIC STEPS

1) Study the announcement

How, then, can you know what subjects to study? Our best answer is: "Learn as much as possible about the class of positions for which you've applied." The exam will test the knowledge, skills and abilities needed to do the work.

Your most valuable source of information about the position you want is the official exam announcement. This announcement lists the training and experience qualifications. Check these standards and apply only if you come reasonably close to meeting them.

The brief description of the position in the examination announcement offers some clues to the subjects which will be tested. Think about the job itself. Review the duties in your mind. Can you perform them, or are there some in which you are rusty? Fill in the blank spots in your preparation.

Many jurisdictions preview the written test in the exam announcement by including a section called "Knowledge and Abilities Required," "Scope of the Examination," or some similar heading. Here you will find out specifically what fields will be tested.

2) Review your own background

Once you learn in general what the position is all about, and what you need to know to do the work, ask yourself which subjects you already know fairly well and which need improvement. You may wonder whether to concentrate on improving your strong areas or on building some background in your fields of weakness. When the announcement has specified "some knowledge" or "considerable knowledge," or has used adjectives like "beginning principles of…" or "advanced … methods," you can get a clue as to the number and difficulty of questions to be asked in any given field. More questions, and hence broader coverage, would be included for those subjects which are more important in the work. Now weigh your strengths and weaknesses against the job requirements and prepare accordingly.

3) Determine the level of the position

Another way to tell how intensively you should prepare is to understand the level of the job for which you are applying. Is it the entering level? In other words, is this the position in which beginners in a field of work are hired? Or is it an intermediate or advanced level? Sometimes this is indicated by such words as "Junior" or "Senior" in the class title. Other jurisdictions use Roman numerals to designate the level – Clerk I, Clerk II, for example. The word "Supervisor" sometimes appears in the title. If the level is not indicated by the title, check the description of duties. Will you be working under very close supervision, or will you have responsibility for independent decisions in this work?

4) Choose appropriate study materials

Now that you know the subjects to be examined and the relative amount of each subject to be covered, you can choose suitable study materials. For beginning level jobs, or even advanced ones, if you have a pronounced weakness in some aspect of your training, read a modern, standard textbook in that field. Be sure it is up to date and has general coverage. Such books are normally available at your library, and the librarian will be glad to help you locate one. For entry-level positions, questions of appropriate difficulty are chosen – neither highly advanced questions, nor those too simple. Such questions require careful thought but not advanced training.

If the position for which you are applying is technical or advanced, you will read more advanced, specialized material. If you are already familiar with the basic principles of your field, elementary textbooks would waste your time. Concentrate on advanced textbooks and technical periodicals. Think through the concepts and review difficult problems in your field.

These are all general sources. You can get more ideas on your own initiative, following these leads. For example, training manuals and publications of the government agency which employs workers in your field can be useful, particularly for technical and professional positions. A letter or visit to the government department involved may result in more specific study suggestions, and certainly will provide you with a more definite idea of the exact nature of the position you are seeking.

III. KINDS OF TESTS

Tests are used for purposes other than measuring knowledge and ability to perform specified duties. For some positions, it is equally important to test ability to make adjustments to new situations or to profit from training. In others, basic mental abilities not dependent on information are essential. Questions which test these things may not appear as pertinent to the duties of the position as those which test for knowledge and information. Yet they are often highly important parts of a fair examination. For very general questions, it is almost impossible to help you direct your study efforts. What we can do is to point out some of the more common of these general abilities needed in public service positions and describe some typical questions.

1) General information

Broad, general information has been found useful for predicting job success in some kinds of work. This is tested in a variety of ways, from vocabulary lists to questions about current events. Basic background in some field of work, such as sociology or economics, may be sampled in a group of questions. Often these are principles which have become familiar to most persons through exposure rather than through formal training. It is difficult to advise you how to study for these questions; being alert to the world around you is our best suggestion.

2) Verbal ability

An example of an ability needed in many positions is verbal or language ability. Verbal ability is, in brief, the ability to use and understand words. Vocabulary and grammar tests are typical measures of this ability. Reading comprehension or paragraph interpretation questions are common in many kinds of civil service tests. You are given a paragraph of written material and asked to find its central meaning.

3) Numerical ability

Number skills can be tested by the familiar arithmetic problem, by checking paired lists of numbers to see which are alike and which are different, or by interpreting charts and graphs. In the latter test, a graph may be printed in the test booklet which you are asked to use as the basis for answering questions.

4) Observation

A popular test for law-enforcement positions is the observation test. A picture is shown to you for several minutes, then taken away. Questions about the picture test your ability to observe both details and larger elements.

5) Following directions

In many positions in the public service, the employee must be able to carry out written instructions dependably and accurately. You may be given a chart with several columns, each column listing a variety of information. The questions require you to carry out directions involving the information given in the chart.

6) Skills and aptitudes

Performance tests effectively measure some manual skills and aptitudes. When the skill is one in which you are trained, such as typing or shorthand, you can practice. These tests are often very much like those given in business school or high school courses. For many of the other skills and aptitudes, however, no short-time preparation can be made. Skills and abilities natural to you or that you have developed throughout your lifetime are being tested.

Many of the general questions just described provide all the data needed to answer the questions and ask you to use your reasoning ability to find the answers. Your best preparation for these tests, as well as for tests of facts and ideas, is to be at your physical and mental best. You, no doubt, have your own methods of getting into an exam-taking mood and keeping "in shape." The next section lists some ideas on this subject.

IV. KINDS OF QUESTIONS

Only rarely is the "essay" question, which you answer in narrative form, used in civil service tests. Civil service tests are usually of the short-answer type. Full instructions for answering these questions will be given to you at the examination. But in case this is your first experience with short-answer questions and separate answer sheets, here is what you need to know:

1) Multiple-choice Questions

Most popular of the short-answer questions is the "multiple choice" or "best answer" question. It can be used, for example, to test for factual knowledge, ability to solve problems or judgment in meeting situations found at work.

A multiple-choice question is normally one of three types—

- It can begin with an incomplete statement followed by several possible endings. You are to find the one ending which *best* completes the statement, although some of the others may not be entirely wrong.
- It can also be a complete statement in the form of a question which is answered by choosing one of the statements listed.
- It can be in the form of a problem – again you select the best answer.

Here is an example of a multiple-choice question with a discussion which should give you some clues as to the method for choosing the right answer:

When an employee has a complaint about his assignment, the action which will *best* help him overcome his difficulty is to
- A. discuss his difficulty with his coworkers
- B. take the problem to the head of the organization
- C. take the problem to the person who gave him the assignment
- D. say nothing to anyone about his complaint

In answering this question, you should study each of the choices to find which is best. Consider choice "A" – Certainly an employee may discuss his complaint with fellow employees, but no change or improvement can result, and the complaint remains unresolved. Choice "B" is a poor choice since the head of the organization probably does not know what assignment you have been given, and taking your problem to him is known as "going over the head" of the supervisor. The supervisor, or person who made the assignment, is the person who can clarify it or correct any injustice. Choice "C" is, therefore, correct. To say nothing, as in choice "D," is unwise. Supervisors have and interest in knowing the problems employees are facing, and the employee is seeking a solution to his problem.

2) True/False Questions

The "true/false" or "right/wrong" form of question is sometimes used. Here a complete statement is given. Your job is to decide whether the statement is right or wrong.

SAMPLE: A roaming cell-phone call to a nearby city costs less than a non-roaming call to a distant city.

This statement is wrong, or false, since roaming calls are more expensive.
This is not a complete list of all possible question forms, although most of the others are variations of these common types. You will always get complete directions for

answering questions. Be sure you understand *how* to mark your answers – ask questions until you do.

V. RECORDING YOUR ANSWERS

Computer terminals are used more and more today for many different kinds of exams.

For an examination with very few applicants, you may be told to record your answers in the test booklet itself. Separate answer sheets are much more common. If this separate answer sheet is to be scored by machine – and this is often the case – it is highly important that you mark your answers correctly in order to get credit.

An electronic scoring machine is often used in civil service offices because of the speed with which papers can be scored. Machine-scored answer sheets must be marked with a pencil, which will be given to you. This pencil has a high graphite content which responds to the electronic scoring machine. As a matter of fact, stray dots may register as answers, so do not let your pencil rest on the answer sheet while you are pondering the correct answer. Also, if your pencil lead breaks or is otherwise defective, ask for another.

Since the answer sheet will be dropped in a slot in the scoring machine, be careful not to bend the corners or get the paper crumpled.

The answer sheet normally has five vertical columns of numbers, with 30 numbers to a column. These numbers correspond to the question numbers in your test booklet. After each number, going across the page are four or five pairs of dotted lines. These short dotted lines have small letters or numbers above them. The first two pairs may also have a "T" or "F" above the letters. This indicates that the first two pairs only are to be used if the questions are of the true-false type. If the questions are multiple choice, disregard the "T" and "F" and pay attention only to the small letters or numbers.

Answer your questions in the manner of the sample that follows:

32. The largest city in the United States is
     A. Washington, D.C.
     B. New York City
     C. Chicago
     D. Detroit
     E. San Francisco

1) Choose the answer you think is best. (New York City is the largest, so "B" is correct.)
2) Find the row of dotted lines numbered the same as the question you are answering. (Find row number 32)
3) Find the pair of dotted lines corresponding to the answer. (Find the pair of lines under the mark "B.")
4) Make a solid black mark between the dotted lines.

VI. BEFORE THE TEST

Common sense will help you find procedures to follow to get ready for an examination. Too many of us, however, overlook these sensible measures. Indeed, nervousness and fatigue have been found to be the most serious reasons why applicants fail to do their best on civil service tests. Here is a list of reminders:

- Begin your preparation early – Don't wait until the last minute to go scurrying around for books and materials or to find out what the position is all about.
- Prepare continuously – An hour a night for a week is better than an all-night cram session. This has been definitely established. What is more, a night a week for a month will return better dividends than crowding your study into a shorter period of time.
- Locate the place of the exam – You have been sent a notice telling you when and where to report for the examination. If the location is in a different town or otherwise unfamiliar to you, it would be well to inquire the best route and learn something about the building.
- Relax the night before the test – Allow your mind to rest. Do not study at all that night. Plan some mild recreation or diversion; then go to bed early and get a good night's sleep.
- Get up early enough to make a leisurely trip to the place for the test – This way unforeseen events, traffic snarls, unfamiliar buildings, etc. will not upset you.
- Dress comfortably – A written test is not a fashion show. You will be known by number and not by name, so wear something comfortable.
- Leave excess paraphernalia at home – Shopping bags and odd bundles will get in your way. You need bring only the items mentioned in the official notice you received; usually everything you need is provided. Do not bring reference books to the exam. They will only confuse those last minutes and be taken away from you when in the test room.
- Arrive somewhat ahead of time – If because of transportation schedules you must get there very early, bring a newspaper or magazine to take your mind off yourself while waiting.
- Locate the examination room – When you have found the proper room, you will be directed to the seat or part of the room where you will sit. Sometimes you are given a sheet of instructions to read while you are waiting. Do not fill out any forms until you are told to do so; just read them and be prepared.
- Relax and prepare to listen to the instructions
- If you have any physical problem that may keep you from doing your best, be sure to tell the test administrator. If you are sick or in poor health, you really cannot do your best on the exam. You can come back and take the test some other time.

VII. AT THE TEST

The day of the test is here and you have the test booklet in your hand. The temptation to get going is very strong. Caution! There is more to success than knowing the right answers. You must know how to identify your papers and understand variations in the type of short-answer question used in this particular examination. Follow these suggestions for maximum results from your efforts:

1) Cooperate with the monitor

The test administrator has a duty to create a situation in which you can be as much at ease as possible. He will give instructions, tell you when to begin, check to see that you are marking your answer sheet correctly, and so on. He is not there to guard you, although he will see that your competitors do not take unfair advantage. He wants to help you do your best.

2) Listen to all instructions

Don't jump the gun! Wait until you understand all directions. In most civil service tests you get more time than you need to answer the questions. So don't be in a hurry. Read each word of instructions until you clearly understand the meaning. Study the examples, listen to all announcements and follow directions. Ask questions if you do not understand what to do.

3) Identify your papers

Civil service exams are usually identified by number only. You will be assigned a number; you must not put your name on your test papers. Be sure to copy your number correctly. Since more than one exam may be given, copy your exact examination title.

4) Plan your time

Unless you are told that a test is a "speed" or "rate of work" test, speed itself is usually not important. Time enough to answer all the questions will be provided, but this does not mean that you have all day. An overall time limit has been set. Divide the total time (in minutes) by the number of questions to determine the approximate time you have for each question.

5) Do not linger over difficult questions

If you come across a difficult question, mark it with a paper clip (useful to have along) and come back to it when you have been through the booklet. One caution if you do this – be sure to skip a number on your answer sheet as well. Check often to be sure that you have not lost your place and that you are marking in the row numbered the same as the question you are answering.

6) Read the questions

Be sure you know what the question asks! Many capable people are unsuccessful because they failed to *read* the questions correctly.

7) Answer all questions

Unless you have been instructed that a penalty will be deducted for incorrect answers, it is better to guess than to omit a question.

8) Speed tests

It is often better NOT to guess on speed tests. It has been found that on timed tests people are tempted to spend the last few seconds before time is called in marking answers at random – without even reading them – in the hope of picking up a few extra points. To discourage this practice, the instructions may warn you that your score will be "corrected" for guessing. That is, a penalty will be applied. The incorrect answers will be deducted from the correct ones, or some other penalty formula will be used.

9) Review your answers

If you finish before time is called, go back to the questions you guessed or omitted to give them further thought. Review other answers if you have time.

10) Return your test materials

If you are ready to leave before others have finished or time is called, take ALL your materials to the monitor and leave quietly. Never take any test material with you. The monitor can discover whose papers are not complete, and taking a test booklet may be grounds for disqualification.

VIII. EXAMINATION TECHNIQUES

1) Read the general instructions carefully. These are usually printed on the first page of the exam booklet. As a rule, these instructions refer to the timing of the examination; the fact that you should not start work until the signal and must stop work at a signal, etc. If there are any *special* instructions, such as a choice of questions to be answered, make sure that you note this instruction carefully.

2) When you are ready to start work on the examination, that is as soon as the signal has been given, read the instructions to each question booklet, underline any key words or phrases, such as *least, best, outline, describe* and the like. In this way you will tend to answer as requested rather than discover on reviewing your paper that you *listed without describing*, that you selected the *worst* choice rather than the *best* choice, etc.

3) If the examination is of the objective or multiple-choice type – that is, each question will also give a series of possible answers: A, B, C or D, and you are called upon to select the best answer and write the letter next to that answer on your answer paper – it is advisable to start answering each question in turn. There may be anywhere from 50 to 100 such questions in the three or four hours allotted and you can see how much time would be taken if you read through all the questions before beginning to answer any. Furthermore, if you come across a question or group of questions which you know would be difficult to answer, it would undoubtedly affect your handling of all the other questions.

4) If the examination is of the essay type and contains but a few questions, it is a moot point as to whether you should read all the questions before starting to answer any one. Of course, if you are given a choice – say five out of seven and the like – then it is essential to read all the questions so you can eliminate the two that are most difficult. If, however, you are asked to answer all the questions, there may be danger in trying to answer the easiest one first because you may find that you will spend too much time on it. The best technique is to answer the first question, then proceed to the second, etc.

5) Time your answers. Before the exam begins, write down the time it started, then add the time allowed for the examination and write down the time it must be completed, then divide the time available somewhat as follows:

- If 3-1/2 hours are allowed, that would be 210 minutes. If you have 80 objective-type questions, that would be an average of 2-1/2 minutes per question. Allow yourself no more than 2 minutes per question, or a total of 160 minutes, which will permit about 50 minutes to review.
- If for the time allotment of 210 minutes there are 7 essay questions to answer, that would average about 30 minutes a question. Give yourself only 25 minutes per question so that you have about 35 minutes to review.

6) The most important instruction is to *read each question* and make sure you know what is wanted. The second most important instruction is to *time yourself properly* so that you answer every question. The third most important instruction is to *answer every question*. Guess if you have to but include something for each question. Remember that you will receive no credit for a blank and will probably receive some credit if you write something in answer to an essay question. If you guess a letter – say "B" for a multiple-choice question – you may have guessed right. If you leave a blank as an answer to a multiple-choice question, the examiners may respect your feelings but it will not add a point to your score. Some exams may penalize you for wrong answers, so in such cases *only*, you may not want to guess unless you have some basis for your answer.

7) Suggestions
   a. Objective-type questions
      1. Examine the question booklet for proper sequence of pages and questions
      2. Read all instructions carefully
      3. Skip any question which seems too difficult; return to it after all other questions have been answered
      4. Apportion your time properly; do not spend too much time on any single question or group of questions
      5. Note and underline key words – *all, most, fewest, least, best, worst, same, opposite,* etc.
      6. Pay particular attention to negatives
      7. Note unusual option, e.g., unduly long, short, complex, different or similar in content to the body of the question
      8. Observe the use of "hedging" words – *probably, may, most likely,* etc.
      9. Make sure that your answer is put next to the same number as the question
      10. Do not second-guess unless you have good reason to believe the second answer is definitely more correct
      11. Cross out original answer if you decide another answer is more accurate; do not erase until you are ready to hand your paper in
      12. Answer all questions; guess unless instructed otherwise
      13. Leave time for review

   b. Essay questions
      1. Read each question carefully
      2. Determine exactly what is wanted. Underline key words or phrases.
      3. Decide on outline or paragraph answer

4. Include many different points and elements unless asked to develop any one or two points or elements
5. Show impartiality by giving pros and cons unless directed to select one side only
6. Make and write down any assumptions you find necessary to answer the questions
7. Watch your English, grammar, punctuation and choice of words
8. Time your answers; don't crowd material

8) Answering the essay question

Most essay questions can be answered by framing the specific response around several key words or ideas. Here are a few such key words or ideas:

M's: manpower, materials, methods, money, management
P's: purpose, program, policy, plan, procedure, practice, problems, pitfalls, personnel, public relations

a. Six basic steps in handling problems:
   1. Preliminary plan and background development
   2. Collect information, data and facts
   3. Analyze and interpret information, data and facts
   4. Analyze and develop solutions as well as make recommendations
   5. Prepare report and sell recommendations
   6. Install recommendations and follow up effectiveness

b. Pitfalls to avoid
   1. *Taking things for granted* – A statement of the situation does not necessarily imply that each of the elements is necessarily true; for example, a complaint may be invalid and biased so that all that can be taken for granted is that a complaint has been registered
   2. *Considering only one side of a situation* – Wherever possible, indicate several alternatives and then point out the reasons you selected the best one
   3. *Failing to indicate follow up* – Whenever your answer indicates action on your part, make certain that you will take proper follow-up action to see how successful your recommendations, procedures or actions turn out to be
   4. *Taking too long in answering any single question* – Remember to time your answers properly

IX. AFTER THE TEST

Scoring procedures differ in detail among civil service jurisdictions although the general principles are the same. Whether the papers are hand-scored or graded by machine we have described, they are nearly always graded by number. That is, the person who marks the paper knows only the number – never the name – of the applicant. Not until all the papers have been graded will they be matched with names. If other tests, such as training and experience or oral interview ratings have been given, scores will be combined. Different parts of the examination usually have different weights. For example, the written test might count 60 percent of the final grade, and a rating of training and experience 40 percent. In many jurisdictions, veterans will have a certain number of points added to their grades.

After the final grade has been determined, the names are placed in grade order and an eligible list is established. There are various methods for resolving ties between those who get the same final grade – probably the most common is to place first the name of the person whose application was received first. Job offers are made from the eligible list in the order the names appear on it. You will be notified of your grade and your rank as soon as all these computations have been made. This will be done as rapidly as possible.

People who are found to meet the requirements in the announcement are called "eligibles." Their names are put on a list of eligible candidates. An eligible's chances of getting a job depend on how high he stands on this list and how fast agencies are filling jobs from the list.

When a job is to be filled from a list of eligibles, the agency asks for the names of people on the list of eligibles for that job. When the civil service commission receives this request, it sends to the agency the names of the three people highest on this list. Or, if the job to be filled has specialized requirements, the office sends the agency the names of the top three persons who meet these requirements from the general list.

The appointing officer makes a choice from among the three people whose names were sent to him. If the selected person accepts the appointment, the names of the others are put back on the list to be considered for future openings.

That is the rule in hiring from all kinds of eligible lists, whether they are for typist, carpenter, chemist, or something else. For every vacancy, the appointing officer has his choice of any one of the top three eligibles on the list. This explains why the person whose name is on top of the list sometimes does not get an appointment when some of the persons lower on the list do. If the appointing officer chooses the second or third eligible, the No. 1 eligible does not get a job at once, but stays on the list until he is appointed or the list is terminated.

X. HOW TO PASS THE INTERVIEW TEST

The examination for which you applied requires an oral interview test. You have already taken the written test and you are now being called for the interview test – the final part of the formal examination.

You may think that it is not possible to prepare for an interview test and that there are no procedures to follow during an interview. Our purpose is to point out some things you can do in advance that will help you and some good rules to follow and pitfalls to avoid while you are being interviewed.

What is an interview supposed to test?

The written examination is designed to test the technical knowledge and competence of the candidate; the oral is designed to evaluate intangible qualities, not readily measured otherwise, and to establish a list showing the relative fitness of each candidate – as measured against his competitors – for the position sought. Scoring is not on the basis of "right" and "wrong," but on a sliding scale of values ranging from "not passable" to "outstanding." As a matter of fact, it is possible to achieve a relatively low score without a single "incorrect" answer because of evident weakness in the qualities being measured.

Occasionally, an examination may consist entirely of an oral test – either an individual or a group oral. In such cases, information is sought concerning the technical knowledges and abilities of the candidate, since there has been no written examination for this purpose. More commonly, however, an oral test is used to supplement a written examination.

Who conducts interviews?

The composition of oral boards varies among different jurisdictions. In nearly all, a representative of the personnel department serves as chairman. One of the members of the board may be a representative of the department in which the candidate would work. In some cases, "outside experts" are used, and, frequently, a businessman or some other representative of the general public is asked to serve. Labor and management or other special groups may be represented. The aim is to secure the services of experts in the appropriate field.

However the board is composed, it is a good idea (and not at all improper or unethical) to ascertain in advance of the interview who the members are and what groups they represent. When you are introduced to them, you will have some idea of their backgrounds and interests, and at least you will not stutter and stammer over their names.

What should be done before the interview?

While knowledge about the board members is useful and takes some of the surprise element out of the interview, there is other preparation which is more substantive. It *is* possible to prepare for an oral interview – in several ways:

1) Keep a copy of your application and review it carefully before the interview

This may be the only document before the oral board, and the starting point of the interview. Know what education and experience you have listed there, and the sequence and dates of all of it. Sometimes the board will ask you to review the highlights of your experience for them; you should not have to hem and haw doing it.

2) Study the class specification and the examination announcement

Usually, the oral board has one or both of these to guide them. The qualities, characteristics or knowledges required by the position sought are stated in these documents. They offer valuable clues as to the nature of the oral interview. For example, if the job involves supervisory responsibilities, the announcement will usually indicate that knowledge of modern supervisory methods and the qualifications of the candidate as a supervisor will be tested. If so, you can expect such questions, frequently in the form of a hypothetical situation which you are expected to solve. NEVER go into an oral without knowledge of the duties and responsibilities of the job you seek.

3) Think through each qualification required

Try to visualize the kind of questions you would ask if you were a board member. How well could you answer them? Try especially to appraise your own knowledge and background in each area, *measured against the job sought*, and identify any areas in which you are weak. Be critical and realistic – do not flatter yourself.

4) Do some general reading in areas in which you feel you may be weak

For example, if the job involves supervision and your past experience has NOT, some general reading in supervisory methods and practices, particularly in the field of human relations, might be useful. Do NOT study agency procedures or detailed manuals. The oral board will be testing your understanding and capacity, not your memory.

5) Get a good night's sleep and watch your general health and mental attitude

You will want a clear head at the interview. Take care of a cold or any other minor ailment, and of course, no hangovers.

What should be done on the day of the interview?

Now comes the day of the interview itself. Give yourself plenty of time to get there. Plan to arrive somewhat ahead of the scheduled time, particularly if your appointment is in the fore part of the day. If a previous candidate fails to appear, the board might be ready for you a bit early. By early afternoon an oral board is almost invariably behind schedule if there are many candidates, and you may have to wait. Take along a book or magazine to read, or your application to review, but leave any extraneous material in the waiting room when you go in for your interview. In any event, relax and compose yourself.

The matter of dress is important. The board is forming impressions about you – from your experience, your manners, your attitude, and your appearance. Give your personal appearance careful attention. Dress your best, but not your flashiest. Choose conservative, appropriate clothing, and be sure it is immaculate. This is a business interview, and your appearance should indicate that you regard it as such. Besides, being well groomed and properly dressed will help boost your confidence.

Sooner or later, someone will call your name and escort you into the interview room. *This is it.* From here on you are on your own. It is too late for any more preparation. But remember, you asked for this opportunity to prove your fitness, and you are here because your request was granted.

What happens when you go in?

The usual sequence of events will be as follows: The clerk (who is often the board stenographer) will introduce you to the chairman of the oral board, who will introduce you to the other members of the board. Acknowledge the introductions before you sit down. Do not be surprised if you find a microphone facing you or a stenotypist sitting by. Oral interviews are usually recorded in the event of an appeal or other review.

Usually the chairman of the board will open the interview by reviewing the highlights of your education and work experience from your application – primarily for the benefit of the other members of the board, as well as to get the material into the record. Do not interrupt or comment unless there is an error or significant misinterpretation; if that is the case, do not hesitate. But do not quibble about insignificant matters. Also, he will usually ask you some question about your education, experience or your present job – partly to get you to start talking and to establish the interviewing "rapport." He may start the actual questioning, or turn it over to one of the other members. Frequently, each member undertakes the questioning on a particular area, one in which he is perhaps most competent, so you can expect each member to participate in the examination. Because time is limited, you may also expect some rather abrupt switches in the direction the questioning takes, so do not be upset by it. Normally, a board member will not pursue a single line of questioning unless he discovers a particular strength or weakness.

After each member has participated, the chairman will usually ask whether any member has any further questions, then will ask you if you have anything you wish to add. Unless you are expecting this question, it may floor you. Worse, it may start you off on an extended, extemporaneous speech. The board is not usually seeking more information. The question is principally to offer you a last opportunity to present further qualifications or to indicate that you have nothing to add. So, if you feel that a significant qualification or characteristic has been overlooked, it is proper to point it out in a sentence or so. Do not compliment the board on the thoroughness of their examination – they have been sketchy, and you know it. If you wish, merely say, "No thank you, I have nothing further to add." This is a point where you can "talk yourself out" of a good impression or fail to present an important bit of information. Remember, *you close the interview yourself.*

The chairman will then say, "That is all, Mr. _____, thank you." Do not be startled; the interview is over, and quicker than you think. Thank him, gather your belongings and take your leave. Save your sigh of relief for the other side of the door.

How to put your best foot forward

Throughout this entire process, you may feel that the board individually and collectively is trying to pierce your defenses, seek out your hidden weaknesses and embarrass and confuse you. Actually, this is not true. They are obliged to make an appraisal of your qualifications for the job you are seeking, and they want to see you in your best light. Remember, they must interview all candidates and a non-cooperative candidate may become a failure in spite of their best efforts to bring out his qualifications. Here are 15 suggestions that will help you:

1) Be natural – Keep your attitude confident, not cocky

If you are not confident that you can do the job, do not expect the board to be. Do not apologize for your weaknesses, try to bring out your strong points. The board is interested in a positive, not negative, presentation. Cockiness will antagonize any board member and make him wonder if you are covering up a weakness by a false show of strength.

2) Get comfortable, but don't lounge or sprawl

Sit erectly but not stiffly. A careless posture may lead the board to conclude that you are careless in other things, or at least that you are not impressed by the importance of the occasion. Either conclusion is natural, even if incorrect. Do not fuss with your clothing, a pencil or an ashtray. Your hands may occasionally be useful to emphasize a point; do not let them become a point of distraction.

3) Do not wisecrack or make small talk

This is a serious situation, and your attitude should show that you consider it as such. Further, the time of the board is limited – they do not want to waste it, and neither should you.

4) Do not exaggerate your experience or abilities

In the first place, from information in the application or other interviews and sources, the board may know more about you than you think. Secondly, you probably will not get away with it. An experienced board is rather adept at spotting such a situation, so do not take the chance.

5) If you know a board member, do not make a point of it, yet do not hide it

Certainly you are not fooling him, and probably not the other members of the board. Do not try to take advantage of your acquaintanceship – it will probably do you little good.

6) Do not dominate the interview

Let the board do that. They will give you the clues – do not assume that you have to do all the talking. Realize that the board has a number of questions to ask you, and do not try to take up all the interview time by showing off your extensive knowledge of the answer to the first one.

7) Be attentive

You only have 20 minutes or so, and you should keep your attention at its sharpest throughout. When a member is addressing a problem or question to you, give him your undivided attention. Address your reply principally to him, but do not exclude the other board members.

8) Do not interrupt

A board member may be stating a problem for you to analyze. He will ask you a question when the time comes. Let him state the problem, and wait for the question.

9) Make sure you understand the question

Do not try to answer until you are sure what the question is. If it is not clear, restate it in your own words or ask the board member to clarify it for you. However, do not haggle about minor elements.

10) Reply promptly but not hastily

A common entry on oral board rating sheets is "candidate responded readily," or "candidate hesitated in replies." Respond as promptly and quickly as you can, but do not jump to a hasty, ill-considered answer.

11) Do not be peremptory in your answers

A brief answer is proper – but do not fire your answer back. That is a losing game from your point of view. The board member can probably ask questions much faster than you can answer them.

12) Do not try to create the answer you think the board member wants

He is interested in what kind of mind you have and how it works – not in playing games. Furthermore, he can usually spot this practice and will actually grade you down on it.

13) Do not switch sides in your reply merely to agree with a board member

Frequently, a member will take a contrary position merely to draw you out and to see if you are willing and able to defend your point of view. Do not start a debate, yet do not surrender a good position. If a position is worth taking, it is worth defending.

14) Do not be afraid to admit an error in judgment if you are shown to be wrong

The board knows that you are forced to reply without any opportunity for careful consideration. Your answer may be demonstrably wrong. If so, admit it and get on with the interview.

15) Do not dwell at length on your present job

The opening question may relate to your present assignment. Answer the question but do not go into an extended discussion. You are being examined for a *new* job, not your present one. As a matter of fact, try to phrase ALL your answers in terms of the job for which you are being examined.

Basis of Rating

Probably you will forget most of these "do's" and "don'ts" when you walk into the oral interview room. Even remembering them all will not ensure you a passing grade. Perhaps you did not have the qualifications in the first place. But remembering them will help you to put your best foot forward, without treading on the toes of the board members.

Rumor and popular opinion to the contrary notwithstanding, an oral board wants you to make the best appearance possible. They know you are under pressure – but they also want to see how you respond to it as a guide to what your reaction would be under the pressures of the job you seek. They will be influenced by the degree of poise you display, the personal traits you show and the manner in which you respond.

ABOUT THIS BOOK

This book contains tests divided into Examination Sections. Go through each test, answering every question in the margin. At the end of each test look at the answer key and check your answers. On the ones you got wrong, look at the right answer choice and learn. Do not fill in the answers first. Do not memorize the questions and answers, but understand the answer and principles involved. On your test, the questions will likely be different from the samples. Questions are changed and new ones added. If you understand these past questions you should have success with any changes that arise. Tests may consist of several types of questions. We have additional books on each subject should more study be advisable or necessary for you. Finally, the more you study, the better prepared you will be. This book is intended to be the last thing you study before you walk into the examination room. Prior study of relevant texts is also recommended. NLC publishes some of these in our Fundamental Series. Knowledge and good sense are important factors in passing your exam. Good luck also helps. So now study this Passbook, absorb the material contained within and take that knowledge into the examination. Then do your best to pass that exam.

———

EXAMINATION SECTION

EVALUATING CONCLUSIONS BASED ON FACTUAL INFORMATION

Test material will be presented in a multiple-choice question format.

Test Task: You will be given a set of statements and a conclusion based on the statements. You are to assume the statements are true. The conclusion is reached from these statements *only-not* on what you may happen to know about the subject discussed. Each question has three possible answers. You must then select the correct answer in the following manner:

Select A, if the statements prove that the conclusion is true.
Select B, if the statements prove that the conclusion is false.
Select C, if the statements are inadequate to prove the conclusion either true or false.

SAMPLE QUESTION #1:

STATEMENTS: All uniforms are cleaned by the Conroy Company. Blue uniforms are cleaned on Mondays or Fridays; green or brown uniforms are cleaned on Wednesdays Alan and Jean have blue uniforms, Gary has green uniforms and Ryan has brown uniforms.

CONCLUSION: Jean's uniforms are cleaned on Wednesdays.
   A. statements prove the conclusion TRUE
   B. statements prove the conclusion FALSE
   C. statements are INADEQUATE to prove the conclusion

The correct answer to this sample question is Choice B.

Solution:

The last sentence of the statements says that jean has blue uniforms. the second sentence of the statements says that blue uniforms are cleaned on Monday or Friday.
the conclusion says jean's uniforms are cleaned on Wednesday. Wednesday is neither Monday or Friday. Therefore, the conclusion must be false (choice B).

SAMPLE QUESTION #2:

STATEMENTS: If Beth works overtime, the assignment will be completed. If the assignment is completed, then all unit employees will receive a bonus. Beth works overtime.

CONCLUSION: A bonus will be given to all employees in the unit.
    A. statement prove the conclusion TRUE
    B. statements prove the conclusion FALSE
    C. statements are INADEQUATE to prove the conclusion

The correct answer to this sample question is Choice A.

Solution:

The conclusion follows necessarily from the statements. Beth works overtime. The assignment is completed. Therefore, all unit employees will receive a bonus.

SAMPLE QUESTION #3:

STATEMENTS: Bill is older than Wanda. Edna is older than Bill. Sarah is twice as old as Wanda.

CONCLUSION: Sarah is older than Edna.

    A. statement prove the conclusion TRUE
    B. statements prove the conclusion FALSE
    C. statements are INADEQUATE to prove the conclusion

The correct answer to this sample question is Choice C.

Solution:

We know from the statements that both Sarah and Edna are older than Wanda. We do not have any other information about Sarah and Edna. Therefore, no conclusion about whether or not Sarah is older than Edna can be made.

Evaluating Conclusions in Light of Known Facts

EXAMINATION SECTION
TEST 1

DIRECTIONS: Each question or incomplete statement is followed by several suggested answers or completions. Select the one that BEST answers the question or completes the statement. *PRINT THE LETTER OF THE CORRECT ANSWER IN THE SPACE AT THE RIGHT.*

Questions 1-9.

DIRECTIONS: In questions 1-9, you will read a set of facts and a conclusion drawn from them. The conclusion may be valid or invalid, based on the facts—it's your task to determine the validity of the conclusion.

For each question, select the letter before the statement that BEST expresses the relationship between the given facts and the conclusion that has been drawn from them. Your choices are:
A. The facts prove the conclusion
B. The facts disprove the conclusion; or
C. The facts neither prove nor disprove the conclusion.

1. FACTS: If the supervisor retires, James, the assistant supervisor, will not be transferred to another department. James will be promoted to supervisor if he is not transferred. The supervisor retired.

   CONCLUSION: James will be promoted to supervisor.

   A. The facts prove the conclusion.
   B. The facts disprove the conclusion.
   C. The facts neither prove nor disprove the conclusion.

1.____

2. FACTS: In the town of Luray, every player on the softball team works at Luray National Bank. In addition, every player on the Luray softball team wears glasses.

   CONCLUSION: At least some of the people who work at Luray National Bank wear glasses.

   A. The facts prove the conclusion.
   B. The facts disprove the conclusion.
   C. The facts neither prove nor disprove the conclusion.

2.____

3. FACTS: The only time Henry and June go out to dinner is on an evening when they have childbirth classes. Their childbirth classes meet on Tuesdays and Thursdays.

   CONCLUSION: Henry and June never go out to dinner on Friday or Saturday.

   A. The facts prove the conclusion.
   B. The facts disprove the conclusion.
   C. The facts neither prove nor disprove the conclusion.

3.____

4. FACTS: Every player on the field hockey team has at least one bruise. Everyone on the field hockey team also has scarred knees.

4._____

CONCLUSION: Most people with both bruises and scarred knees are field hockey players.

   A. The facts prove the conclusion.
   B. The facts disprove the conclusion.
   C. The facts neither prove nor disprove the conclusion.

5. FACTS: In the chess tournament, Lance will win his match against Jane if Jane wins her match against Mathias. If Lance wins his match against Jane, Christine will not win her match against Jane.

5._____

CONCLUSION: Christine will not win her match against Jane if Jane wins her match against Mathias.

   A. The facts prove the conclusion.
   B. The facts disprove the conclusion.
   C. The facts neither prove nor disprove the conclusion.

6. FACTS: No green lights on the machine are indicators for the belt drive status. Not all of the lights on the machine's upper panel are green. Some lights on the machine's lower panel are green.

6._____

CONCLUSION: The green lights on the machine's lower panel may be indicators for the belt drive status.

   A. The facts prove the conclusion.
   B. The facts disprove the conclusion.
   C. The facts neither prove nor disprove the conclusion.

7. FACTS: At a small, one-room country school, there are eight students: Amy, Ben, Carla, Dan, Elliot, Francine, Greg, and Hannah. Each student is in either the 6th, 7th, or 8th grade. Either two or three students are in each grade. Amy, Dan, and Francine are all in different grades. Ben and Elliot are both in the 7th grade. Hannah and Carl are in the same grade.

7._____

CONCLUSION: Exactly three students are in the 7th grade.

   A. The facts prove the conclusion.
   B. The facts disprove the conclusion.
   C. The facts neither prove nor disprove the conclusion.

8. FACTS: Two married couples are having lunch together. Two of the four people are German and two are Russian, but in each couple the nationality of a spouse is not necessarily the same as the other's. One person in the group is a teacher, the other a lawyer, one an engineer, and the other a writer. The teacher is a Russian man. The writer is Russian, and her husband is an engineer. One of the people, Mr. Stern, is German.

8._____

CONCLUSION: Mr. Stern's wife is a writer.

4

A. The facts prove the conclusion.
B. The facts disprove the conclusion.
C. The facts neither prove nor disprove the conclusion.

9. FACTS: The flume ride at the county fair is open only to children who are at least 36 inches tall. Lisa is 30 inches tall. John is shorter than Henry, but more than 10 inches taller than Lisa.

9.____

CONCLUSION: Lisa is the only one who can't ride the flume ride.

A. The facts prove the conclusion.
B. The facts disprove the conclusion.
C. The facts neither prove nor disprove the conclusion.

Questions 10-17.

DIRECTIONS: Questions 10-17 are based on the following reading passage. It is not your knowledge of the particular topic that is being tested, but your ability to reason based on what you have read. The passage is likely to detail several proposed courses of action and factors affecting these proposals. The reading passage is followed by a conclusion or outcome based on the facts in the passage, or a description of a decision taken regarding the situation. The conclusion is followed by a number of statements that have a possible connection to the conclusion. For each statement, you are to determine whether:

A. The statement proves the conclusion.
B. The statement supports the conclusion but does not prove it.
C. The statement disproves the conclusion.
D. The statement weakens the conclusion but does not disprove it.
E. The statement has no relevance to the conclusion.

Remember that the conclusion after the passage is to be accepted as the outcome of what actually happened, and that you are being asked to evaluate the impact each statement would have had on the conclusion.

PASSAGE:

The Grand Army of Foreign Wars, a national veteran's organization, is struggling to maintain its National Home, where the widowed spouses and orphans of deceased members are housed together in a small village-like community. The Home is open to spouses and children who are bereaved for any reason, regardless of whether the member's death was related to military service, but a new global conflict has led to a dramatic surge in the number of members' deaths: many veterans who re-enlisted for the conflict have been killed in action.

The Grand Army of Foreign Wars is considering several options for handling the increased number of applications for housing at the National Home, which has been traditionally supported by membership dues. At its national convention, it will choose only one of the following:

The first idea is a one-time $50 tax on all members, above and beyond the dues they pay already. Since the organization has more than a million members, this tax should be sufficient for the construction and maintenance of new housing for applicants on the existing grounds of the National Home. The idea is opposed, however, by some older members who live on fixed incomes. These members object in principle to the taxation of Grand Army members. The Grand Army has never imposed a tax on its members.

The second idea is to launch a national fund-raising drive and public relations campaign that will attract donations for the National Home. Several national celebrities are members of the organization, and other celebrities could be attracted to the cause. Many Grand Army members are wary of this approach, however: in the past, the net receipts of some fund-raising efforts have been relatively insignificant, given the costs of staging them.

A third approach, suggested by many of the younger members, is to have new applicants share some of the costs of construction and maintenance. The spouses and children would pay an up-front "enrollment" fee, based on a sliding scale proportionate to their income and assets, and then a monthly fee adjusted similarly to contribute to maintenance costs. Many older members are strongly opposed to this idea, as it is in direct contradiction to the principles on which the organization was founded more than a century ago.

The fourth option is simply to maintain the status quo, focus the organization's efforts on supporting the families who already live at the National Home, and wait to accept new applicants based on attrition.

CONCLUSION: At its annual national convention, the Grand Army of Foreign Wars votes to impose a one-time tax of $10 on each member for the purpose of expanding and supporting the National Home to welcome a larger number of applicants. The tax is considered to be the solution most likely to produce the funds needed to accommodate the growing number of applicants.

10. Actuarial studies have shown that because the Grand Army's membership consists mostly of older veterans from earlier wars, the organization's membership will suffer a precipitous decline in numbers in about five years.

    10.____

    A.
    B.
    C.
    D.
    E.

11. After passage of the funding measure, a splinter group of older members appeals for the "sliding scale" provision to be applied to the tax, so that some members may be allowed to contribute less based on their income.

    11.____

    A.
    B.
    C.
    D.
    E.

12. The original charter of the Grand Army of Foreign Wars specifically states that the organization will not levy any taxes or duties on its members beyond its modest annual dues. It takes a super-majority of attending delegates at the national convention to make alterations to the charter.

    A.
    B.
    C.
    D.
    E.

12.____

13. Six months before Grand Army of Foreign Wars' national convention, the Internal Revenue Service rules that because it is an organization that engages in political lobbying, the Grand Army must no longer enjoy its own federal tax-exempt status.

    A.
    B.
    C.
    D.
    E.

13.____

14. Two months before the national convention, Dirk Rockwell, arguably the country's most famous film actor, announces in a nationally televised interview that he has been saddened to learn of the plight of the National Home, and that he is going to make it his own personal crusade to see that it is able to house and support a greater number of widowed spouses and orphans in the future.

    A.
    B.
    C.
    D.
    E.

14.____

15. The Grand Army's final estimate is that the cost of expanding the National Home to accommodate the increased number of applicants will be about $61 million.

    A.
    B.
    C.
    D.
    E.

15.____

16. Just before the national convention, the federal Department of Veterans Affairs announces steep cuts in the benefits package that is currently offered to the widowed spouses and orphans of veterans.

    A.
    B.
    C.
    D.

16.____

17. After the national convention, the Grand Army of Foreign Wars begins charging a modest   17._____
    "start-up" fee to all families who apply for residence at the national home.

    A.
    B.
    C.
    D.
    E.

Questions 18-25.

DIRECTIONS: Questions 18-25 each provide four factual statements and a conclusion based
on these statements. After reading the entire question, you will decide
whether:
  A. The conclusion is proved by statements 1-4;
  B. The conclusion is disproved by statements 1-4; or
  C. The facts are not sufficient to prove or disprove the conclusion.

18. FACTUAL STATEMENTS: 18._____

1. In the Field Day high jump competition, Martha jumped higher than Frank.
2. Carl jumped higher than Ignacio.
3. Ignacio jumped higher than Frank.
4. Dan jumped higher than Carl.

CONCLUSION: Frank finished last in the high jump competition.

  A. The conclusion is proved by statements 1-4.
  B. The conclusion is disproved by statements 1-4.
  C. The facts are not sufficient to prove or disprove the conclusion.

19. FACTUAL STATEMENTS: 19._____

1. The door to the hammer mill chamber is locked if light 6 is red.
2. The door to the hammer mill chamber is locked only when the mill is operating.
3. If the mill is not operating, light 6 is blue.
4. Light 6 is blue.

CONCLUSION: The door to the hammer mill chamber is locked.

  A. The conclusion is proved by statements 1-4.
  B. The conclusion is disproved by statements 1-4.
  C. The facts are not sufficient to prove or disprove the conclusion.

20. FACTUAL STATEMENTS: 20.____

    1. Ziegfried, the lion tamer at the circus, has demanded ten additional minutes of performance time during each show.
    2. If Ziegfried is allowed his ten additional minutes per show, he will attempt to teach Kimba the tiger to shoot a basketball.
    3. If Kimba learns how to shoot a basketball, then Ziegfried was not given his ten additional minutes.
    4. Ziegfried was given his ten additional minutes.

CONCLUSION: Despite Ziegfried's efforts, Kimba did not learn how to shoot a basketball.

    A.   The conclusion is proved by statements 1-4.
    B.   The conclusion is disproved by statements 1-4.
    C.   The facts are not sufficient to prove or disprove the conclusion.

21. FACTUAL STATEMENTS: 21.____

    1. If Stan goes to counseling, Sara won't divorce him.
    2. If Sara divorces Stan, she'll move back to Texas.
    3. If Sara doesn't divorce Stan, Irene will be disappointed.
    4. Stan goes to counseling.

CONCLUSION: Irene will be disappointed.

    A.   The conclusion is proved by statements 1-4.
    B.   The conclusion is disproved by statements 1-4.
    C.   The facts are not sufficient to prove or disprove the conclusion.

22. FACTUAL STATEMENTS: 22.____

    1. If Delia is promoted to district manager, Claudia will have to be promoted to team leader.
    2. Delia will be promoted to district manager unless she misses her fourth-quarter sales quota.
    3. If Claudia is promoted to team leader, Thomas will be promoted to assistant team leader.
    4. Delia meets her fourth-quarter sales quota.

CONCLUSION: Thomas is promoted to assistant team leader.

    A.   The conclusion is proved by statements 1-4.
    B.   The conclusion is disproved by statements 1-4.
    C.   The facts are not sufficient to prove or disprove the conclusion.

23. FACTUAL STATEMENTS: 23._____

1. Clone D is identical to Clone B.
2. Clone B is not identical to Clone A.
3. Clone D is not identical to Clone C.
4. Clone E is not identical to the clones that are identical to Clone B.

CONCLUSION: Clone E is identical to Clone D.

   A.   The conclusion is proved by statements 1-4.
   B.   The conclusion is disproved by statements 1-4.
   C.   The facts are not sufficient to prove or disprove the conclusion.

24. FACTUAL STATEMENTS: 24._____

1. In the Stafford Tower, each floor is occupied by a single business.
2. Big G Staffing is on a floor between CyberGraphics and MainEvent.
3. Gasco is on the floor directly below CyberGraphics and three floors above Treehorn Audio.
4. MainEvent is five floors below EZ Tax and four floors below Treehorn Audio.

CONCLUSION: EZ Tax is on a floor between Gasco and MainEvent.

   A.   The conclusion is proved by statements 1-4.
   B.   The conclusion is disproved by statements 1-4.
   C.   The facts are not sufficient to prove or disprove the conclusion.

25. FACTUAL STATEMENTS: 25._____

1. Only county roads lead to Nicodemus.
2. All the roads from Hill City to Graham County are federal highways.
3. Some of the roads from Plainville lead to Nicodemus.
4. Some of the roads running from Hill City lead to Strong City.

CONCLUSION: Some of the roads from Plainville are county roads.

   A.   The conclusion is proved by statements 1-4.
   B.   The conclusion is disproved by statements 1-4.
   C.   The facts are not sufficient to prove or disprove the conclusion.

KEY (CORRECT ANSWERS)

1.	A	11.	A
2.	A	12.	D
3.	A	13.	E
4.	C	14.	D
5.	A	15.	B
6.	B	16.	B
7.	A	17.	C
8.	A	18.	A
9.	A	19.	B
10.	E	20.	A

21.	A
22.	A
23.	B
24.	A
25.	A

———

SOLUTIONS TO PROBLEMS

1) (A) Given statement 3, we deduce that James will not be transferred to another department. By statement 2, we can conclude that James will be promoted.

2) (A) Since every player on the softball team wears glasses, these individuals compose some of the people who work at the bank. Although not every person who works at the bank plays softball, those bank employees who do play softball wear glasses.

3) (A) If Henry and June go out to dinner, we conclude that it must be on Tuesday or Thursday, which are the only two days when they have childbirth classes. This implies that if it is not Tuesday or Thursday, then this couple does not go out to dinner.

4) (C) We can only conclude that if a person plays on the field hockey team, then he or she has both bruises and scarred knees. But there are probably a great number of people who have both bruises and scarred knees but do not play on the field hockey team. The given conclusion can neither be proven or disproven.

5) (A) From statement 1, if Jane beats Mathias, then Lance will beat Jane. Using statement 2, we can then conclude that Christine will not win her match against Jane.

6) (B) Statement 1 tells us that no green light can be an indicator of the belt drive status. Thus, the given conclusion must be false.

7) (A) We already know that Ben and Elliot are in the 7th grade. Even though Hannah and Carl are in the same grade, it cannot be the 7th grade because we would then have at least four students in this 7th grade. This would contradict the third statement, which states that either two or three students are in each grade. Since Amy, Dan, and Francine are in different grades, exactly one of them must be in the 7th grade. Thus, Ben, Elliot and exactly one of Amy, Dan, and Francine are the three students in the 7th grade.

8) (A) One man is a teacher, who is Russian. We know that the writer is female and is Russian. Since her husband is an engineer, he cannot be the Russian teacher. Thus, her husband is of German descent, namely Mr. Stern. This means that Mr. Stern's wife is the writer. Note that one couple consists of a male Russian teacher and a female German lawyer. The other couple consists of a male German engineer and a female Russian writer.

9) (A) Since John is more than 10 inches taller than Lisa, his height is at least 46 inches. Also, John is shorter than Henry, so Henry's height must be greater than 46 inches. Thus, Lisa is the only one whose height is less than 36 inches. Therefore, she is the only one who is not allowed on the flume ride.

18) (A) Dan jumped higher than Carl, who jumped higher than Ignacio, who jumped higher than Frank. Since Martha jumped higher than Frank, every person jumped higher than Frank. Thus, Frank finished last.

19) (B) If the light is red, then the door is locked. If the door is locked, then the mill is operating. Reversing the logical sequence of these statements, if the mill is not operating, then the door is not locked, which means that the light is blue. Thus, the given conclusion is disproved.

20) (A) Using the contrapositive of statement 3, if Ziegfried was given his ten additional minutes, then Kimba did not learn how to shoot a basketball. Since statement 4 is factual, the conclusion is proved.

21) (A) From statements 4 and 1, we conclude that Sara doesn't divorce Stan. Then statement 3 reveals that Irene will be disappointed. Thus the conclusion is proved.

22) (A) Statement 2 can be rewritten as "Delia is promoted to district manager or she misses her sales quota." Furthermore, this statement is equivalent to "If Delia makes her sales quota, then she is promoted to district manager." From statement 1, we conclude that Claudia is promoted to team leader. Finally, by statement 3, Thomas is promoted to assistant team leader. The conclusion is proved.

23) (B) By statement 4, Clone E is not identical to any clones identical to clone B. Statement 1 tells us that clones B and D are identical. Therefore, clone E cannot be identical to clone D. The conclusion is disproved.

24) (A) Based on all four statements, CyberGraphics is somewhere below Main Event. Gasco is one floor below CyberGraphics. EZ Tax is two floors below Gasco. Treehorn Audio is one floor below EZ Tax. Main Event is four floors below Treehorn Audio. Thus, EZ Tax is two floors below Gasco and five floors above Main Event. The conclusion is proved.

25) (A) From statement 3, we know that some of the roads from Plainville lead to Nicodemus. But statement 1 tells us that only county roads lead to Nicodemus. Therefore, some of the roads from Plainville must be county roads. The conclusion is proved.

TEST 2

DIRECTIONS: Each question or incomplete statement is followed by several suggested answers or completions. Select the one that BEST answers the question or completes the statement. *PRINT THE LETTER OF THE CORRECT ANSWER IN THE SPACE AT THE RIGHT.*

Questions 1-9.

DIRECTIONS: In questions 1-9, you will read a set of facts and a conclusion drawn from them. The conclusion may be valid or invalid, based on the facts-it's your task to determine the validity of the conclusion.

For each question, select the letter before the statement that BEST expresses the relationship between the given facts and the conclusion that has been drawn from them. Your choices are:
A.   The facts prove the conclusion
B.   The facts disprove the conclusion; or
C.   The facts neither prove nor disprove the conclusion.

1.   FACTS: Some employees in the testing department are statisticians. Most of the statisti-   1.____
     cians who work in the testing department are projection specialists. Tom Wilks works in
     the testing department.

     CONCLUSION: Tom Wilks is a statistician.

     A.   The facts prove the conclusion.
     B.   The facts disprove the conclusion.
     C.   The facts neither prove nor disprove the conclusion.

2.   FACTS: Ten coins are split among Hank, Lawrence, and Gail. If Lawrence gives his coins   2.____
     to Hank, then Hank will have more coins than Gail. If Gail gives her coins to Lawrence,
     then Lawrence will have more coins than Hank.

     CONCLUSION: Hank has six coins.

     A.   The facts prove the conclusion.
     B.   The facts disprove the conclusion.
     C.   The facts neither prove nor disprove the conclusion.

3.   FACTS: Nobody loves everybody. Janet loves Ken. Ken loves everybody who loves   3.____
     Janet.

     CONCLUSION: Everybody loves Janet.

     A.   The facts prove the conclusion.
     B.   The facts disprove the conclusion.
     C.   The facts neither prove nor disprove the conclusion.

4. FACTS: Most of the Torres family lives in East Los Angeles. Many people in East Los Angeles celebrate Cinco de Mayo. Joe is a member of the Torres family.

   CONCLUSION: Joe lives in East Los Angeles.

   A. The facts prove the conclusion.
   B. The facts disprove the conclusion.
   C. The facts neither prove nor disprove the conclusion.

   4.____

5. FACTS: Five professionals each occupy one story of a five-story office building. Dr. Kane's office is above Dr. Assad's. Dr. Johnson's office is between Dr. Kane's and Dr. Conlon's. Dr. Steen's office is between Dr. Conlon's and Dr. Assad's. Dr. Johnson is on the fourth story.

   CONCLUSION: Dr. Kane occupies the top story.

   A. The facts prove the conclusion.
   B. The facts disprove the conclusion.
   C. The facts neither prove nor disprove the conclusion.

   5.____

6. FACTS: To be eligible for membership in the Yukon Society, a person must be able to either tunnel through a snowbank while wearing only a T-shirt and shorts, or hold his breath for two minutes under water that is 50° F. Ray can only hold his breath for a minute and a half.

   CONCLUSION: Ray can still become a member of the Yukon Society by tunneling through a snowbank while wearing a T-shirt and shorts.

   A. The facts prove the conclusion.
   B. The facts disprove the conclusion.
   C. The facts neither prove nor disprove the conclusion.

   6.____

7. FACTS: A mark is worth five plunks. You can exchange four sharps for a tinplot. It takes eight marks to buy a sharp.

   CONCLUSION: A sharp is the most valuable.

   A. The facts prove the conclusion.
   B. The facts disprove the conclusion.
   C. The facts neither prove nor disprove the conclusion.

   7.____

8. FACTS: There are gibbons, as well as lemurs, who like to play in the trees at the monkey house. All those who like to play in the trees at the monkey house are fed lettuce and bananas.

   CONCLUSION: Lemurs and gibbons are types of monkeys.

   A. The facts prove the conclusion.
   B. The facts disprove the conclusion.
   C. The facts neither prove nor disprove the conclusion.

   8.____

9. FACTS: None of the Blackfoot tribes is a Salishan Indian tribe. Sal-ishan Indians came   9.____
    from the northern Pacific Coast. All Salishan Indians live east of the Continental Divide.

    CONCLUSION: No Blackfoot tribes live east of the Continental Divide.

    A. The facts prove the conclusion.
    B. The facts disprove the conclusion.
    C. The facts neither prove nor disprove the conclusion.

Questions 10-17.

DIRECTIONS: Questions 10-17 are based on the following reading passage. It is not your
              knowledge of the particular topic that is being tested, but your ability to reason
              based on what you have read. The passage is likely to detail several proposed
              courses of action and factors affecting these proposals. The reading passage
              is followed by a conclusion or outcome based on the facts in the passage, or a
              description of a decision taken regarding the situation. The conclusion is fol-
              lowed by a number of statements that have a possible connection to the con-
              clusion. For each statement, you are to determine whether:

              A. The statement proves the conclusion.
              B. The statement supports the conclusion but does not prove it.
              C. The statement disproves the conclusion.
              D. The statement weakens the conclusion but does not disprove it.
              E. The statement has no relevance to the conclusion.

Remember that the conclusion after the passage is to be accepted as the outcome of
what actually happened, and that you are being asked to evaluate the impact each statement would have had on the conclusion.

PASSAGE:

On August 12, Beverly Willey reported that she was in the elevator late on the previous
evening after leaving her office on the 16th floor of a large office building. In her report,
she states that a man got on the elevator at the 11th floor, pulled her off the elevator,
assaulted her, and stole her purse. Ms. Willey reported that she had seen the man in the
elevators and hallways of the building before. She believes that the man works in the
building. Her description of him is as follows: he is tall, unshaven, with wavy brown hair
and a scar on his left cheek. He walks with a pronounced limp, often dragging his left foot
behind his right.

CONCLUSION: After Beverly Willey makes her report, the police arrest a 43-year-man,
Barton Black, and charge him with her assault.

10. Barton Black is a former Marine who served in Vietnam, where he sustained shrapnel   10.____
     wounds to the left side of his face and suffered nerve damage in his left leg.

     A.
     B.
     C.
     D.
     E.

16

11. When they arrived at his residence to question him, detectives were greeted at the door   11.____
by Barton Black, who was tall and clean-shaven.

    A.
    B.
    C.
    D.
    E.

12. Barton Black was booked into the county jail several days after Beverly Willey's assault.   12.____

    A.
    B.
    C.
    D.
    E.

13. Upon further investigation, detectives discover that Beverly Willey does not work at the   13.____
office building.

    A.
    B.
    C.
    D.
    E.

14. Upon further investigation, detectives discover that Barton Black does not work at the   14.____
office building.

    A.
    B.
    C.
    D.
    E.

15. In the spring of the following year, Barton Black is convicted of assaulting Beverly Willey   15.____
on August 11.

    A.
    B.
    C.
    D.
    E.

16. During their investigation of the assault, detectives determine that Beverly Willey was   16.____
assaulted on the 12th floor of the office building.

    A.
    B.
    C.
    D.
    E.

17. The day after Beverly Willey's assault, Barton Black fled the area and was never seen   17.____
    again.

    A.
    B.
    C.
    D.
    E.

Questions 18-25.

DIRECTIONS: Questions 18-25 each provide four factual statements and a conclusion based
               on these statements. After reading the entire question, you will decide
               whether:

    A.   The conclusion is proved by statements 1-4;
    B.   The conclusion is disproved by statements 1-4; or
    C.   The facts are not sufficient to prove or disprove the conclusion.

18.   FACTUAL STATEMENTS: 18.____

    1. Among five spice jars on the shelf, the sage is to the right of the parsley.
    2. The pepper is to the left of the basil.
    3. The nutmeg is between the sage and the pepper.
    4. The pepper is the second spice from the left.

    CONCLUSION: The sage is the farthest to the right.

    A.   The conclusion is proved by statements 1-4.
    B.   The conclusion is disproved by statements 1-4.
    C.   The facts are not sufficient to prove or disprove the conclusion.

19.   FACTUAL STATEMENTS: 19.____

    1. Gear X rotates in a clockwise direction if Switch C is in the OFF position
    2. Gear X will rotate in a counter-clockwise direction if Switch C is ON.
    3. If Gear X is rotating in a clockwise direction, then Gear Y will not be rotating at all.
    4. Switch C is ON.

    CONCLUSION: Gear X is rotating in a counter-clockwise direction.

    A.   The conclusion is proved by statements 1-4.
    B.   The conclusion is disproved by statements 1-4.
    C.   The facts are not sufficient to prove or disprove the conclusion.

20. FACTUAL STATEMENTS:

    20.____

    1. Lane will leave for the Toronto meeting today only if Terence, Rourke, and Jackson all file their marketing reports by the end of the work day.

    2. Rourke will file her report on time only if Ganz submits last quarter's data.

    3. If Terence attends the security meeting, he will attend it with Jackson, and they will not file their marketing reports by the end of the work day.

    4. Ganz submits last quarter's data to Rourke.

    CONCLUSION: Lane will leave for the Toronto meeting today.

    A. The conclusion is proved by statements 1-4.
    B. The conclusion is disproved by statements 1-4.
    C. The facts are not sufficient to prove or disprove the conclusion.

21. FACTUAL STATEMENTS:

    21.____

    1. Bob is in second place in the Boston Marathon.

    2. Gregory is winning the Boston Marathon.

    3. There are four miles to go in the race, and Bob is gaining on Gregory at the rate of 100 yards every minute.

    4. There are 1760 yards in a mile, and Gregory's usual pace during the Boston Marathon is one mile every six minutes.

    CONCLUSION: Bob wins the Boston Marathon.

    A. The conclusion is proved by statements 1-4.
    B. The conclusion is disproved by statements 1-4.
    C. The facts are not sufficient to prove or disprove the conclusion.

22. FACTUAL STATEMENTS:

    22.____

    1. Four brothers are named Earl, John, Gary, and Pete.

    2. Earl and Pete are unmarried.

    3. John is shorter than the youngest of the four.

    4. The oldest brother is married, and is also the tallest.

    CONCLUSION: Gary is the oldest brother.

    A. The conclusion is proved by statements 1-4.
    B. The conclusion is disproved by statements 1-4.
    C. The facts are not sufficient to prove or disprove the conclusion.

23. FACTUAL STATEMENTS:

    23.____

    1. Brigade X is ten miles from the demilitarized zone.

    2. If General Woundwort gives the order, Brigade X will advance to the demilitarized zone, but not quickly enough to reach the zone before the conflict begins.

    3. Brigade Y, five miles behind Brigade X, will not advance unless General Woundwort gives the order.

    4. Brigade Y advances.

    CONCLUSION: Brigade X reaches the demilitarized zone before the conflict begins.

A. The conclusion is proved by statements 1-4.
B. The conclusion is disproved by statements 1-4.
C. The facts are not sufficient to prove or disprove the conclusion.

24. FACTUAL STATEMENTS:

24._____

1. Jerry has decided to take a cab from Fullerton to Elverton.
2. Chubby Cab charges $5 plus $3 a mile.
3. Orange Cab charges $7.50 but gives free mileage for the first 5 miles.
4. After the first 5 miles, Orange Cab charges $2.50 a mile.

CONCLUSION: Orange Cab is the cheaper fare from Fullerton to Elverton.

A. The conclusion is proved by statements 1-4.
B. The conclusion is disproved by statements 1-4.
C. The facts are not sufficient to prove or disprove the conclusion.

25. FACTUAL STATEMENTS:

25._____

1. Dan is never in class when his friend Lucy is absent.
2. Lucy is never absent unless her mother is sick.
3. If Lucy is in class, Sergio is in class also
4. Sergio is never in class when Dalton is absent.

CONCLUSION: If Lucy is absent, Dalton may be in class.

A. The conclusion is proved by statements 1-4.
B. The conclusion is disproved by statements 1-4.
C. The facts are not sufficient to prove or disprove the conclusion.

KEY (CORRECT ANSWERS)

1.	C		11.	E
2.	B		12.	B
3.	B		13.	D
4.	C		14.	E
5.	A		15.	A
6.	A		16.	E
7.	B		17.	C
8.	C		18.	B
9.	C		19.	A
10.	B		20.	C

21.	C
22.	A
23.	B
24.	A
25.	B

SOLUTIONS TO PROBLEMS

1) (C) Statement 1 only tells us that some employees who work in the Testing Department are statisticians. This means that we need to allow the possibility that at least one person in this department is not a statistician. Thus, if a person works in the Testing Department, we cannot conclude whether or not this individual is a statistician.

2) (B) If Hank had six coins, then the total of Gails collection and Lawrence's collection would be four. Thus, if Gail gave all her coins to Lawrence, Lawrence would only have four coins. Thus, it would be impossible for Lawrence to have more coins than Hank.

3) (B) Statement 1 tells us that nobody loves everybody. If everybody loved Janet, then Statement 3 would imply that Ken loves everybody. This would contradict statement 1. The conclusion is disproved.

4) (C) Although most of the Torres family lives in East Los Angeles, we can assume that some members of this family do not live in East Los Angeles. Thus, we cannot prove or disprove that Joe, who is a member of the Torres family, lives in East Los Angeles.

5) (A) Since Dr. Johnson is on the 4th floor, either (a) Dr. Kane is on the 5th floor and Dr. Conlon is on the 3rd floor, or (b) Dr. Kane is on the 3rd floor and Dr. Conlon is on the 5th floor. If option (b) were correct, then since Dr. Assad would be on the 1st floor, it would be impossible for Dr. Steen's office to be between Dr. Conlon and Dr. Assad's office. Therefore, Dr. Kane's office must be on the 5th floor. The order of the doctors' offices, from 5th floor down to the 1st floor is: Dr. Kane, Dr. Johnson, Dr. Conlon, Dr. Steen, Dr. Assad.

6) (A) Ray does not satisfy the requirement of holding his breath for two minutes under water, since he can only hold his breath for one minute in that setting. But if he tunnels through a snowbank with just a T-shirt and shorts, he will satisfy the eligibility requirement. Note that the eligibility requirement contains the key word "or." So only one of the two clauses separated by "or" need to be fulfilled.

7) (B) Statement 2 says that four sharps is equivalent to one tinplot. This means that a tinplot is worth more than a sharp. The conclusion is disproved. We note that the order of these items, from most valuable to least valuable are: tinplot, sharp, mark, plunk.

8) (C) We can only conclude that gibbons and lemurs are fed lettuce and bananas. We can neither prove or disprove that these animals are types of monkeys.

9) (C) We know that all Salishan Indians live east of the Continental Divide. But some nonmembers of this tribe of Indians may also live east of the Continental Divide. Since none of the members of the Blackfoot tribe belong to the Salishan Indian tribe, we cannot draw any conclusion about the location of the Blackfoot tribe with respect to the Continental Divide.

18) (B) Since the pepper is second from the left and the nutmeg is between the sage and the pepper, the positions 2, 3, and 4 (from the left) are pepper, nutmeg, sage. By statement 2, the basil must be in position 5, which implies that the parsley is in position 1. Therefore, the basil, not the sage is farthest to the right. The conclusion disproved.

19) (A) Statement 2 assures us that if switch C is ON, then Gear X is rotating in a counterclockwise direction. The conclusion is proved.

20) (C) Based on Statement 4, followed by Statement 2, we conclude that Ganz and Rourke will file their reports on time. Statement 3 reveals that if Terence and Jackson attend the security meeting, they will fail to file their reports on time. We have no further information if Terence and Jackson attended the security meeting, so we are not able to either confirm or deny that their reports were filed on time. This implies that we cannot know for certain that Lane will leave for his meeting in Toronto.

21) (C) Although Bob is in second place behind Gregory, we cannot deduce how far behind Gregory he is running. At Gregory's current pace, he will cover four miles in 24 minutes. If Bob were only 100 yards behind Gregory, he would catch up to Gregory in one minute. But if Bob were very far behind Gregory, for example 5 miles, this is the equivalent of $(5)(1760) = 8800$ yards. Then Bob would need $8800/100 = 88$ minutes to catch up to Gregory. Thus, the given facts are not sufficient to draw a conclusion.

22) (A) Statement 2 tells us that neither Earl nor Pete could be the oldest; also, either John or Gary is married. Statement 4 reveals that the oldest brother is both married and the tallest. By statement 3, John cannot be the tallest. Since John is not the tallest, he is not the oldest. Thus, the oldest brother must be Gary. The conclusion is proved.

23) (B) By statements 3 and 4, General Woundwort must have given the order to advance. Statement 2 then tells us that Brigade X will advance to the demilitarized zone, but not soon enough before the conflict begins. Thus, the conclusion is disproved.

24) (A) If the distance is 5 miles or less, then the cost for the Orange Cab is only $7.50, whereas the cost for the Chubby Cab is $5 + 3x$, where x represents the number of miles traveled. For 1 to 5 miles, the cost of the Chubby Cab is between $8 and $20. This means that for a distance of 5 miles, the Orange Cab costs $7.50, whereas the Chubby Cab costs $20. After 5 miles, the cost per mile of the Chubby Cab exceeds the cost per mile of the Orange Cab. Thus, regardless of the actual distance between Fullerton and Elverton, the cost for the Orange Cab will be cheaper than that of the Chubby Cab.

25) (B) It looks like "Dalton" should be replaced by "Dan in the conclusion. Then by statement 1, if Lucy is absent, Dan is never in class. Thus, the conclusion is disproved.

LOGICAL REASONING
EVALUATING CONCLUSIONS IN LIGHT OF KNOWN FACTS

EXAMINATION SECTION
TEST 1
COMMENTARY

This section is designed to provide practice questions in evaluating conclusions when you are given specific data to work with.

We suggest you do the questions three at a time, consulting the answer key and then the solution section for any questions you may have missed. It's a good idea to try the questions again a week before the exam.

In the validity of conclusion type of question, you are first given a reading passage which describes a particular situation. The passage may be on any topic, as it is not your knowledge of the topic that is being tested, but your reasoning abilities. The passage is likely to detail several proposed courses of action and factors affecting these proposals. The reading passage is followed by a conclusion based on the facts in the passage, or a description of a decision taken regarding the situation. The conclusion is followed by a number of statements which have a possible connection to the conclusion. For each statement, you are to determine whether:

A. The statement proves the conclusion.
B. The statement supports the conclusion but does not prove it.
C. The statement disproves the conclusion.
D. The statement weakens the conclusion but does not disprove it.
E. The statement has no relevance to the conclusion.

Remember that the conclusion after the passage is to be accepted as the outcome of what actually happened, and that you are being asked to evaluate the impact each statement would have had on the conclusion.

Questions 1-8 are based on the following paragraph.

In May of 1993, Mr. Bryan inherited a clothing store on Main Street in a small New England town. The store has specialized in selling quality men's and women's clothing since 1885. Business has been stable throughout the years, neither increasing nor decreasing. He has an opportunity to buy two adjacent stores which would enable him to add a wider range and style of clothing. In order to do this, he would have to borrow a substantial amount of money. He also risks losing the goodwill of his present clientele.

CONCLUSION: On November 7, 1993, Mr. Bryan tells the owner of the two adjacent stores that he has decided not to purchase them. He feels that it would be best to simply maintain his present marketing position, as there would not be enough new business to support an expansion.

A. The statement proves the conclusion.
B. The statement supports the conclusion but does not prove it.
C. The statement disproves the conclusion.
D. The statement weakens the conclusion.
E. The statement is irrelevant to the conclusion.

1. A large new branch of the county's community college holds its first classes in September of 1993.

      1.____

2. The town's largest factory shuts down with no indication that it will reopen.

      2.____

3. The 1990 United States Census showed that the number of children per household dropped from 2.4 to 2.1 since the 1980 census.

      3.____

4. Mr. Bryan's brother tells him of a new clothing boutique specializing in casual women's clothing which is opening soon.

      4.____

5. Mr. Bryan's sister buys her baby several items for Christmas at Mr. Bryan's store.

      5.____

6. Mrs. McIntyre, the President of the Town Council, brings Mr. Bryan a home-baked pumpkin pie in honor of his store's 100th anniversary. They discuss the changes that have taken place in the town, and she comments on how his store has maintained the same look and feel over the years.

      6.____

7. In October of 1993, Mr. Bryan's aunt lends him $50,000.

      7.____

8. The Town Council has just announced that the town is eligible for funding from a federal project designed to encourage the location of new businesses in the central districts of cities and towns.

      8.____

Questions 9-18 are based on the following paragraph.

A proposal has been put before the legislative body of a small European country to require air bags in all automobiles manufactured for domestic use in that country after 1999. The air bag, made of nylon or plastic, is designed to inflate automatically within a car at the impact of a collision, thus protecting front-seat occupants from being thrown forward. There has been much support of the measure from consumer groups, the insurance industry, key legislators, and the general public. The country's automobile manufacturers, who contend the new crash equipment would add up to $1,000 to car prices and provide no more protection than existing seat belts, are against the proposed legislation.

CONCLUSION: On April 21, 1994, the legislature passed legislation requiring air bags in all automobiles manufactured for domestic use in that country after 1999.

    A. The statement proves the conclusion.
    B. The statement supports the conclusion but does not prove it.
    C. The statement disproves the conclusion.
    D. The statement weakens the conclusion.
    E. The statement is irrelevant to the conclusion.

9. A study has shown that 59% of car occupants do not use seat belts.

      9.____

10. The country's Department of Transportation has estimated that the crash protection equipment would save up to 5,900 lives each year.

      10.____

11. On April 27, 1993, Augusta Raneoni was named head of an advisory committee to gather and analyze data on the costs, benefits, and feasibility of the proposed legislation on air bags in automobiles.

      11.____

12. Consumer groups and the insurance industry accuse the legislature of rejecting passage   12.____
of the regulation for political reasons.

13. A study by the Committee on Imports and Exports projected that the sales of imported   13.____
cars would rise dramatically in 1999 because imported cars do not have to include air
bags, and can be sold more cheaply.

14. Research has shown that air bags, if produced on a large scale, would cost about $200   14.____
apiece, and would provide more reliable protection than any other type of seat belt.

15. Auto sales in 1991 have increased 3% over the previous year.   15.____

16. A Department of Transportation report in July of 2000 credits a drop in automobile   16.____
deaths of 4,100 to the use of air bags.

17. In June of 1994, the lobbyist of the largest insurance company receives a bonus for her   17.____
work on the passage of the air bag legislation.

18. In 2000, the stock in crash protection equipment has risen three-fold over the previous   18.____
year.

Questions 19-25 are based on the following paragraph.

On a national television talk show, Joan Rivera, a famous comedienne, has recently
insulted the physical appearances of a famous actress and the dead wife of an ex-Presi-
dent. There has been a flurry of controversy over her comments, and much discussion of
the incident has appeared in the press. Most of the comments have been negative. It
appears that this time she might have gone too far. There have been cancellations of two
of her five scheduled performances in the two weeks since the show was televised, and
Joan's been receiving a lot of negative mail. Because of the controversy, she has an
interview with a national news magazine at the end of the week, and her press agent is
strongly urging her to apologize publicly. She feels strongly that her comments were no
worse than any other she has ever made, and that the whole incident will *blow over* soon.
She respects her press agent's judgment, however, as his assessment of public sentiment tends to be very accurate.

CONCLUSION: Joan does not apologize publicly, and during the interview she challenges the actress to a weight-losing contest. For every pound the actress loses, Joan
says she will donate $1 to the Cellulite Prevention League.

    A. The statement proves the conclusion.
    B. The statement supports the conclusion but does not prove it.
    C. The statement disproves the conclusion.
    D. The statement weakens the conclusion.
    E. The statement is irrelevant to the conclusion.

19. Joan's mother, who she is very fond of, is very upset about Joan's comments.   19.____

20. Six months after the interview, Joan's income has doubled.   20.____

21. Joan's agent is pleased with the way Joan handles the interview.   21.____

22. Joan's sister has been appointed Treasurer of the Cellulite Prevention League. In her   22.____
     report, she states that Joan's $12 contribution is the only amount that has been donated
     to the League in its first six months.

23. The magazine receives many letters commending Joan for the courage it took for her to   23.____
     apologize publicly in the interview.

24. Immediately after the interview appears, another one of Joan's performances is can-   24.____
     celled.

25. Due to a printers strike, the article was not published until the following week.   25.____

Questions 26-30 are based on the following paragraph.

The law-making body of Country X must decide what to do about the issue of videotaping television shows for home use. There is currently no law against taping shows
directly from the TV as long as the videotapes are not used for commercial purposes.
The increasing popularity of pay TV and satellite systems, combined with the increasing
number of homes that own video-cassette recorders, has caused a great deal of concern
in some segments of the entertainment industry. Companies that own the rights to films,
popular television shows, and sporting events feel that their copyright privileges are
being violated, and they are seeking compensation or the banning of TV home videotaping. Legislation has been introduced to make it illegal to videotape television programs for home use. Separate proposed legislation is also pending that would continue
to allow videotaping of TV shows for home use, but would place a tax of 10% on each
videocassette that is purchased for home use. The income from that tax would then be
proportionately distributed as royalties to those owning the rights to programs being
aired. A weighted point system coupled with the averaging of several national viewing
rating systems would be used to determine the royalties. There is a great deal of lobbying
being done for both bills, as the manufacturers of videocassette recorders and videocassettes are against the passage of the bills.

CONCLUSION: The legislature of Country X rejects both bills by a wide margin.

    A.   The statement proves the conclusion.
    B.   The statement supports the conclusion but does not prove it.
    C.   The statement disproves the conclusion.
    D.   The statement weakens the conclusion.
    E.   The statement is irrelevant to the conclusion.

26. Country X's Department of Taxation hires 500 new employees to handle the increased   26.____
     paperwork created by the new tax on videocassettes.

27. A study conducted by the country's most prestigious accounting firm shows that the cost   27.____
     of implementing the proposed new videocassette tax would be greater than the income
     expected from it.

28. It is estimated that 80% of all those working in the entertainment industry, excluding per-   28.____
formers, own video-cassette recorders.

29. The head of Country X's law enforcement agency states that legislation banning the   29.____
home taping of TV shows would be unenforceable.

30. Financial experts predict that unless a tax is placed on videocassettes, several large   30.____
companies in the entertainment industry will have to file for bankruptcy.

Questions 31-38.

DIRECTIONS: The following questions 31 through 38 are variations on the type of question
you just had. It is important that you read the question very carefully to determine exactly what is required.

31. In this question, select the choice that is most relevant to the conclusion.   31.____

1.   The Buffalo Bills football team is in second place in its division.
2.   The New England Patriots are in first place in the same division.
3.   There are two games left to play in the season, and the Bills will not play the Patriots again.
4.   The New England Patriots won ten games and lost four games, and the Buffalo
Bills have won eight games and lost six games.

CONCLUSION: The Buffalo Bills win their division.

A.   The conclusion is proved by sentences 1-4.
B.   The conclusion is disproved by sentences 1-4.
C.   The facts are not sufficient to prove or disprove the conclusion.

32. In this question, select the choice that is most relevant to the conclusion.   32.____

1.   On the planet of Zeinon there are only two different eye colors and only two different hair colors.
2.   Half of those beings with purple hair have golden eyes.
3.   There are more inhabitants with purple hair than there are inhabitants with silver
hair.
4.   One-third of those with silver hair have green eyes.

CONCLUSION: There are more golden-eyed beings on Zeinon than green-eyed ones.

A.   The conclusion is proved by sentences 1-4.
B.   The conclusion is disproved by sentences 1-4.
C.   The facts are not sufficient to prove or disprove the conclusion.

33. In this question, select the choice that is most relevant to the conclusion.   33.____
John and Kevin are leaving Amaranth to go to school in Bethany. They've decided to
rent a small truck to move their possessions. Joe's Truck Rental charges $100 plus
30¢ a mile. National Movers charges $50 more but gives free mileage for the first 100
miles. After the first 100 miles, they charge 25¢ a mile.

CONCLUSION: John and Kevin rent their truck from National Movers because it is cheaper.

    A.   The conclusion is proved by the facts in the above paragraph.
    B.   The conclusion is disproved by the facts in the above paragraph.
    C.   The facts are not sufficient to prove or disprove the conclusion.

34.   For this question, select the choice that supports the information given in the passage.   34.____

Municipalities in Country X are divided into villages, towns, and cities. A village has a population of 5,000 or less. The population of a town ranges from 5,001 to 15,000. In order to be incorporated as a city, the municipality must have a population over 15,000. If, after a village becomes a town, or a town becomes a city, the population drops below the minimum required (for example, the population of a city goes below 15,000), and stays below the minimum for more than ten years, it loses its current status, and drops to the next category. As soon as a municipality rises in population to the next category (village to town, for example), however, it is immediately reclassified to the next category.

In the 1970 census, Plainfield had a population of 12,000. Between 1970 and 1980, Plainfield grew 10%, and between 1980 and 1990 Plainfield grew another 20%. The population of Springdale doubled from 1970 to 1980, and increased 25% from 1980 to 1990. The city of Smallville's population, 20,283, has not changed significantly in recent years. Granton had a population of 25,000 people in 1960, and has decreased 25% in each ten year period since then. Ellenville had a population of 4,283 in 1960, and grew 5% in each ten year period since 1960.

In 1990,

    A.   Plainfield, Smallville, and Granton are cities
    B.   Smallville is a city, Granton is a town, and Ellenville is a village
    C.   Springdale, Granton, and Ellenville are towns
    D.   Plainfield and Smallville are cities, and Ellenville is a town

35.   For this question, select the choice that is most relevant to the conclusion.   35.____

A study was done for a major food distributing firm to determine if there is any difference in the kind of caffeine containing products used by people of different ages. A sample of one thousand people between the ages of twenty and fifty were drawn from selected areas in the country. They were divided equally into three groups.
Those individuals who were 20-29 were designated Group A, those 30-39 were Group B, and those 40-50 were placed in Group C.
It was found that on the average, Group A drank 1.8 cups of coffee, Group B 3.1, and Group C 2.5 cups of coffee daily. Group A drank 2.1 cups of tea, Group B drank 1.2, and Group C drank 2.6 cups of tea daily. Group A drank 3.1 8-ounce glasses of cola, Group B drank 1.9, and Group C drank 1.5 glasses of cola daily.

CONCLUSION: According to the study, the average person in the 20-29 age group drinks less tea daily than the average person in the 40-50 age group, but drinks more coffee daily than the average person in the 30-39 age group drinks cola.

    A.   The conclusion is proved by the facts in the above paragraph.
    B.   The conclusion is disproved by the facts in the above paragraph.
    C.   The facts are not sufficient to prove or disprove the conclusion.

36. For this question, select the choice that is most relevant to the conclusion.   36.____

    1. Mary is taller than Jane but shorter than Dale.
    2. Fred is taller than Mary but shorter than Steven.
    3. Dale is shorter than Steven but taller than Elizabeth.
    4. Elizabeth is taller than Mary but not as tall as Fred.

CONCLUSION: Dale is taller than Fred.

    A. The conclusion is proved by sentences 1-4.
    B. The conclusion is disproved by sentences 1-4.
    C. The facts are not sufficient to prove or disprove the conclusion.

37. For this question, select the choice that is most relevant to the conclusion.   37.____

    1. Main Street is between Spring Street and Glenn Blvd.
    2. Hawley Avenue is one block south of Spring Street and three blocks north of Main Street.
    3. Glenn Street is five blocks south of Elm and four blocks south of Main.
    4. All the streets mentioned are parallel to one another.

CONCLUSION: Elm Street is between Hawley Avenue and Glenn Blvd.

    A. The conclusion is proved by the facts in sentences 1-4.
    B. The conclusion is disproved by the facts in sentences 1-4.
    C. The facts are not sufficient to prove or disprove the conclusion.

38. For this question, select the choice that is most relevant to the conclusion.   38.____

    1. Train A leaves the town of Hampshire every day at 5:50 A.M. and arrives in New London at 6:42 A.M.
    2. Train A leaves New London at 7:00 A.M. and arrives in Kellogsville at 8:42 A.M.
    3. Train B leaves Kellogsville at 8:00 A.M. and arrives in Hampshire at 10:42 A.M.
    4. Due to the need for repairs, there is just one railroad track between New London and Hampshire.

CONCLUSION: It is impossible for Train A and Train B to follow these schedules without colliding.

    A. The conclusion is proved by the facts in the above paragraph.
    B. The conclusion is disproved by the facts in the above passage.
    C. The facts are not sufficient to prove or disprove the conclusion.

KEY (CORRECT ANSWERS)

1.	D	11.	C	21.	D	31.	C
2.	B	12.	C	22.	A	32.	A
3.	E	13.	D	23.	C	33.	C
4.	B	14.	B	24.	B	34.	B
5.	C	15.	E	25.	E	35.	B
6.	D	16.	B	26.	C	36.	C
7.	B	17.	A	27.	B	37.	A
8.	A	18.	B	28.	E	38.	B
9.	B	19.	D	29.	B		
10.	B	20.	E	30.	D		

———

SOLUTIONS TO QUESTIONS

1. The answer is D. This statement weakens the conclusion, but does not disprove it. If a new branch of the community college opened in September, it could possibly bring in new business for Mr. Bryant. Since it states in the conclusion that Mr. Bryant felt there would not be enough new business to support the additional stores, this would tend to disprove the conclusion. Choice C would not be correct because it's possible that he felt that the students would not have enough additional money to support his new venture, or would not be interested in his clothing styles. It's also possible that the majority of the students already live in the area, so that they wouldn't really be a new customer population. This type of question is tricky, and can initially be very confusing, so don't feel badly if you missed it. Most people need to practice with a few of these types of questions before they feel comfortable recognizing exactly what they're being asked to do.

2. The answer is B. It supports the conclusion because the closing of the factory would probably take money and customers out of the town, causing Mr. Bryant to lose some of his present business. It doesn't prove the conclusion, however, because we don't know how large the factory was. It's possible that only a small percentage of the population was employed there, or that they found other jobs.

3. The answer is E. The fact that the number of children per household dropped slightly nationwide from 1970 to 1980 is irrelevant. Statistics showing a drop nationwide doesn't mean that there was a drop in the number of children per household in Mr. Bryant's hometown. This is a tricky question, as choice B, supporting the conclusion but not proving it, may seem reasonable. If the number of children per household declined nationwide, then it may not seem unreasonable to feel that this would support Mr. Bryant's decision not to expand his business. However, we're preparing you for promotional exams, not "real life." One of the difficult things about taking exams is that sometimes you're forced to make a choice between two statements that both seem like they could be the possible answer. What you need to do in that case is choose the <u>best</u> choice. Becoming annoyed or frustrated with the question won't really help much. If there's a review of the exam, you can certainly appeal the question. There have been many cases where, after an appeal, two possible choices have been allowed as correct answers. We've included this question, however, to help you see what to do should you get a question like this. It's most important not to get rattled, and to select the <u>best</u> choice. In this case, the connection between the statistical information and Mr. Bryant's decision is pretty remote. If the question had said that the number of children in Mr. Bryant's <u>town</u> had decreased, then choice B would have been a more reasonable choice. It could also help in this situation to visualize the situation. Picture Mr. Bryant in his armchair reading that, nationwide, the average number of children per household has declined slightly. How likely would this be to influence his decision, especially since he sells men's and women's clothing? It would take a while for this decline in population to show up, and we're not even sure if it applies to Mr. Bryant's hometown. Don't feel badly if you missed this, it was tricky. The more of these you do, the more comfortable you'll feel.

4. The answer is B. If a new clothing boutique specializing in casual women's clothing were to open soon, this would lend support to Mr. Bryant's decision not to expand, but would not prove that he had actually made the decision not to expand. A new women's clothing boutique would most likely be in competition with his existing business, thus making any possible expansion a riskier venture. We can't be sure from this, however, that he didn't go ahead and expand his business despite the increased competition. Choice A, proves the conclusion, would only be the answer if we could be absolutely sure from the statement that Mr. Bryant had actually <u>not</u> expanded his business.

5. The answer is C. This statement disproves the conclusion. In order for his sister to buy several items for her baby at Mr. Bryant's store, he would have to have changed his business to include children's clothing.

6. The answer is A. It definitely proves the conclusion. The passage states that Mr. Bryant's store had been in business since 1885. A pie baked in honor of his store's 100th anniversary would have to be presented sometime in 1985. The conclusion states that he made his decision not to expand on November 7, 1983. If, more than a year later Mrs. MacIntyre comments that his store has maintained the same look and feel over the years, it could not have been expanded, or otherwise significantly changed.

7. The answer is D. If Mr. Bryant's aunt lent him $50,000 in October, this would tend to weaken the conclusion, which took place in November. Because it was stated that Mr. Bryant would need to borrow money in order to expand his business, it would be logical to assume that if he borrowed money he had decided to expand his business, weakening the conclusion. The reason C, disproves the conclusion, is not the correct answer is because we can't be sure Mr. Bryant didn't borrow the money for another reason.

8. The answer is B. If Mr. Bryant's town is eligible for federal funds to encourage the location of new businesses in the central district, this would tend to support his decision not to expand his business. Funds to encourage new business would increase the likelihood of there being additional competition for Mr. Bryant's store to contend with. Since we can't say for sure that there would be direct competition from a new business, however, choice A would be incorrect. Note that this is also a tricky question. You might have thought that the new funds weakened the conclusion because it would mean that Mr. Bryant could easily get the money he needed. Mr. Bryant is expanding his present business, not creating a <u>new</u> business. Therefore he is not eligible for the funding.

9. The answer is B. This is a very tricky question. It's stated that 59% of car occupants don't use seat belts. The legislature is considering the use of air bags because of safety issues. The advantage of air bags over seat belts is that they inflate upon impact, and don't require car occupants to do anything with them ahead of time. Since the population has strongly resisted using seat belts, the air bags could become even more important in saving lives. Since saving lives is the purpose of the proposed legislation, the information that a small percentage of people use seat belts could be helpful to the passage of the legislation. We can't be sure that this is reason enough for the legislature to vote for the legislation, however, so choice A is incorrect.

10. The answer is B, as the information that 5,900 lives could be saved would tend to support the conclusion. Saving that many lives through the use of air bags could be a very persuasive reason to vote for the legislation. Since we don't know for sure that it's enough of a compelling reason for the legislature to vote for the legislation, however, choice A could not be the answer.

11. The answer is C, disproves the conclusion. If the legislation had been passed as stated in the conclusion, there would be no reason to appoint someone head of an advisory committee six days later to analyze the "feasibility of the proposed legislation." The key word here is "proposed." If it has been proposed, it means it hasn't been passed. This contradicts the conclusion and therefore disproves it.

12. The answer is C, disproves the conclusion. If the legislation had passed, there would be no reason for supporters of the legislation to accuse the legislature of rejecting the legislation for political reasons. This question may have seemed so obvious that you might have thought there was a trick to it. Exams usually have a few obvious questions, which will trip you up if you begin reading too much into them.

13. The answer is D, as this would tend to disprove the conclusion. A projected dramatic rise in imported cars could be very harmful to the country's economy and could be a very good reason for some legislators to vote against the proposed legislation. It would be assuming too much to choose C, however, because we don't know if they actually did vote against it.

14. The answer is B. This information would tend to support the passage of the legislation. The estimate of the cost of the air bags is $800 less than the cost estimated by opponents, and it's stated that the protection would be more reliable than any other type of seat belt. Both of these would be good arguments in favor of passing the legislation. Since we don't know for sure, however, how persuasive they actually were, choice A would not be the correct choice.

15. The answer is E, as this is irrelevant information. It really doesn't matter whether auto sales in 1981 have increased slightly over the previous year. If the air bag legislation were to go into effect in 1984, that might make the information somehow more relevant. But the air bag legislation would not take effect until 1989, so the information is irrelevant, since it tells us nothing about the state of the auto industry then.

16. The answer is B, supports the conclusion. This is a tricky question. While at first it might seem to prove the conclusion, we can't be sure that the air bag legislation is responsible for the drop in automobile deaths. It's possible air bags came into popular use without the legislation, or with different legislation. There's no way we can be sure that it was the proposed legislation mandating the use of air bags that was responsible.

17. The answer is A. If, in June of 1984, the lobbyist received a bonus "for her work on the air bag legislation," we can be sure that the legislation passed. This proves the conclusion.

18. The answer is B. This is another tricky question. A three fold stock increase would strongly suggest that the legislation had been passed, but it's possible that factors other than the air bag legislation caused the increase. Note that the stock is in "crash protection equipment." Nowhere in the statement does it say air bags. Seat belts, motorcycle helmets, and collapsible bumpers are all crash protection equipment and could have contributed to the increase. This is just another reminder to read carefully because the questions are often designed to mislead you.

19. The answer is D. This would tend to weaken the conclusion because Marsha is very fond of her mother and she would not want to upset her unnecessarily. It does not prove it, however, because if Marsha strongly feels she is right, she probably wouldn't let her mother's opinion sway her. Choice E would also not be correct, because we cannot assume that Marsha's mother's opinion is of so little importance to her as to be considered irrelevant.

20. The answer is E. The statement is irrelevant. We are told that Marsha's income has doubled but we are not told why. The phrase "six months after the interview" can be misleading in that it leads us to assume that the increase and the interview are related. Her income could have doubled because she regained her popularity but it could also have come from stocks or some other business venture. Because we are not given any reason for her income doubling, it would be impossible to say whether or not this statement proves or disproves the conclusion. Choice E is the best choice of the five possible choices. One of the problems with promotional exams is that sometimes you need to select a choice you're not crazy about. In this case, "not having enough information to make a determination" would be the best choice. However, that's not an option, so you're forced to work with what you've got. On these exams it's sometimes like voting for President, you have to pick the "lesser of the two evils" or the least awful choice. In this case, the information is more irrelevant to the conclusion than it is anything else.

21. The answer is D, weakens the conclusion. We've been told that Marsha's agent feels that she should apologize. If he is pleased with her interview, then it would tend to weaken the conclusion but not disprove it. We can't be sure that he hasn't had a change of heart, or that there weren't other parts of the interview he liked so much that they outweighed her unwillingness to apologize.

22. The answer is A. The conclusion states that Marsha will donate $1 to the Cellulite Prevention League for every pound the actress loses. Marsha's sister's financial report on the League's activities directly supports and proves the conclusion.

23. The answer is C, disproves the conclusion. If the magazine receives many letters commending Marsha for her courage in apologizing, this directly contradicts the conclusion, which states that Marsha didn't apologize.

24. The answer is B. It was stated in the passage that two of Marsha's performances were cancelled after the controversy first occurred. The cancellation of another performance immediately after her interview was published would tend to support the conclusion that she refused to apologize. Because we can't be sure, however, that her performance wasn't cancelled for another reason, choice A would be incorrect.

25. The answer is E, as this information is irrelevant. Postponing the article an extra week does not affect Marsha's decision or the public's reaction to it.

26. The answer is C. If 500 new employees are hired to handle the "increased paperwork created by the new tax on videocassettes", this would directly contradict the conclusion, which states that the legislature defeated both bills. (They should all be this easy.)

27. The answer is B. The results of the study would support the conclusion. If implementing the legislation was going to be so costly, it is likely that the legislature would vote against it. Choice A is not the answer, however, because we can't be sure that the legislature didn't pass it anyway.

28. The answer is E. It's irrelevant to the conclusion that 80% of all those working in the entertainment industry own videocassette recorders. Sometimes if you're not sure about these, it can help a lot to try and visualize the situation. Why would someone voting on this legislation care about this fact? It doesn't seem to be the kind of information that would make any difference or impact upon the conclusion.

29. The answer is B. The head of the law enforcement agency's statement that the legislation would be unenforceable would support the conclusion. It's possible that many legislators would question why they should bother to pass legislation that would be impossible to enforce. Choice A would be incorrect however, because we can't be sure that the legislation wasn't passed in spite of his statement.

30. The answer is D. This would tend to weaken the conclusion because the prospect of several large companies going bankrupt would seem to be a good argument in favor of the legislation. The possible loss of jobs and businesses would be a good reason for some people to vote for the legislation. We can't be sure, however, that this would be a compelling enough reason to ensure passage of the legislation so choice C is incorrect.

This concludes our section on the "Validity of Conclusion" type of questions.

We hope these weren't too horrible for you. It's important to keep in mind _exactly_ what you've been given and _exactly_ what they want you to do with it. It's also necessary to remember that you may have to choose between two possible answers. In that case you must choose the one that seems the best. Sometimes you may think there is no good answer. You will probably be right but you can't let that upset you. Just choose the one you dislike the least.

We want to repeat that it is unlikely that this exact format will appear on the exam. The skills required to answer these questions, however, are the same as those you'll need for the exam so we suggest that you review this section before taking the actual exam.

31. The answer is C. This next set of questions requires you to "switch gears" slightly, and get used to different formats. In this type of question, you have to decide whether the conclusion is proved by the facts given, disproved by the facts given, or neither because not enough information has been provided. Fortunately, unlike the previous questions, you don't have to decide whether particular facts support or don't support the conclusion. This type of question is more straight forward, but the reasoning behind it is the same. We are told that the Bills have won two games less than the Patriots, and that the Patriots are in first place and the Bills are in second place. We are also told that there are two games left to play, and that they won't play each other again. The conclusion states that the Bills won the division. Is there anything in the four statements that would prove this? We have no idea what the outcome of the last two games of the season was. The

Bills and Patriots could have ended up tied at the end of the season, or the Bills could have lost both or one of their last games while the Patriots did the same. There might even be another team tied for first or second place with the Bills or Patriots. Since we don't know for sure, Choice A is incorrect. Choice B is trickier. It might seem at first glance that the best the Bills could do would be to tie the Patriots if the Patriots lost their last two games and the Bills won their last two games. But it would be too much to assume that there is no procedure for a tiebreaker that wouldn't give the Bills the division championship. Since we don't know what the rules are in the event of a tie (for example, what if a tie was decided on the results of what happened when the two teams had played each other, or on the best record in the division, or on most points scored?), we can't say for sure that it would be impossible for the Bills to win their division. For this reason, choice C is the answer, as we don't have enough information to prove or disprove the conclusion. This question looked more difficult than it actually was. It's important to disregard any factors outside of the actual question, and to focus only on what you've been given. In this case, as on all of these types of questions, what you know or don't know about a subject is actually irrelevant. It's best to concentrate only on the actual facts given.

32.   The answer is A. The conclusion is proved by the facts given.

In this type of problem it is usually best to pull as many facts as possible from the sentences and then put them into a simpler form. The phrasing and the order of exam questions are designed to be confusing so you need to restate things as clearly as possible by eliminating the extras.

Sentence 1 tells us that there are only two possible colors for eyes and two for hair. Looking at the other sentences we learn that eyes are either green or gold and that hair is either silver or purple. If half the beings with purple hair have golden eyes then the other half must have green eyes since it is the only other eye color. Likewise, if one-third of those with silver hair have green eyes the other two-thirds must have golden eyes.

This information makes it clear that there are more golden-eyed beings on Zeinon than green-eyed ones. It doesn't matter that we don't know exactly how many are actually living on the planet. The number of those with gold eyes (1/2 plus 2/3) will always be greater than the number of those with green eyes (1/2 plus 1/3), no matter what the actual figures might be. Sentence 3 is totally irrelevant because even if there were more silver-haired inhabitants it would not affect the conclusion.

33.   The answer is C. The conclusion is neither proved nor disproved by the facts because we don't know how many miles Bethany is from Amoranth.

With this type of question, if you're not sure how to approach it you can always substitute in a range of "real numbers" to see what the result would be. If they were 200 miles apart Joe's Truck Rental would be cheaper because they would charge a total of $160 while National Movers would charge $175.

Joe's - $100 plus .30 x 200 (or $60) = $160
National - $150 plus .25 x 100 (or $25) = $175

If the towns were 600 miles apart, however, National Movers would be cheaper. The cost of renting from National would be $275 compared to the $280 charged by Joe's Trucking.

Joe's - $100 plus .30 x 600 (or $180) = $280
National - $150 plus .25 x 500 (or $125) = $275

34. The answer is B. We've varied the format once more, but the reasoning is similar. This is a tedious question that is more like a math question, but we wanted to give you some practice with this type, just in case. You won't be able to do this question if you've forgotten how to do percents. Many exams require this knowledge, so if you feel you need a review we suggest you read Booklets 1, 2 or 3 in this series.

The only way to attack this problem is to go through each choice until you find the one that is correct. Choice A states that Plainfield, Smallville and Granton are cities. Let's begin with Plainfield. The passage states that in 1960 Plainfield had a population of 12,000, and that it grew 10% between 1960 and 1970, and another 20% between 1970 and 1980. Ten percent of 12,000 is 1200 (12,000 x .10 = 1200). Therefore, the population grew from 12,000 in 1960 to 12,000 + 1200 between 1960 and 1970. At the time of the 1970 Census, Plainfield's population was 13,200. It then grew another 20% between 1970 and 1980, so, 13,200 x .20 = 2640. 13,200 plus the additional increase of 2640 would make the population of Plainfield 15,840. This would qualify it as a city, since its population is over 15,000. Since a change upward in the population of a municipality is re-classified immediately, Plainfield would have become a city right away. So far, statement A is true. The passage states that Smallville's population has not changed significantly in the last twenty years. Since Smallville's population was 20,283, Smallville would still be a city. Granton had a population of 25,000 (what a coincidence that so many of these places have such nice, even numbers) in 1950. The population has decreased 25% in each ten year period since that time. So from 1950 to 1960 the population decreased 25%. 25,000 x .25 = 6,250. 25,000 minus 6,250 = 18,750. So the population of Granton in 1960 would have been 18,750. (Or you could have saved a step and multiplied 25,000 by .75 to get 18,750.) The population from 1960 to 1970 decreased an additional 25%. So: 18,750 x .25 = 4687.50. 18,750 minus 4687.50 = 14,062.50. Or: 18,750 x .75 = 14,062.50. (Don't let the fact that a half of a person is involved confuse you, these are exam questions, not real life.) From 1970 to 1980 the population decreased an additional 25%. This would mean that Granton's population was below 15,000 for more than ten years, so it's status as a city would have changed to that of a town, which would make choice A incorrect, since it states that Granton is a city.

Choice B states that Smallville is a city and Granton is a town which we know to be true from the information above. Choice B is correct so far. We next need to determine if Ellenville is a village. Ellenville had a population of 4,283 in 1950, and increased 5% in each ten year period since 1950. 4,283 x .05 = 214.15. 4,283 plus 214.15 = 4,497.15, so Ellenville's population from 1950 to 1960 increased to 4,497.15. (Or: 4,283 x 1.05 - 4,497.15.) From 1960 to 1970 Ellenville's population increased another 5%: 4,497.15 x .05 = 224.86. 4,497.15 plus 224.86 = 4,772.01 (or: 4,497.15 x 1.05 = 4,722.01.) From 1970 to 1980, Ellenville's population increased another 5%: 4,722.01 x .05 = 236.1. 4722.01 plus 236.10 = 4958.11. (Or: 4,722.01 x 1.05 = 4958.11.).

Ellenville's population is still under 5,000 in 1980 so it would continue to be classified as a village. Since all three statements in choice B are true, Choice B must be the answer. However, we'll go through the other choices. Choice C states that Springdale is a town. The passage tells us that the population of Springdale doubled from 1960 to 1970, and increased

25% from 1970 to 1980. It doesn't give us any actual population figures, however, so it's impossible to know what the population of Springdale is, making Choice C incorrect. Choice C also states that Granton is a town, which is true, and that Ellenville is a town, which is false (from Choice B we know it's a village). Choice D states that Plainfield and Smallville are cities, which is information we already know is true, and that Ellenville is a town. Since Ellenville is a village, Choice D is also incorrect.

This was a lot of work for just one question and we doubt you'll get one like this on this section of the exam, but we included it just in case. On an exam, you can always put a check mark next to a question like this and come back to it later, if you feel you're pressed for time and could spend your time more productively on other, less time consuming problems.

35. The answer is B. This question requires very careful reading. It's best to break the conclusion down into smaller parts in order to solve the problem. The first half of the conclusion states that the average person in the 20-29 age group (Group A) drinks less tea daily than the average person in the 40-50 age group (Group C). The average person in Group A drinks 2.1 cups of tea daily, while the average person in Group C drinks 2.6 cups of tea daily. Since 2.1 is less than 2.6, the conclusion is correct so far. The second half of the conclusion states that the average person in Group A drinks more coffee daily than the average person in the 30-39 age group (Group B) drinks cola. The average person in Group A drinks 1.8 cups of coffee daily while the average person in Group B drinks 1.9 glasses of cola. This disproves the conclusion, which states that the average person in Group A drinks more coffee daily than the average person in Group B drinks cola.

36. The answer is C. The easiest way to approach a problem that deals with the relationship between a number of different people or things is to set up a diagram. This type of problem is usually too confusing to do in your head. For this particular problem the "diagram" could be a line, one end of which would be labelled tall and the other end labelled short. Then, taking one sentence at a time, place the people on the line to see where they fall in relation to one another.

The diagram of the first sentence would look like this:

```
Tall _____Dale_____Mary_____Jane_____Short
(left)                                       (right)
```

Mary is taller than Jane but shorter than Dale so she would fall somewhere between the two of them. We have placed tall on the left and labelled it left just to make the explanation easier. You could just as easily have reversed the position.

The second sentence places Fred somewhere to the left of Mary because he is taller than she is. Steven would be to the left of Fred for the same reason. At this point we don't know whether Steven and Fred are taller or shorter than Dale. The new diagram would look like this:

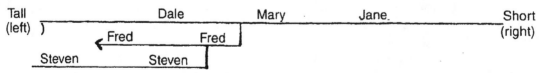

The third stentence introduces Elizabeth, presenting a new problem. Elizabeth can be anywhere to the right of Dale. Don't make the mistake of assuming she falls between Dale and Mary. At this point we don't know where she fits in relation to Mary, Jane, or even Fred.

We do get information about Steven, however. He is taller than Dale so he would be to the left of Dale. Since he is also taller than Fred (see sentence two) we know that Steven is the tallest person thus far. The diagram would now look like this:

| Tall (left) | | Dale | Mary | Jane. | | Short (right) |

Fred ← Fred

Steven Steven

Fred's height is somewhere between Steven and Mary, Elizabeth's anywhere between Dale and the end of the line.

The fourth sentence tells us where Elizabeth stands, in relation to Fred and the others in the problem. The fact that she is taller than Mary means she is also taller than Jane. The final diagram would look like this:

| Tall (left) | Steven | Dale | Elizabeth | Mary | Jane | Short (right) |

Fred

We still don't know whether Dale or Fred is taller, however. Therefore, the conclusion that Dale is taller than Fred can't be proved. It also can't be disproved because we don't know for sure that he isn't. The answer has to be Choice C, as the conclusion can't be proved or disproved.

37. The answer is A. This is another problem that is easiest for most people if they make a diagram. Sentence 1 states that Main Street is between Spring Street and Glenn Blvd. At this point we don't know if they are next to each other or if they are separated by a number of streets. Therefore, you should leave space between streets as you plot your first diagram.

The order of the streets could go either:

Spring St.	or	Glenn Blvd.
Main St.		Main St.
Glenn Blvd.		Spring St.

Sentence 2 states that Hawley Street is one block south of Spring Street and 3 blocks north of Main Street. Because most people think in terms of north as above and south as below and because it was stated that Hawley is one block south of Spring Street and three blocks north of Main Street, the next diagram could look like this:

Spring
Hawley

———

———

Main
Glenn

The third sentence states that Glenn Street is five blocks south of Elm and four blocks south of Main. It could look like this:

41

Spring
Hawley
_____
Elm
Main
_____
_____
_____
Glenn

The conclusion states that Elm Street is between Hawley Avenue and Glenn Blvd. From the above diagram we can see that this is the case.

38. The answer is B. For most people the best way to do this problem is to draw a diagram, plotting the course of both trains. Sentence 1 states that train A leaves Hampshire at 5:50 a.m. and reaches New London at 6:42. Your first diagram might look like this:

38.____

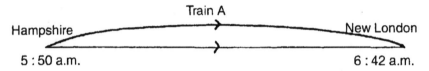

Sentence 2 states that the train leaves New London at 7:00 a.m. and arrives in Kellogsville at 8:42 a.m. The diagram might now look like this:

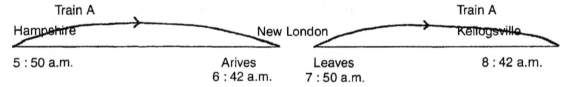

Sentence 3 gives us the rest of the information that must be included in the diagram. It introduces Train B, which moves in the opposite direction, leaving Kellogsville at 8:00 a.m. and arriving at Hampshire at 10:42 a.m. The final diagram might look like this:

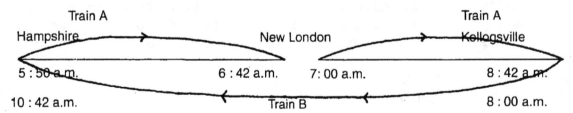

As you can see from the diagram, the routes of the two trains will overlap somewhere between Kellogsville and New London. If you read sentence 4 quickly and assumed that that was the section with only one track, you probably would have assumed that there would have had to be a collision. Sentence 4 states, however, that there is only one rail-road track between New London and Hampshire. That is the only section, then, where the two trains could collide. By the time Train B gets to that section, however, Train A will have passed it. The two trains will pass each other somewhere between New London and Kellogsville, not New London and Hampshire.

EVALUATING INFORMATION AND EVIDENCE
EXAMINATION SECTION
TEST 1

DIRECTIONS: Each question or incomplete statement is followed by several suggested answers or completions. Select the one that BEST answers the question or completes the statement. *PRINT THE LETTER OF THE CORRECT ANSWER IN THE SPACE AT THE RIGHT.*

Questions 1 -9

Questions 1 through 9 measure your ability to (1) determine whether statements from witnesses say essentially the same thing and (2) determine the evidence needed to make it reasonably certain that a particular conclusion is true.

1. Which of the following pairs of statements say essentially the same thing in two different ways?
    I. All Hoxie steelworkers are at least six feet tall. No steelworker is less than six feet tall.
    II. Some neutered pit bulls are not dangerous dogs. Some dangerous dogs are neutered pit bulls.

   A. I only
   B. I and II
   C. II only
   D. Neither I nor II

1.____

2. Which of the following pairs of statements say essentially the same thing in two different ways?
    I. If we are in training today, it is definitely Wednesday. Every Wednesday there is training.
    II. You may go out tonight only after you clean your room. If you clean your room, you may go out tonight.

   A. I only
   B. I and II
   C. II only
   D. Neither I nor II

2.____

3. Which of the following pairs of statements say essentially the same thing in two different ways?
    I. The case will be dismissed if either the defendant pleads guilty and agrees to perform community service, or the defendant pleads guilty and makes a full apology to the victim.
The case will be dismissed if the defendant pleads guilty and either agrees to perform community service or makes a full apology to the victim.
    II. Long books are fun to read.
Books that aren't fun to read aren't long.

   A. I only
   B. I and II
   C. II only
   D. Neither I nor II

3.____

4. Which of the following pairs of statements say essentially the same thing in two different ways?   4.____

    I.   If you live in a mansion, you have a big heating bill. If you do not have a big heating bill, you do not live in a mansion.
    II. Some clerks can both type and read shorthand. Some clerks can neither type nor read shorthand.

    A. I only
    B. I and II
    C. II only
    D. Neither I nor II

5. Summary of Evidence Collected to Date: 5.____

    I.   Three students - Bob, Mary and Stan - each received a grade of A, C and F on the civil service exam.
    II. Stan did not receive an F on the exam.

    Prematurely Drawn Conclusion: Stan received an A.
    Which of the following pieces of evidence, if any, would make it *reasonably certain* that the conclusion drawn is true?

    A. Bob received an F
    B. Mary received a C
    C. Bob did not receive an A
    D. None of these

6. Summary of Evidence Collected to Date: 6.____

    I.   At Walco, all the employees who work the morning shift work the evening shift as well.
    II. Some Walco employees who work the evening shift also work the afternoon shift.

    Prematurely Drawn Conclusion: If Ron, a Walco employee, works the morning shift, he does not work the afternoon shift.
    Which of the following pieces of evidence, if any, would make it *reasonably certain* that the conclusion drawn is true?

    A. Ron works only two shifts
    B. Ron works the evening shift
    C. All Walco employees work at least one shift
    D. None of these

7. Summary of Evidence Collected to Date: 7.____

    All the family counselors at the agency have an MTF certification and an advanced degree.

    Prematurely Drawn Conclusion: Any employee of the agency who has an advanced degree is a family counselor.

    Which of the following pieces of evidence, if any, would make it *reasonably certain* that the conclusion drawn is true?

A. Nobody at the agency who has an advanced degree is employed as anything other than a family counselor
B. Everyone who has an MTF certification is a family counselor
C. Each person at the agency who has an MTF certification also has an advanced degree
D. None of these

8. <u>Summary of Evidence Collected to Date:</u>   8.____
Margery, a worker at the elder agency, is working on recreational programs.
<u>Prematurely Drawn Conclusion:</u> Margery is not working on cases of elder abuse.
Which of the following pieces of evidence, if any, would make it *reasonably certain* that the conclusion drawn is true?

A. Elder abuse and recreational programs are unrelated fields
B. Nobody at the elder agency who works on cases of elder abuse works on recreation programs
C. Nobody at the elder agency who works on recreational programs works on cases of elder abuse
D. None of these

9. <u>Summary of Evidence Collected to Date:</u>   9.____
   I. St. Leo's Cathedral is not as tall as the FarCorp building.
   II. The FarCorp building and the Hyatt Uptown are the same height.
<u>Prematurely Drawn Conclusion:</u> The FarCorp building is not in Springfield.
Which of the following pieces of evidence, if any, would make it *reasonably certain* that the conclusion drawn is true?

A. No buildings in Springfield are as tall as the Hyatt Uptown
B. The Hyatt Uptown is not in Springfield
C. St. Leo's Cathedral is the oldest building in Springfield
D. None of these

Questions 10-14

Questions 10 through 14 refer to Map #1 and measure your ability to orient yourself within a given section of town, neighborhood or particular area. Each of the questions describes a starting point and a destination. Assume that you are driving a car in the area shown on the map accompanying the questions. Use the map as a basis for the shortest way to get from one point to another without breaking the law.

On the map, a street marked by arrows, or by arrows and the words "One Way," indicates one-way travel, and should be assumed to be one-way for the entire length, even when there are breaks or jogs in the street.

45

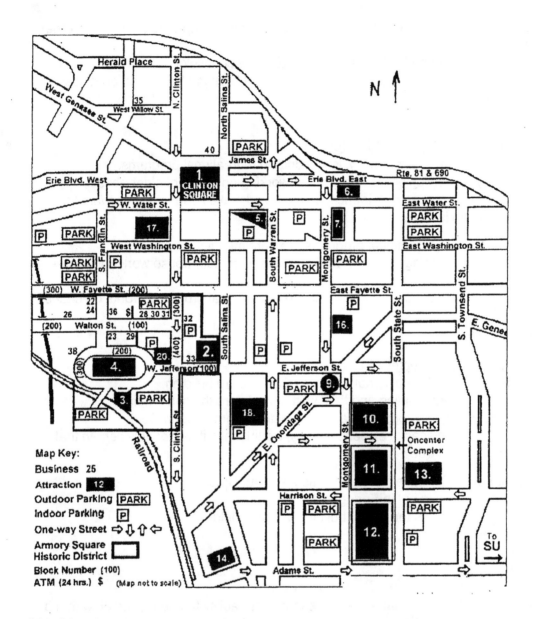

Map#1

1. Clinton Square
2. Landmark Theatre
3. OnTrack Commuter Rail Service
4. Museum of Science and Technology
5. Hanover Square
6. Erie Canal Museum
7. City Hall
9. Columbus Circle

10. Mulroy Civic Center Theaters
11. War Memorial
12. Convention Center
13. Everson Museum of Art
14. Convention and Visitors Bureau
16. Onondaga Historical Association
17. Federal Plaza
18. Galleries of Syracuse

10. The shortest legal way from Columbus Circle to Federal Plaza is   10.____

    A. west on Jefferson St., north on Salina St., west on Water St.
    B. east on Jefferson St., north on State St., west on Washington St.
    C. north on Montgomery St., west on Washington St.
    D. south on Montgomery St., west on Harrison St., north on Salina St., west on Washington St.

11. The shortest legal way from Clinton Square to the Museum of Science and Technology is   11.____

    A. south on Clinton St., west on Fayette St., south on Franklin St.
    B. west on Erie Blvd., south on Franklin St.
    C. south on Clinton St., west on Water St., south on Franklin St.
    D. south on Clinton St., west on Jefferson St.

12. The shortest legal way from Hanover Square to Landmark Theatre is   12.____

    A. west on Water St., south on Salina St.
    B. east on Water St., south on Montgomery St., west on Fayette St., south on Salina St.
    C. east on Water St., south on Montgomery St., west on Fayette St., south on Clinton St., east on Jefferson St.
    D. south on Warren St., west on Jefferson St.

13. The shortest legal way from the Convention Center to the Erie Canal Museum is   13.____

    A. north on State St., west on Washington St., north on Montgomery St.
    B. north on Montgomery St., jog west on Jefferson St., north on Montgomery St.
    C. north on State St., west on Fayette St., north on Warren St., east on Water St.
    D. north on State St., west on Water St.

14. The shortest legal way from City Hall to Clinton Square is   14.____

    A. west on Washington St., north on Salina St.
    B. south on Montgomery St., west on Fayette St., north on Salina St.
    C. north on Montgomery St., west on Erie Blvd.
    D. west on Water St.

Questions 15-19

Questions 15 through 19 refer to Figure #1, on the following page, and measure your ability to understand written descriptions of events. Each question presents a description of an accident or event and asks you which of the five drawings in Figure #1 BEST represents it.

In the drawings, the following symbols are used:

Moving vehicle: 　　　　⌂　　　　　Non-moving vehicle: 　　　　▲

Pedestrian or bicycle: 　　　　●

The path and direction of travel of a vehicle or pedestrian is indicated by a solid line.

The path and direction of travel of each vehicle or pedestrian directly involved in a collision from the point of impact is indicated by a dotted line.

In the space at the right, print the letter of the drawing that best fits the descriptions written below:

15. A driver heading north on Elm sideswipes a parked car, veers into the oncoming lane and travels through the intersection of Elm and Main. He then sideswipes an oncoming car, veers back into the northbound lane and flees.　　　15.＿＿＿

16. A driver heading south on Elm sideswipes a car parked in the southbound lane, then loses control and veers through the intersection of Elm and Main. The driver then collides with the rear of another parked car, which is knocked forward after the impact.　　　16.＿＿＿

17. A driver heading north on Elm strikes the rear of a parked car, which is knocked through the intersection of Elm and Main and strikes a parked car in the southbound lane head-on.　　　17.＿＿＿

18. A driver heading north on Elm strikes the rear of a car that is stopped at a traffic light. The car at the light is knocked through the intersection of Elm and Main and strikes a parked car in the rear.　　　18.＿＿＿

19. A driver heading south on Elm loses control and crosses into the other lane of traffic, where he sideswipes a car parked in the northbound lane, then veers back into the southbound lane, travels through the intersection of Elm and Main and collides with the rear end of a parked car.　　　19.＿＿＿

FIGURE #1

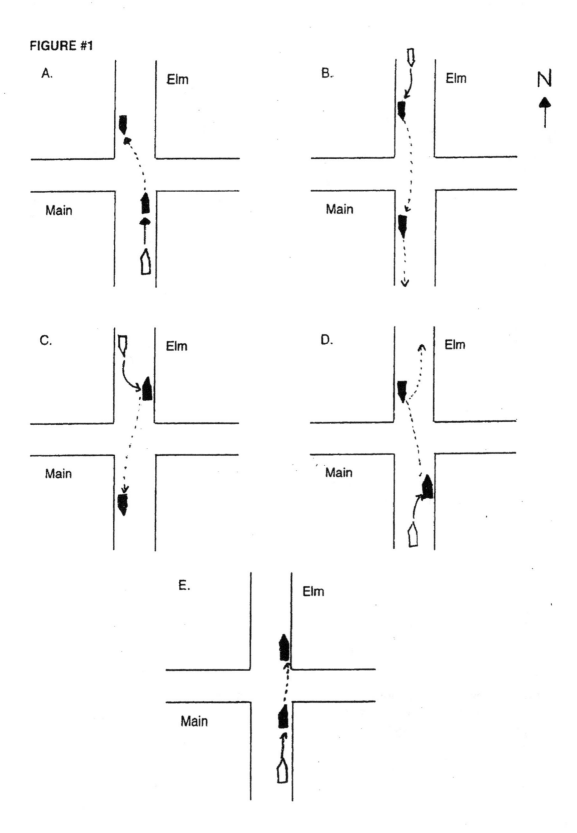

Questions 20-22

In questions 20 through 22, choose the word or phrase CLOSEST in meaning to the word or phrase printed in capital letters.

20. REDRESS   20.____

    A. suspend
    B. repeat
    C. compensate
    D. subdue

21. PRECEDENT   21.____

    A. cohort
    B. example
    C. obstruction
    D. elder

22. ADJUDICATION   22.____

    A. case
    B. judgment
    C. claim
    D. defendant

Questions 23-25

Questions 23 through 25 measure your ability to do fieldwork-related arithmetic. Each question presents a separate arithmetic problem for you to solve.

23. The Department of Sanitation purchased seven vehicles in the last year. Four of the vehi-   23.____
cles were street sweepers that cost $95,000 each. Three were garbage compactors that
cost $160,000 each. The average price of a vehicle purchased by the Department in the
last year was about

    A. $98,000
    B. $108,000
    C. $122,000
    D. $145,000

24. Agent Frederick, whose car gets about 24 miles to the gallon, drives to Buffalo, 260 miles   24.____
away. The average price of gasoline is $2.30 a gallon. How much did Agent Frederick
spend on gas for the trip to Buffalo?

    A. $11   B. $25   C. $55   D. $113

25. Over the last four days, Precinct 11 has had 20 misdemeanor arrests each day. If the   25.____
precinct records 15 misdemeanor arrests on the fifth day, what will its average daily number of misdemeanor arrests be?

    A. 16   B. 17   C. 18   D. 19

KEY (CORRECT ANSWERS)

1.	D		11.	A
2.	C		12.	B
3.	A		13.	C
4.	A		14.	A
5.	B		15.	D
6.	A		16.	B
7.	A		17.	A
8.	C		18.	E
9.	A		19.	C
10.	B		20.	C

21.	B
22.	B
23.	C
24.	B
25.	D

TEST 2

DIRECTIONS: Each question or incomplete statement is followed by several suggested answers or completions. Select the one that BEST answers the question or completes the statement. *PRINT THE LETTER OF THE CORRECT ANSWER IN THE SPACE AT THE RIGHT.*

Questions 1-9

Questions 1 through 9 measure your ability to (1) determine whether statements from witnesses say essentially the same thing and (2) determine the evidence needed to make it reasonably certain that a particular conclusion is true.

To do well on this part of the test, you do NOT have to have a working knowledge of police procedures and techniques. Nor do you have to have any more familiarity with criminals and criminal behavior than that acquired from reading newspapers, listening to radio or watching TV. To do well in this part, you must read and reason carefully.

1. Which of the following pairs of statements say essentially the same thing in two different ways?   1.____

     I. All of the teachers at the school are wise, but some have proven to be bad-tempered.
       Teachers at the school are either wise or bad-tempered.
     II. If John can both type and do long division, he is qualified for this job.
       If John applies for this job, he can both type and do long division.

    A. I only
    B. I and II
    C. II only
    D. Neither I nor II

2. Which of the following pairs of statements say essentially the same thing in two different ways?   2.____

     I. If Carl rides the A train, the C train is down.
       Carl doesn't ride the A train unless the C train is down.
     II. If the three sides of a triangle are equal, the triangle is equilateral.
       A triangle is equilateral if the three sides are equal.

    A. I only
    B. I and II
    C. II only
    D. Neither I nor II

3. Which of the following pairs of statements say essentially the same thing in two different ways?   3.____

     I. If this dog has a red collar, it must be Slim.
       If this dog does not have a red collar, it can't be Slim.
     II. Dr. Slouka is not in his office during lunchtime.
       If it's not lunchtime, Dr. Slouka is in his office.

    A. I only
    B. I and II
    C. II only
    D. Neither I nor II

4. Which of the following pairs of statements say essentially the same thing in two different ways?   4.____

       I.   At least one caseworker at Social Services has a degree in psychology.
           Not all the caseworkers at Social Services have a degree in psychology.
      II.   If an officer doesn't pass the physical fitness test, he cannot be promoted.
           If an officer is not promoted, he hasn't passed the physical fitness test.

    A.   I only   B.   I and II
    C.   II only   D.   Neither I nor II

5. Summary of Evidence Collected to Date: 5.____

       I.   All the Class II inspectors use multiplication when they inspect escalators.
      II.   On some days, Fred, a Class II inspector, doesn't use multiplication at all.
     III.   Fred's friend, Garth, uses multiplication every day.

Prematurely Drawn Conclusion: Garth inspects escalators every day.

Which of the following pieces of evidence, if any, would make it *reasonably certain* that the conclusion drawn is true?

    A.   Garth is a Class II inspector
    B.   Fred never inspects escalators
    C.   Fred usually doesn't inspect escalators
    D.   None of these

6. Summary of Evidence Collected to Date: 6.____

       I.   Every one of the shelter's male pit bulls has been neutered.
      II.   Some male pit bulls have also been muzzled.

Prematurely Drawn Conclusion: Rex has been neutered.

Which of the following pieces of evidence, if any, would make it *reasonably certain* that the conclusion drawn is true?

    A.   Rex, a pit bull at the shelter, has been muzzled
    B.   All of the pit bulls at the shelter are males
    C.   Rex is one of the shelter's male pit bulls
    D.   None of these

7. Summary of Evidence Collected to Date: 7.____

       I.   Some of the social workers at the clinic have been welfare recipients.
      II.   Some of the social workers at the clinic are college graduates.

Prematurely Drawn Conclusion: Some of the social workers at the clinic who are college graduates have never received welfare benefits.

Which of the following pieces of evidence, if any, would make it *reasonably certain* that the conclusion drawn is true?

    A.   There are more college graduates at the clinic than those who have received welfare benefits
    B.   There is an odd number of social workers at the clinic
    C.   The number of college graduates and former welfare recipients at the clinic is the same
    D.   None of these

8. <u>Summary of Evidence Collected to Date:</u>   8._____
   Everyone who works at the library has read *War and Peace*. Most people who have read *War and Peace* have also read *Anna Karenina*.
   <u>Prematurely Drawn Conclusion:</u> Marco has read *War and Peace*.
   Which of the following pieces of evidence, if any, would make it *reasonably certain* that the conclusion drawn is true?

   A. Marco works at the library
   B. Marco has probably read *Anna Karenina*
   C. Everyone who has read *Anna Karenina* has read *War and Peace*
   D. None of these

9. <u>Summary of Evidence Collected to Date:</u>   9._____
   Officer Skiles is working on the Martin investigation.
   <u>Prematurely Drawn Conclusion:</u> Skiles is also working on the Bartlett case.
   Which of the following pieces of evidence, if any, would make it *reasonably certain* that the conclusion drawn is true?

   A. Everyone who is working on the Martin investigation is also working on the Bartlett investigation
   B. Everyone who is working on the Bartlett investigation is also working on the Martin investigation
   C. The Martin investigation and Bartlett investigation are being conducted at the same time
   D. None of these

Questions 10-14

Questions 10 through 14 refer to Map #2 and measure your ability to orient yourself within a given section of town, neighborhood or particular area. Each of the questions describes a starting point and a destination. Assume that you are driving a car in the area shown on the map accompanying the questions. Use the map as a basis for the shortest way to get from one point to another without breaking the law.

On the map, a street marked by arrows, or by arrows and the words "One Way," indicates one-way travel, and should be assumed to be one-way for the entire length, even when there are breaks or jogs in the street. EXCEPTION: A street that does not have the same name over the full length.

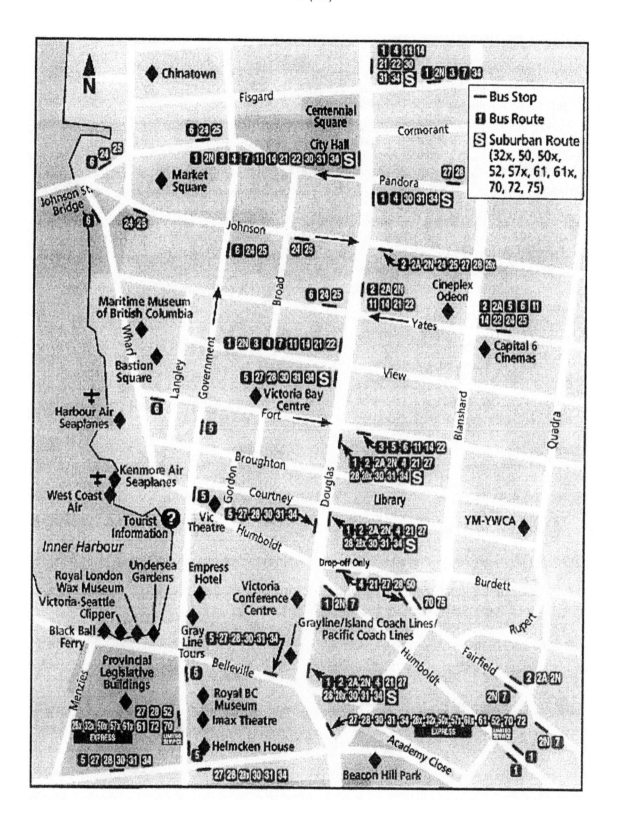

Map #2

10. The shortest legal way from the Royal London Wax Museum to the Chinatown block is   10.____

    A. east on Belleville, north on Douglas, west on Broughton, north on Government
    B. east on Belleville, north on Government
    C. east on Belleville, north on Government, west on Yates, north on Wharf
    D. east on Belleville, north on Douglas, west on Fisgard

11. The shortest legal way from the Maritime Museum of British Columbia to the Victoria   11.____
Conference Centre is

    A. north on Wharf, east on Yates, south on Douglas
    B. south and west on Wharf, north on Government, east on Broughton, south on Douglas
    C. south on Wharf, east on Fort, south on Douglas
    D. south and west on Wharf, south on Government, east on Belleville, north on Douglas

12. The shortest legal way from Market Square to City Hall is   12.____

    A. north on Government, east on Fisgard, south on Douglas
    B. east on Pandora, north on Douglas
    C. east on Johnson, north on Blanshard, west on Pandora, north on Douglas
    D. east on Johnson, north on Douglas

13. The shortest legal way from the Victoria Bay Centre to Bastion Square is   13.____

    A. east on Fort, south on Douglas, west on Broughton, north on Wharf
    B. west on Fort, north on Government, west on Yates, south on Wharf
    C. west on Fort, north on Wharf
    D. east on Fort, north on Douglas, west on Johnson, south on Wharf

14. The shortest legal way from The Empress Hotel to the YM-YWCA is   14.____

    A. north on Government, east on Broughton
    B. north on Government, east on Courtney
    C. north on Government, southeast on Humboldt, north on Quadra
    D. north on Government, west on Courtney

Questions 15-19

Questions 15 through 19 refer to Figure #2, on the following page, and measure your ability to understand written descriptions of events. Each question presents a description of an accident or event and asks you which of the five drawings in Figure #2 BEST represents it.

In the drawings, the following symbols are used:

Moving vehicle: ⬠   Non-moving vehicle: ▲

Pedestrian or bicycle: ●

The path and direction of travel of a vehicle or pedestrian is indicated by a solid line.

The path and direction of travel of each vehicle or pedestrian directly involved in a collision from the point of impact is indicated by a dotted line.

In the space at the right, print the letter of the drawing that best fits the descriptions written below:

15. A driver traveling north on Taylor strikes a parked car in the rear and knocks it forward, where it collides with a pedestrian in the crosswalk.   15.____

16. A driver headed south on Taylor strikes another car that is traveling east through the intersection of Taylor and Hayes. After the impact, the eastbound car veers to the right and strikes a pedestrian in the crosswalk on Jones.   16.____

17. A driver headed south on Taylor runs a red light and strikes another car that is headed east on Hayes. The eastbound car is knocked into a pedestrian that is using the crosswalk on Taylor   17.____

18. A driver traveling south on Taylor makes a sudden left turn onto Hayes. In the intersection, he strikes the front of an oncoming car and veers onto Hayes, where he strikes a pedestrian in the crosswalk.   18.____

19. A driver headed west on Hayes strikes a car that is traveling east through the intersection of Taylor and Hayes. After the impact, the eastbound car veers to the right and strikes a pedestrian in the crosswalk on Jones.   19.____

FIGURE #2

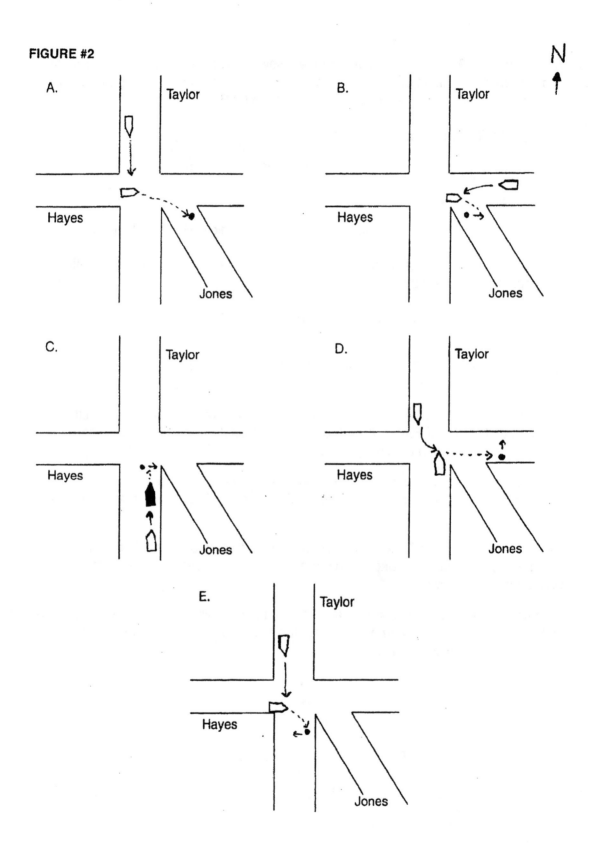

Questions 20-22

In questions 20 through 22, choose the word or phrase CLOSEST in meaning to the word or phrase printed in capital letters.

20. SEQUESTER   20._____

    A. follow
    B. separate
    C. endorse
    D. punish

21. EXECUTE   21._____

    A. carry out
    B. advance
    C. impede
    D. occur

22. SUPPRESS   22._____

    A. uphold
    B. convict
    C. forbid
    D. compensate

Questions 23-25

Questions 23 through 25 measure your ability to do fieldwork-related arithmetic. Each question presents a separate arithmetic problem for you to solve..

23. In the election for the presidency of Local Union 1134, Stan Fitz received 542 votes, Eliz-   23._____
abeth Stuckey received 430 votes and Gene Sterner received 130 votes. Ninety percent of those eligible to vote did so. What was the number of eligible voters?

    A. 900
    B. 992
    C. 1102
    D. 1224

24. The Department of Records wants to sort its files alphabetically into boxes that hold an   24._____
average of 50 files each. The Department has 1,140 records, an amount that is expected to double in the next ten years. To have enough boxes ten years from now, the Department should buy at least _____ boxes.

    A. 23   B. 38   C. 45   D. 47

25. The office's petty cash fund contains a total of $433 on Wednesday. At the beginning of   25._____
the day, Arnold reimburses $270 that he had previously borrowed from the fund. Then Janet withdraws $158 for office supplies; Hank spends $87 on lunch for a committee meeting; and at the end of the day, Ernestine buys a new office calendar for $12. How much remains in the petty cash fund at the end of the day on Wednesday?

    A. $94   B. $257   C. $446   D. $527

_____

KEY (CORRECT ANSWERS)

1.	D		11.	C
2.	B		12.	D
3.	A		13.	A
4.	D		14.	B
5.	A		15.	C
6.	C		16.	A
7.	D		17.	E
8.	A		18.	D
9.	A		19.	B
10.	B		20.	B

21.	A
22.	C
23.	D
24.	D
25.	C

EVALUATING INFORMATION AND EVIDENCE

EXAMINATION SECTION

TEST 1

DIRECTIONS: Each question or incomplete statement is followed by several suggested answers or completions. Select the one that BEST answers the question or completes the statement. *PRINT THE LETTER OF THE CORRECT ANSWER IN THE SPACE AT THE RIGHT.*

Questions 1-9

Questions 1 through 9 measure your ability to (1) determine whether statements say essentially the same thing and (2) determine the evidence needed to make it reasonably certain that a particular conclusion is true.

1. Which of the following pairs of statements say essentially the same thing in two different ways?

    I. Some employees at the water department have fully vested pensions. At least one employee at the water department has a pension that is not fully vested.
    II. All swans are white birds. A bird that is not white is not a swan.

    A. I only
    B. I and II
    C. II only
    D. Neither I nor II

1. _____

2. Which of the following pairs of statements say essentially the same thing in two different ways?

    I. If you live in Humboldt County, your property taxes are high. If your property taxes are high, you live in Humboldt County.
    II. All the Hutchinsons live in Lindsborg. At least some Hutchinsons do not live in Lindsborg.

    A. I only
    B. I and II
    C. II only
    D. Neither I nor II

2. _____

3. Which of the following pairs of statements say essentially the same thing   3._____
in two different ways?

   I.   Although Spike is a friendly dog, he is also one of the most unpopular
   dogs on the block.
        Although Spike is one of the most unpopular dogs on the block, he is
   a friendly dog.
   II. Everyone in Precinct 19 is taller than Officer Banks.
        Nobody in Precinct 19 is shorter than Officer Banks.

      A. I only
      B. I and II
      C. II only
      D. Neither I nor II

4. Which of the following pairs of statements say essentially the same thing   4._____
in two different ways?

   I.   On Friday, every officer in Precinct 1 is assigned parking duty or
   crowd control, or both.
        If a Precinct 1 officer has been assigned neither parking duty nor
   crowd control, it is not Friday.
   II. Because the farmer mowed the hay fields today, his house will have
   mice tomorrow.
        Whenever the farmer mows his hay fields, his house has mice the
   next day.

      A. I only
      B. I and II
      C. II only
      D. Neither I nor II

5. <u>Summary of Evidence Collected to Date:</u>   5._____

   I.   Fishing in the Little Pony River is against the law.
   II. Captain Rick caught an 8-inch trout and ate it for dinner.

   <u>Prematurely Drawn Conclusion:</u> Captain Rick broke the law.

   Which of the following pieces of evidence, if any, would make it
   reasonably certain that the conclusion drawn is true?

      A. Captain Rick caught his trout in the Little Pony River
      B. There is no size limit on trout mentioned in the law
      C. A trout is a species of fish
      D. None of these

6. <u>Summary of Evidence Collected to Date:</u>   6._____

    I.   Some of the doctors in the ICU have been sued for malpractice
    II. Some of the doctors in the ICU are pediatricians

<u>Prematurely Drawn Conclusion:</u> Some of the pediatricians in the ICU have never been sued for malpractice

Which of the following pieces of evidence, if any, would make it *reasonably certain* that the conclusion drawn is true?

    A. The number of pediatricians in the ICU is the same as the number of doctors who have been sued for malpractice
    B. The number of pediatricians in the ICU is smaller than the number of doctors who have been sued for malpractice
    C. The number of ICU doctors who have been sued for malpractice is smaller than the number who are pediatricians
    D. None of these

7. <u>Summary of Evidence Collected to Date:</u>   7._____

    I.   Along Paseo Boulevard, there are five convenience stores
    II. EZ-Go is east of Pop-a-Shop
    III. Kwik-E-Mart is west of Bob's Market
    IV. The Nightwatch is between EZ-Go and Kwik-E-Mart

<u>Prematurely Drawn Conclusion:</u> Pop-a-Shop is the westernmost convenience store on Paseo Boulevard

Which of the following pieces of evidence, if any, would make it *reasonably certain* that the conclusion drawn is true?

    A. Bob's Market is the easternmost convenience store on Paseo
    B. Kwik-E-Mart is the second store from the west
    C. The Nightwatch is west of the EZ-Go
    D. None of these

8. <u>Summary of Evidence Collected to Date:</u>   8._____

Stark drove home from work at 70 miles an hour and wasn't breaking the law

<u>Prematurely Drawn Conclusion:</u> Stark was either on an interstate highway or in the state of Montana

Which of the following pieces of evidence, if any, would make it *reasonably certain* that the conclusion drawn is true?

    A. There are no interstate highways in Montana
    B. Montana is the only state that allows a speed of 70 miles an hour on roads other than interstate highways
    C. Most states don't allow speed of 70 miles an hour on state highways
    D. None of these

9. <u>Summary of Evidence Collected to Date:</u>   9._____

    I.   Margaret, owner of *MetroWoman* magazine, signed a contract with each of her salespeople promising an automatic $200 bonus to any employee who sells more than 60 subscriptions in a calendar month
II. Lynn sold 82 subscriptions to *MetroWoman* in the month of December

<u>Prematurely Drawn Conclusion:</u> Lynn received a $200 bonus

Which of the following pieces of evidence, if any, would make it *reasonably certain* that the conclusion drawn is true?

    A. Lynn is a salesperson
    B. Lynn works for Margaret
    C. Margaret offered only $200 regardless of the number of subscriptions sold
    D. None of these

Questions 10-14

Questions 10 through 14 refer to Map #3 and measure your ability to orient yourself within a given section of town, neighborhood or particular area. Each of the questions describes a starting point and a destination. Assume that you are driving a car in the area shown on the map accompanying the questions. Use the map as a basis for the shortest way to get from one point to another without breaking the law.

On the map, a street marked by arrows, or by arrows and the words "One Way," indicates one-way travel, and should be assumed to be one-way for the entire length, even when there are breaks or jogs in the street. EXCEPTION: A street that does not have the same name over the full length.

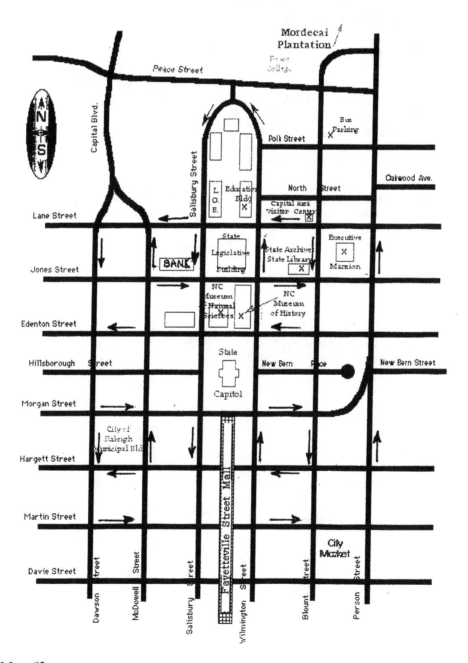

Map #3

10. The shortest legal way from the south end of the Fayetteville Street Mall,   10._____
at Davie Street, to the city of Raleigh Municipal Building is
   A. west on Davie, north on McDowell
   B. west on Davie, north on Dawson
   C. east on Davie, north on Wilmington, west on Morgan
   D. east on Davie, north on Wilmington, west on Hargett

11. The shortest legal way from the City Market to the Education Building is   11._____
   A. north on Blount, west on North
   B. north on Person, west on Lane
   C. north on Blount, west on Lane
   D. west on Martin, north on Wilmington

12. The shortest legal way from the Education Building to the State Capitol is   12._____
   A. south on Wilmington
   B. north on Wilmington, west on Peace, south on Capitol, bear west
      to go south on Dawson, and east on Morgan
   C. west on Lane, south on Salisbury
   D. east on North, south on Blount, west on Edenton

13. The shortest legal way from the State Capitol to Peace College is   13._____
   A. north on Wilmington, jog north, east on Peace
   B. east on Morgan, north on Person, west on Peace
   C. west on Edenton, north on McDowell, north on Capitol Blvd., east
      on Peace
   D. east on Morgan, north on Blount, west on Peace

14. The shortest legal way from the State Legislative Building to the City   14._____
Market is
   A. south on Wilmington, east on Martin
   B. east on Jones, south on Blount
   C. south on Salisbury, east on Davie
   D. east on Lane, south on Blount

Questions 15-19

Questions 15 through 19 refer to Figure #3, on the following page, and measure your ability to understand written descriptions of events. Each question presents a description of an accident or event and asks you which of the five drawings in Figure #3 BEST represents it.

In the drawings, the following symbols are used:

Moving vehicle: ⌂   Non-moving vehicle: ▲

Pedestrian or bicyclist: ●

The path and direction of travel of a vehicle or pedestrian is indicated by a solid line.

The path and direction of travel of each vehicle or pedestrian directly involved in a collision from the point of impact is indicated by a dotted line.

In the space at the right, print the letter of the drawing that best fits the descriptions written below:

15. A driver headed north on Carson veers to the right and strikes a bicyclist who is also heading north. The bicyclist is thrown from the road. The driver flees north on Carson.

15._____

16. A driver heading south on Carson runs the stop sign and barely misses colliding with an eastbound cyclist. The cyclist swerves to avoid the collision and continues traveling east. The driver swerves to avoid the collision and strikes a car parked in the northbound lane on Carson.

16._____

17. A bicyclist heading west on Stone collides with a pedestrian in the crosswalk, then veers through the intersection and collides with the front of a car parked in the southbound lane on Carson.

17._____

18. A driver traveling south on Carson runs over a bicyclist who has run the stop sign, and then flees south on Carson.

18._____

19. A bicyclist heading west on Stone collides with the rear of a car parked in the westbound lane.

19._____

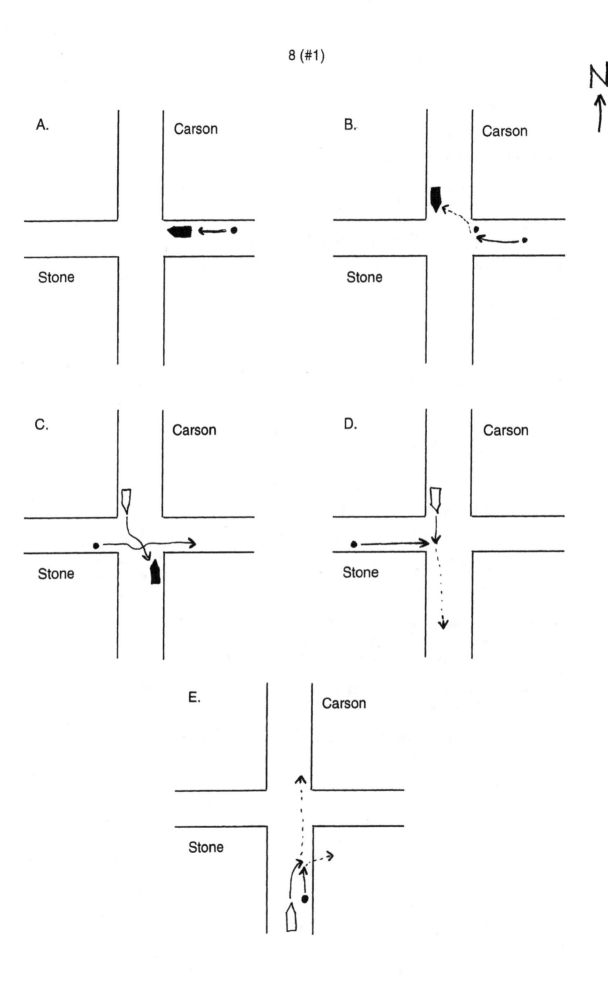

Questions 20-22

In questions 20 through 22, choose the word or phrase CLOSEST in meaning to the word or phrase printed in capital letters.

20. INSOLVENT
    A. bankrupt
    B. vagrant
    C. hazardous
    D. illegal

20._____

21. TENANT
    A. laborer
    B. occupant
    C. owner
    D. creditor

21._____

22. INFRACTION
    A. portion
    B. violation
    C. remark
    D. detour

22._____

Questions 23-25

Questions 23 through 25 measure your ability to do fieldwork-related arithmetic. Each question presents a separate arithmetic problem for you to solve.

23. Officer Jones has served on the police force longer than Smith. Smith has served longer than Moore. Moore has served less time than Jones, and Park has served longer than Jones.
    Which officer has served the longest on the police force?
    A. Jones
    B. Smith
    C. Moore
    D. Park

23._____

24. A car wash has raised the price of an outside-only wash from $4 to $5. The car wash applies the same percentage increase to its inside-and-out wash, which was $10. What is the new cost of the inside-and-out wash?
    A. $8   B. $11   C. $12.50   D. $15

24._____

25. Ron and James, college students, make $10 an hour working at the restaurant. Ron works 13 hours a week and James works 20 hours a week. To make the same amount that Ron earns in a year, James would work about _____ weeks.
    A. 18   B. 27   C. 34   D. 45

25._____

KEY (CORRECT ANSWERS)

1. C	11. B	21. B
2. D	12. C	22. B
3. B	13. A	23. D
4. B	14. B	24. C
5. A	15. E	25. C
6. D	16. C	
7. B	17. B	
8. B	18. D	
9. B	19. A	
10. A	20. A	

SOLUTIONS TO QUESTIONS 1-9

P implies Q = original statement

Not Q implies not P = contrapositive of the original statement. A statement and its contrapositive are logically equivalent.

Q implies P = converse of the original statement.

Not P implies not Q = inverse of the original statement. The converse and inverse of an original statement are logically equivalent.

P implies Q = Not P or Q.

#1. The correct answer is **C**. Item I is wrong because "some employees" means "at least one employee" and possibly "all employees. If it is true that all employees have fully vested pensions, then the second statement is false. Item II is correct because the second statement is the contrapositive of the first statement.

#2. The correct answer is **D**. Item I is wrong because the converse of a statement does not necessarily follow from the original statement. Item II is wrong because statement I implies that there are no Hutchinson family members who live outside Lindsborg.

#3. The correct answer is **B**. Item I is correct because it is composed of the same two compound statements that are simply mentioned in a different order. Item II is correct because if each person is taller than Officer Banks, then there is no person in that precinct who can possibly be shorter than Officer Banks.

#4. The correct answer is **B**. Item I is correct because the second statement is the contrapositive of the first statement. Item II is correct because each statement indicates that mowing the hay fields on a particular day leads to the presence of mice the next day.

#5. The correct answer is **A**. If Captain Rick caught his trout in the Little Pony River, then we can conclude that he was fishing there. Since statement I says that fishing in the Little Pony River is against the law, we conclude that Captain Rick broke the law.

#6. The correct answer is **D**. The number of doctors in each group, whether the same or not, has no bearing on the conclusion. There is nothing in evidence to suggest that the group of doctors sued for malpractice overlaps with the group of doctors that are pediatricians.

#7. The correct answer is **B**. If we are given that Kwik-E-Mart is the second store from the west, then the order of stores, from west to east, is Pop-a - Shop, Kwik- E - Mart, Nightwatch, EZ- GO, and Bob's Market.

#8. The correct answer is **B**. We are given that Stark drove at 70 miles per hour and didn't break the law. If we also know that Montana is the only state that allows a speed of 70 miles per hour, then we can conclude that Stark must have been driving in Montana or else was driving on some interstate.

#9. The correct answer is **B**. The only additional piece of information needed is that Lynn works for Margaret. This will guarantee that Lynn receives the promised $200 bonus.

TEST 2

DIRECTIONS: Each question or incomplete statement is followed by several suggested answers or completions. Select the one that BEST answers the question or completes the statement. *PRINT THE LETTER OF THE CORRECT ANSWER IN THE SPACE AT THE RIGHT.*

<u>Questions 1-9</u>

Questions 1 through 9 measure your ability to (1) determine whether statements say essentially the same thing and (2) determine the evidence needed to make it reasonably certain that a particular conclusion is true.

1. Which of the following pairs of statements say essentially the same thing in two different ways?   1._____

    I.   All of the teachers at Slater Middle School are intelligent, but some are irrational thinkers.
         Although some teachers at Slater Middle School are irrational thinkers, all of them are intelligent.
    II. Nobody has no friends.
         Everybody has at least one friend.

        A. I only
        B. I and II
        C. II only
        D. Neither I nor II

2. Which of the following pairs of statements say essentially the same thing in two different ways?   2._____

    I.   Although bananas taste good to most people, they are also a healthy food.
         Bananas are a healthy food, but most people eat them because they taste good.
    II. If Dr. Jones is in, we should call at the office.
         Either Dr. Jones is in, or we should not call at the office.

        A. I only
        B. I and II
        C. II only
        D. Neither I nor II

3. Which of the following pairs of statements say essentially the same thing   3._____
   in two different ways?

   I. Some millworkers work two shifts.
       If someone works only one shift, he is probably not a millworker.
   II. If a letter carrier clocks in at nine, he can finish his route by the end of
       the day.
       If a letter carrier does not clock in at nine, he cannot finish his route by
       the end of the day.

   A. I only
   B. I and II
   C. II only
   D. Neither I nor II

4. Which of the following pairs of statements say essentially the same thing   4._____
   in two different ways?

   I. If a member of the swim team attends every practice, he will compete
       in the next meet.
       Either a swim team member will compete in the next meet, or he did
       not attend every practice.
   II. All the engineers in the drafting department who wear glasses know
       how to use AutoCAD.
       If an engineer wears glasses he will know how to use AutoCAD.

   A. I only
   B. I and II
   C. II only
   D. Neither I nor II

5. <u>Summary of Evidence Collected to Date:</u>   5._____

   All of the parents who attend the weekly parenting seminars are high
   school graduates.

   <u>Prematurely Drawn Conclusion:</u> Some parents who attend the weekly
   parenting seminars have been convicted of child abuse.

   Which of the following pieces of evidence, if any, would make it
   reasonably certain that the conclusion drawn is true?

   A. Those convicted of child abuse are often high school graduates
   B. Some high school graduates have been convicted of child abuse
   C. There is no correlation between education level and the incidence
      of child abuse
   D. None of these

6. Summary of Evidence Collected to Date: 6._____

I.   Mr. Cantwell promised to vote for new school buses if he was reelected to the board.
II. If the new school buses are approved by the school board, then Mr. Cantwell was not reelected to the board.

Prematurely Drawn Conclusion: Approval of the new school buses was defeated in spite of Mr. Cantwell's vote.

Which of the following pieces of evidence, if any, would make it *reasonably certain* that the conclusion drawn is true?

    A. Mr. Cantwell decided not to run for reelection
    B. Mr. Cantwell was reelected to the board
    C. Mr. Cantwell changed his mind and voted against the new buses
    D. None of these

7. Summary of Evidence Collected to Date: 7._____

I.   The station employs three detectives: Francis, White and Stern. One of the detectives is a lieutenant, one is a sergeant and one is a major.
II. Francis is not a lieutenant.

Prematurely Drawn Conclusion: Jackson is a lieutenant.

Which of the following pieces of evidence, if any, would make it *reasonably certain* that the conclusion drawn is true?

    A. Stern is not a sergeant
    B. Stern is a major
    C. Francis is a major
    D. None of these

8. Summary of Evidence Collected to Date: 8._____

I.   In the office building, every survival kit that contains a gas mask also contains anthrax vaccine.
II. Some of the kits containing water purification tablets also contain anthrax vaccine.

Prematurely Drawn Conclusion: If the survival kit near the typists' pool contains a gas mask, it does not contain water purification tablets.

Which of the following pieces of evidence, if any, would make it *reasonably certain* that the conclusion drawn is true?

    A. Some survival kits contain all three items
    B. The survival kit near the typists' pool contains anthrax vaccine
    C. The survival kit near the typists' pool contains only two of these items
    D. None of these

9. <u>Summary of Evidence Collected to Date:</u>   9._____

The shrink-wrap mechanism is designed to shut itself off if the heating coil temperature drops below 400° during the twin cycle.

<u>Prematurely Drawn Conclusion:</u> If the machine was operating the twin cycle on Monday, it was not operating properly.

Which of the following pieces of evidence, if any, would make it *reasonably certain* that the conclusion drawn is true?

    A. On Monday the heating coil temperature reached 450°
    B. When the machine performs functions other than the twin cycle, the heating coil temperature sometimes drops below 400°
    C. The shrink-wrap mechanism did not shut itself off on Monday
    D. None of these

Questions 10-14

Questions 10 through 14 refer to Map #4, located on the following page, and measure your ability to orient yourself within a given section of town, neighborhood or particular area. Each of the questions describes a starting point and a destination. Assume that you are driving a car in the area shown on the map accompanying the questions. Use the map as a basis for the shortest way to get from one point to another without breaking the law.

On the map, a street marked by arrows, or by arrows and the words "One Way," indicates one-way travel, and should be assumed to be one-way for the entire length, even when there are breaks or jogs in the street. EXCEPTION: A street that does not have the same name over the full length.

10. The shortest legal way from the State Capitol to Idaho Power is   10._____
    A. south on Capitol Blvd., west on Main, north on 12th
    B. south on 8th, west on Main
    C. west on Jefferson, south on 12th
    D. south on Capitol Blvd., west on Front, north on 12th

11. The shortest legal way from the Jefferson Place Building to the   11._____
    Statesman Building is
    A. east on Jefferson, south on Capitol Blvd.
    B. south on 8th, east on Main
    C. east on Jefferson, south on 4th, west on Main
    D. south on 9th, east on Main

12. The shortest legal way from Julia Davis Park to Owyhee Plaza Hotel is   12._____
    A. north on 5th, west on Front, north on 11th
    B. north on 6th, west on Main
    C. west on Battery, north on 9th, west on Front, north on Main
    D. north on 5th, west on Front, north on 13th, east on Main

13. The shortest legal way from the Big Easy to City Hall is   13._____
    A. north on 9th, east on Main
    B. east on Myrtle, north on Capitol Blvd.
    C. north on 9th, east on Idaho
    D. east on Myrtle, north on 6th

14. The shortest legal way from the Boise Contemporary Theater to the   14._____
    Pioneer Building is
    A. north on 9th, east on Main
    B. north on 9th, east on Myrtle, north on 6th
    C. east on Fulton, north on Capitol Blvd., east on Main
    D. east on Fulton, north on 6th

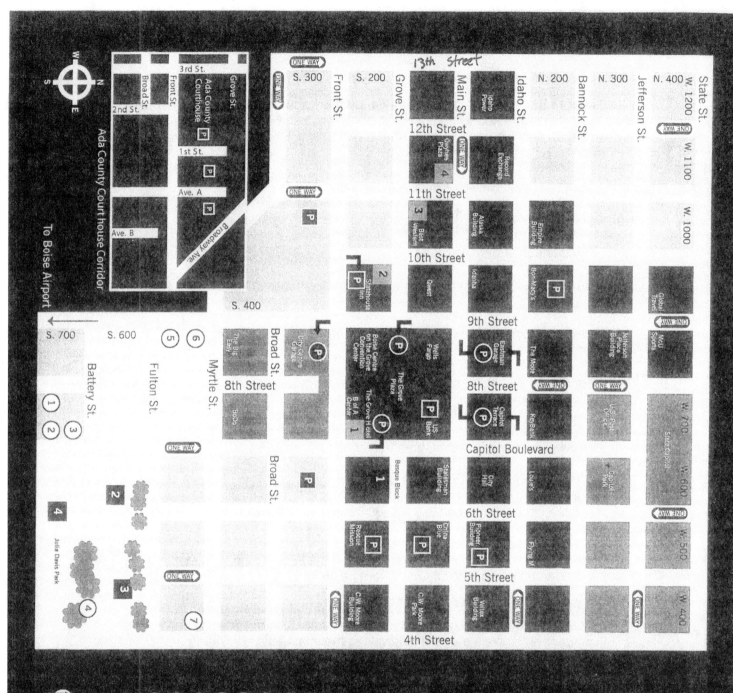

Questions 15-19

Questions 15 through 19 refer to Figure #4, on the following page, and measure your ability to understand written descriptions of events. Each question presents a description of an accident or event and asks you which of the five drawings in Figure #4 BEST represents it.

In the drawings, the following symbols are used:

Moving vehicle: ⬠   Non-moving vehicle: ◢

Pedestrian or bicyclist: ●

The path and direction of travel of a vehicle or pedestrian is indicated by a solid line.

The path and direction of travel of each vehicle or pedestrian directly involved in a collision from the point of impact is indicated by a dotted line.

In the space at the right, print the letter of the drawing that best fits the descriptions written below:

15. A driver headed east on Union strikes a car that is pulling out from between two parked cars, and then continues east.   15._____

16. A driver headed north on Post strikes a car that is pulling out from in front of a parked car, then veers into the oncoming lane and collides head-on with a car that is parked in the southbound lane of Post.   16._____

17. A driver headed east on Union strikes a car that is pulling out from between two parked cars, travels through the intersection, and makes a sudden right turn onto Cherry, where he strikes a parked car in the rear.   17._____

18. A driver headed west on Union strikes a car that is pulling out from between two parked cars, and then swerves to the left. He cuts the corner and travels over the sidewalk at the intersection of Cherry and Post, and then strikes a car that is parked in the northbound lane on Post.   18._____

19. A driver headed east on Union strikes a car that is pulling out from between two parked cars, and then swerves to the left. He cuts the corner and travels over the sidewalk at the intersection of Oak and Post, and then flees north on Post.   19._____

FIGURE #4   8 (#2)

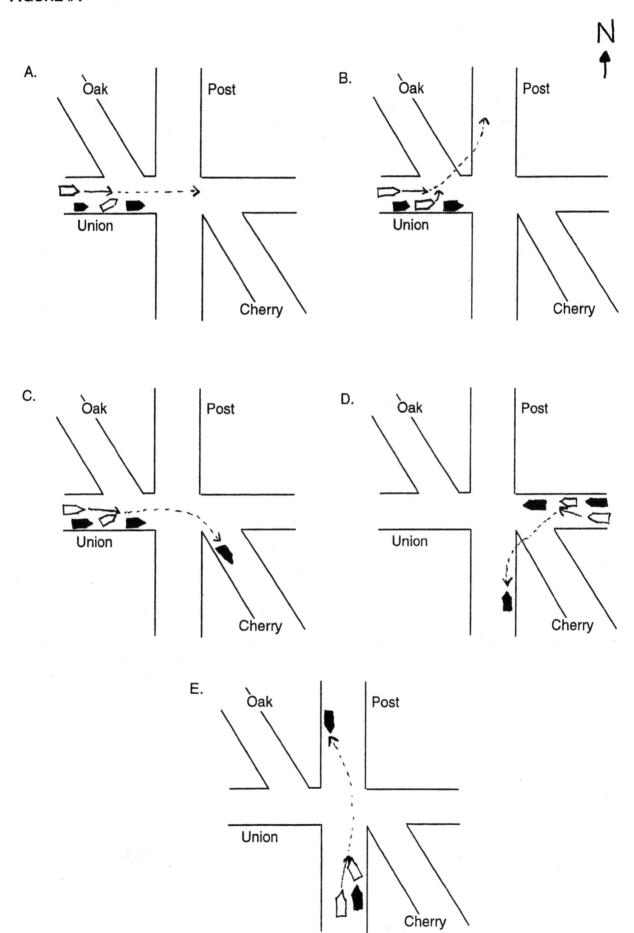

Questions 20-22

In questions 20 through 22, choose the word or phrase CLOSEST in meaning to the word or phrase printed in capital letters.

20. TITLE
    A. danger
    B. ownership
    C. description
    D. treatise

20._____

21. REVOKE
    A. cancel
    B. imagine
    C. solicit
    D. cause

21._____

22. BRIEF
    A. summary
    B. ruling
    C. plea
    D. motion

22._____

Questions 23-25

Questions 23 through 25 measure your ability to do fieldwork-related arithmetic. Each question presents a separate arithmetic problem for you to solve.

23. An investigator plans to drive from his home to Los Angeles, a trip of 2,800 miles. His car has a 24-gallon tank and gets 18 miles to the gallon. If he starts out with a full tank of gasoline, what is the FEWEST number of stops he will have to make for gasoline to complete his trip to Los Angeles?
    A. 4   B. 5   C. 6   D. 7

23._____

24. A caseworker has 24 home visits to schedule for a week. She will visit three homes on Sunday, and on every day that follows she will visit one more home than she visited on the previous day. At the end of the day on _____, the caseworker will have completed all of her home visits.
    A. Wednesday
    B. Thursday
    C. Friday
    D. Saturday

24._____

25. Ms. Langhorn takes a cab from her house to the airport. The cab company charges $3.00 to start the meter and $.50 per mile after that. It's 15 miles from Ms. Langhorn's house to the airport. How much will she have to pay for a cab?
    A. $10.50   B. $11.50   C. $14.00   D. $15.50

25._____

KEY (CORRECT ANSWERS)

1. B	11. D	21. A
2. A	12. A	22. A
3. D	13. B	23. C
4. B	14. C	24. B
5. D	15. A	25. A
6. B	16. E	
7. B	17. C	
8. C	18. D	
9. C	19. B	
10. C	20. B	

SOLUTIONS TO QUESTIONS 1-9

P implies Q = original statement

Not Q implies not P = contrapositive of the original statement. A statement and its contrapositive are logically equivalent.

Q implies P = converse of the original statement.

Not P implies not Q = inverse of the original statement. The converse and inverse of an original statement are logically equivalent.

P implies Q = Not P or Q.

#1. The correct answer is **B**. For item I, the irrational thinking teachers at the Middle School belong the group of all Middle School teachers. Since all teachers at the Middle School are intelligent, this includes the subset of irrational thinkers. For item II, if no one person has no friends, this implies that each person must have at least one friend.

#2. The correct answer is **A**. In item I, both statements state that (a) bananas are healthy and (b) bananas are eaten mainly because they taste good. In item II, the second statement is not equivalent to the first statement. An equivalent statement to the first statement would be "Either Dr. Jones is not in or we should call at the office."

#3. The correct answer is **D**. In item I, given that a person works one shift, we cannot draw any conclusion about whether he/she is a millworker. It is possible that a millworker works one, two, or a number more than two shifts. In item II, the second statement is the inverse of the first statement; they are not logically equivalent.

#4. The correct answer is **B**. In item I, any statement in the form "P implies Q" is equivalent to "Not P or Q." In this case, P = A member of the swim team attends practice, and Q = He will compete in the next meet. In item II, "P implies Q" is equivalent to "all P belongs to Q." In this case, P = Engineer wears glasses, and Q = He will know how to use AutoCAD.

#5. The correct answer is **D**. Because the number of high school graduates is so much larger than the number of convicted child abusers, none of the additional pieces of evidence make it reasonably certain that there are convicted abusers within this group of parents.

#6. The correct answer is **B**. Statement II is equivalent to "If Mr. Cantwell is reelected to the school board, then school buses are not approved. Statement I assures us that Mr. Cantwell will vote for new school buses. The only logical conclusion is that in spite of Mr. Cantwell's reelection to the board and subsequent vote, approval of the buses was still defeated.

#7. The correct answer is **B**. From statement II, we conclude that Francis is either a sergeant or a major. If we also know that Stern is a major, we can deduce that Francis is a sergeant. This means that the third person, Jackson, must be a lieutenant.

#8. The correct answer is **C**. Given that a survival kit contains a gas mask, statement I assures us that it also contains the anthrax vaccine. If the survival kit near the typist pool only contains two items, then we can conclude that the gas mask in this location cannot contain a third item, namely the anthrax vaccine.

#9. The correct answer is **C**. The original statement can be written in "P implies Q" form, where P = The heating coil temperature drops below 400 during the twin cycle, and Q = The mechanism shuts itself off. The contrapositive (which must be true) would be "If the mechanism did not shut itself off, then the heating coil temperature did not drop below 400." We would then conclude that the temperature was too high and therefore the machine did not operate properly.

REPORT WRITING
EXAMINATION SECTION
TEST 1

DIRECTIONS: Each question or incomplete statement is followed by several suggested answers or completions. Select the one that BEST answers the question or completes the statement. *PRINT THE LETTER OF THE CORRECT ANSWER IN THE SPACE AT THE RIGHT.*

Questions 1-4.

DIRECTIONS: Answer Questions 1 through 4 on the basis of the following report which was prepared by a supervisor for inclusion in his agency's annual report.

Line
#
1   On Oct. 13, I was assigned to study the salaries paid
2   to clerical employees in various titles by the city and by
3   private industry in the area.
4   In order to get the data I needed, I called Mr. Johnson at
5   the Bureau of the Budget and the payroll officers at X Corp.—
6   a brokerage house, Y Co.—an insurance company, and Z Inc.—
7   a publishing firm. None of them was available and I had to call
8   all of them again the next day.
9   When I finally got the information I needed, I drew up a
10   chart, which is attached. Note that not all of the companies I
11   contacted employed people at all the different levels used in the
12   city service.
13   The conclusions I draw from analyzing this information is
14   as follows: The city's entry-level salary is about average for
15   the region; middle-level salaries are generally higher in the
16   city government than in private industry; but salaries at the
17   highest levels in private industry are better than city em-
18   ployees' pay.

1. Which of the following criticisms about the style in which this report is written is *most valid*?   1.____

    A. It is too informal.   B. It is too concise.
    C. It is too choppy.   D. The syntax is too complex.

2. Judging from the statements made in the report, the method followed by this employee in performing his research was   2.____

    A. *good;* he contacted a representative sample of businesses in the area
    B. *poor;* he should have drawn more definite conclusions
    C. *good;* he was persistent in collecting information
    D. *poor;* he did not make a thorough study

3. One sentence in this report contains a grammatical error. This sentence *begins* on line number

    A. 4   B. 7   C. 10   D. 13

3._____

4. The type of information given in this report which should be presented in footnotes or in an appendix, is the

    A. purpose of the study
    B. specifics about the businesses contacted
    C. reference to the chart
    D. conclusions drawn by the author

4._____

5. The use of a graph to show statistical data in a report is *superior* to a table because it

    A. features approximations
    B. emphasizes facts and relationships more dramatically
    C. C. presents data more accurately
    D. is easily understood by the average reader

5._____

6. Of the following, the degree of formality required of a written report in tone is *most likely* to depend on the

    A. subject matter of the report
    B. frequency of its occurrence
    C. amount of time available for its preparation
    D. audience for whom the report is intended

6._____

7. Of the following, a distinguishing characteristic of a written report intended for the head of your agency as compared to a report prepared for a lower-echelon staff member, is that the report for the agency head should *usually* include

    A. considerably more detail, especially statistical data
    B. the essential details in an abbreviated form
    C. all available source material
    D. an annotated bibliography

7._____

8. Assume that you are asked to write a lengthy report for use by the administrator of your agency, the subject of which is "The Impact of Proposed New Data Processing Operations on Line Personnel" in your agency. You decide that the *most appropriate* type of report for you to prepare is an analytical report, including recommendations.
The MAIN reason for your decision is that

    A. the subject of the report is extremely complex
    B. large sums of money are involved
    C. the report is being prepared for the administrator
    D. you intend to include charts and graphs

8._____

9. Assume that you are preparing a report based on a survey dealing with the attitudes of employees in Division X regarding proposed new changes in compensating employees for working overtime. Three per cent of the respondents to the survey voluntarily offer an unfavorable opinion on the method of assigning overtime work, a question not specifically asked of the employees.

   On the basis of this information, the *most appropriate* and *significant* of the following comments for you to make in the report with regard to employees' attitudes on assigning overtime work, is that

   A. an insignificant percentage of employees dislike the method of assigning overtime work
   B. three per cent of the employees in Division X dislike the method of assigning overtime work
   C. three per cent of the sample selected for the survey voiced an unfavorable opinion on the method of assigning overtime work
   D. some employees voluntarily voiced negative feelings about the method of assigning overtime work, making it impossible to determine the extent of this attitude

9.____

10. A supervisor should be able to prepare a report that is well-written and unambiguous. Of the following sentences that might appear in a report, select the one which communicates *most clearly* the intent of its author.

   A. When your subordinates speak to a group of people, they should be well-informed.
   B. When he asked him to leave, SanMan King told him that he would refuse the request.
   C. Because he is a good worker, Foreman Jefferson assigned Assistant Foreman D'Agostino to replace him.
   D. Each of us is responsible for the actions of our subordinates.

10.____

11. In some reports, especially longer ones, a list of the resources (books, papers, magazines, etc.) used to prepare it is included. This list is called the

   A. accreditation   B. bibliography
   C. summary   D. glossary

11.____

12. Reports are usually divided into several sections, some of which are more necessary than others.
   Of the following, the section which is ABSOLUTELY necessary to include in a report is

   A. a table of contents   B. the body
   C. an index   D. a bibliography

12.____

13. Suppose you are writing a report on an interview you have just completed with a particularly hostile applicant. Which of the following BEST describes what you should include in this report?

   A. What you think caused the applicant's hostile attitude during the interview
   B. Specific examples of the applicant's hostile remarks and behavior
   C. The relevant information uncovered during the interview
   D. A recommendation that the applicant's request be denied because of his hostility

13.____

14. When including recommendations in a report to your supervisor, which of the following   14._____
is MOST important for you to do?

    A. Provide several alternative courses of action for each recommendation
    B. First present the supporting evidence, then the recommendations
    C. First present the recommendations, then the supporting evidence
    D. Make sure the recommendations arise logically out of the information in the report

15. It is often necessary that the writer of a report present facts and sufficient arguments to   15._____
gain acceptance of the points, conclusions, or recommendations set forth in the report.
Of the following, the LEAST advisable step to take in organizing a report, when such
argumentation is the important factor, is a(n)

    A. elaborate expression of personal belief
    B. businesslike discussion of the problem as a whole
    C. orderly arrangement of convincing data
    D. reasonable explanation of the primary issues

16. In some types of reports, visual aids add interest, meaning, and support. They also pro-   16._____
vide an essential means of effectively communicating the message of the report.
Of the following, the selection of the suitable visual aids to use with a report is LEAST
dependent on the

    A. nature and scope of the report
    B. way in which the aid is to be used
    C. aids used in other reports
    D. prospective readers of the report

17. Visual aids used in a report may be placed either in the text material or in the appendix.   17._____
Deciding where to put a chart, table, or any such aid *should* depend on the

    A. title of the report   B. purpose of the visual aid
    C. title of the visual aid   D. length of the report

18. A report is often revised several times before final preparation and distribution in an effort   18._____
to make certain the report meets the needs of the situation for which it is designed.
Which of the following is the BEST way for the author to be sure that a report covers
the areas he intended?

    A. Obtain a co-worker's opinion
    B. Compare it with a content checklist
    C. Test it on a subordinate
    D. Check his bibliography

19. In which of the following situations is an oral report preferable to a written report? When   19._____
a(n)

    A. recommendation is being made for a future plan of action
    B. department head requests immediate information
    C. long standing policy change is made
    D. analysis of complicated statistical data is involved

20. When an applicant is approved, the supervisor must fill in standard forms with certain   20._____
information.
The GREATEST advantage of using standard forms in this situation rather than having
the supervisor write the report as he sees fit, is that

    A. the report can be acted on quickly
    B. the report can be written without directions from a supervisor
    C. needed information is less likely to be left out of the report
    D. information that is written up this way is more likely to be verified

21. Assume that it is part of your job to prepare a monthly report for your unit head that even-   21._____
tually goes to the director. The report contains information on the number of applicants
you have interviewed that have been approved and the number of applicants you have
interviewed that have been turned down.
Errors on such reports are serious because

    A. you are expected to be able to prove how many applicants you have interviewed
       each month
    B. accurate statistics are needed for effective management of the department
    C. they may not be discovered before the report is transmitted to the director
    D. they may result in loss to the applicants left out of the report

22. The frequency with which job reports are submitted should depend MAINLY on   22._____

    A. how comprehensive the report has to be
    B. the amount of information in the report
    C. the availability of an experienced man to write the report
    D. the importance of changes in the information included in the report

23. The CHIEF purpose in preparing an outline for a report is *usually* to insure that   23._____

    A. the report will be grammatically correct
    B. every point will be given equal emphasis
    C. principal and secondary points will be properly integrated
    D. the language of the report will be of the same level and include the same technical
       terms

24. The MAIN reason for requiring written job reports is to   24._____

    A. avoid the necessity of oral orders
    B. develop better methods of doing the work
    C. provide a permanent record of what was done
    D. increase the amount of work that can be done

25. Assume you are recommending in a report to your supervisor that a radical change in a   25._____
standard maintenance procedure should be adopted.
Of the following, the MOST important information to be included in this report is

    A. a list of the reasons for making this change
    B. the names of others who favor the change
    C. a complete description of the present procedure
    D. amount of training time needed for the new procedure

KEY (CORRECT ANSWERS)

1.	A		11.	B
2.	D		12.	B
3.	D		13.	C
4.	B		14.	D
5.	B		15.	A
6.	D		16.	C
7.	B		17.	B
8.	A		18.	B
9.	D		19.	B
10.	D		20.	C

21.	B
22.	D
23.	C
24.	C
25.	A

TEST 2

DIRECTIONS: Each question or incomplete statement is followed by several suggested answers or completions. Select the one that BEST answers the question or completes the statement. *PRINT THE LETTER OF THE CORRECT ANSWER IN THE SPACE AT THE RIGHT.*

1. It is often necessary that the writer of a report present facts and sufficient arguments to gain acceptance of the points, conclusions, or recommendations set forth in the report. Of the following, the LEAST advisable step to take in organizing a report, when such argumentation is the important factor, is a(n)

    A. elaborate expression of personal belief
    B. businesslike discussion of the problem as a whole
    C. orderly arrangement of convincing data
    D. reasonable explanation of the primary issues

1.____

2. Of the following, the factor which is generally considered to be LEAST characteristic of a good control report is that it

    A. stresses performance that adheres to standard rather than emphasizing the exception
    B. supplies information intended to serve as the basis for corrective action
    C. provides feedback for the planning process
    D. includes data that reflect trends as well as current status

2.____

3. An administrative assistant has been asked by his superior to write a concise, factual report with objective conclusions and recommendations based on facts assembled by other researchers.
Of the following factors, the administrative assistant should give LEAST consideratio to

    A. the educational level of the person or persons for whom the report is being prepared
    B. the use to be made of the report
    C. the complexity of the problem
    D. his own feelings about the importance of the problem

3.____

4. When making a written report, it is often recommended that the findings or conclusions be presented near the beginning of the report.
Of the following, the MOST important reason for doing this is that it

    A. facilitates organizing the material clearly
    B. assures that all the topics will be covered
    C. avoids unnecessary repetition of ideas
    D. prepares the reader for the facts that will follow

4.____

5. You have been asked to write a report on methods of hiring and training new employees. Your report is going to be about ten pages long.
For the convenience of your readers, a brief summary of your findings *should*

    A. appear at the beginning of your report
    B. be appended to the report as a postscript
    C. be circulated in a separate memo
    D. be inserted in tabular form in the middle of your report

5.____

6. In preparing a report, the MAIN reason for writing an outline is *usually* to   6.____

    A. help organize thoughts in a logical sequence
    B. provide a guide for the typing of the report
    C. allow the ultimate user to review the report in advance
    D. ensure that the report is being prepared on schedule

7. The one of the following which is *most appropriate* as a reason for including footnotes in a report is to   7.____

    A. correct capitalization   B. delete passages
    C. improve punctuation   D. cite references

8. A completed formal report may contain all of the following EXCEPT   8.____

    A. a synopsis   B. a preface
    C. marginal notes   D. bibliographical references

9. Of the following, the MAIN use of proofreaders' marks is to   9.____

    A. explain corrections to be made
    B. indicate that a manuscript has been read and approved
    C. let the reader know who proofread the report
    D. indicate the format of the report

10. Informative, readable and concise reports have been found to observe the following rules: 10.____

    Rule I.   Keep the report short and easy to understand.
    Rule II.   Vary the length of sentences.
    Rule III.   Vary the style of sentences so that, for example, they are not all just subject-verb, subject-verb.

Consider this hospital laboratory report: The experiment was started in January. The apparatus was put together in six weeks. At that time the synthesizing process was begun. The synthetic chemicals were separated. Then they were used in tests on patients.

Which one of the following choices MOST accurately classifies the above rules into those which are *violated* by this report and those which are *not*?

    A. II is violated, but I and III are not.
    B. III is violated, but I and II are not.
    C. II and III are violated, but I is not.
    D. I, II, and III are violated.

Questions 11-13.

DIRECTIONS: Questions 11 through 13 are based on the following example of a report. The report consists of eight numbered sentences, some of which are not consistent with the principles of good report writing.

(1) I interviewed Mrs. Loretta Crawford in Room 424 of County Hospital. (2) She had collapsed on the street and been brought into emergency. (3) She is an attractive woman with many friends judging by the cards she had received. (4) She did not know what her husband's last job had been, or what their present income was. (5) The first thing that Mrs. Crawford said was that she had never worked and that her husband was presently unemployed. (6) She did not know if they had any medical coverage or if they could pay the bill. (7) She said that her husband could not be reached by telephone but that he would be in to see her that afternoon. (8) I left word at the nursing station to be called when he arrived.

11. A good report should be arranged in logical order. Which of the following sentences from the report does NOT appear in its proper sequence in the report? Sentence   11._____

    A. 1   B. 4   C. 7   D. 8

12. Only material that is relevant to the main thought of a report should be included. Which of the following sentences from the report contains material which is LEAST relevant to this report? Sentence   12._____

    A. 3   B. 4   C. 6   D. 8

13. Reports should include all essential information.   13._____
Of the following, the MOST important fact that is *missing* from this report is:

    A. Who was involved in the interview
    B. What was discovered at the interview
    C. When the interview took place
    D. Where the interview took place

Questions 14-15.

DIRECTIONS: Each of Questions 14 and 15 consists of four numbered sentences which constitute a paragraph in a report. They are not in the right order. Choose the numbered arrangement appearing after letter A, B, C, or D which is MOST logical and which BEST expresses the thought of the paragraph.

14.   I.   Congress made the commitment explicit in the Housing Act of 1949, establishing   14._____
        as a national goal the realization of a decent home and suitable environment for
        every American family.
    II.   The result has been that the goal of decent home and suitable environment is
        still as far distant as ever for the disadvantaged urban family.
    III.   In spite of this action by Congress, federal housing programs have continued to
        be fragmented and grossly under-funded.
    IV.   The passage of the National Housing Act signaled a new federal commitment to
        provide housing for the nation's citizens.

    A. I, IV, III, II   B. IV, I, III, II
    C. IV, I, III, II   D. II, IV, I, III

15.
   I.   The greater expense does not necessarily involve "exploitation," but it is often per-
       ceived as exploitative and unfair by those who are aware of the price differences
       involved, but unaware of operating costs.
   II. Ghetto residents believe they are "exploited" by local merchants, and evidence
       substantiates some of these beliefs.
  III. However, stores in low-income areas were more likely to be small independents,
       which could not achieve the economies available to supermarket chains and
       were, therefore, more likely to charge higher prices, and the customers were
       more likely to buy smaller-sized packages which are more expensive per unit of
       measure.
  IV. A study conducted in one city showed that distinctly higher prices were charged
       for goods sold in ghetto stores than in other areas.

15.____

   A. IV, II, I, III
   C. II, IV, III, I
   B. IV, I, III, II
   D. II, III, IV, I

16. In organizing data to be presented in a formal report, the FIRST of the following steps
should be

16.____

   A. determining the conclusions to be drawn
   B. establishing the time sequence of the data
   C. sorting and arranging like data into groups
   D. evaluating how consistently the data support the recommendations

17. All reports should be prepared with *at least* one copy so that

17.____

   A. there is one copy for your file
   B. there is a copy for your supervisor
   C. the report can be sent to more than one person
   D. the person getting the report can forward a copy to someone else

18. Before turning in a report of an investigation he has made, a supervisor discovers some
additional information he did not include in this report.
Whether he rewrites this report to include this additional information should PRIMA-
RILY depend on the

18.____

   A. importance of the report itself
   B. number of people who will eventually review this report
   C. established policy covering the subject matter of the report
   D. bearing this new information has on the conclusions of the report

KEY (CORRECT ANSWERS)

1.	A	11.	B
2.	A	12.	A
3.	D	13.	C
4.	D	14.	B
5.	A	15.	C
6.	A	16.	C
7.	D	17.	A
8.	C	18.	D
9.	A		
10.	C		

COMMUNICATION
EXAMINATION SECTION
TEST 1

DIRECTIONS: Each question or incomplete statement is followed by several suggested answers or completions. Select the one that BEST answers the question or completes the statement. *PRINT THE LETTER OF THE CORRECT ANSWER IN THE SPACE AT THE RIGHT.*

1. In some agencies the counsel to the agency head is given the right to bypass the chain of command and issue orders directly to the staff concerning matters that involve certain specific processes and practices.
   This situation *most nearly* illustrates the PRINCIPLE of

   A. the acceptance theory of authority   B. multiple - linear authority
   C. splintered authority   D. functional authority

   1.____

2. It is commonly understood that communication is an important part of the administrative process.
   Which of the following is NOT a valid principle of the communication process in adminis-tration?

   A. The channels of communication should be spontaneous
   B. The lines of communication should be as direct and as short as possible
   C. Communications should be authenticated
   D. The persons serving in communications centers should be competent

   2.____

3. Of the following, the *one* factor which is generally considered LEAST essential to suc-cessful committee operations is

   A. stating a clear definition of the authority and scope of the committee
   B. selecting the committee chairman carefully
   C. limiting the size of the committee to four persons
   D. limiting the subject matter to that which can be handled in group discussion

   3.____

4. Of the following, the failure by line managers to accept and appreciate the benefits and limitations of a new program or system *very frequently* can be traced to the

   A. budgetary problems involved
   B. resultant need to reduce staff
   C. lack of controls it engenders
   D. failure of top management to support its implementation

   4.____

5. If a manager were thinking about using a committee of subordinates to solve an operat-ing problem, which of the following would generally NOT be an *advantage* of such use of the committee approach?

   A. Improved coordination   B. Low cost
   C. Increased motivation   D. Integrated judgment

   5.____

6. Every supervisor has many occasions to lead a conference or participate in a conference of some sort.
Of the following statements that pertain to conferences and conference leadership, which is generally considered to be MOST valid?

   A. Since World War II, the trend has been toward fewer shared decisions and more conferences.
   B. The most important part of a conference leader's job is to direct discussion.
   C. In providing opportunities for group interaction, management should avoid consideration of its past management philosophy.
   D. A good administrator cannot lead a good conference if he is a poor public speaker.

6._____

7. Of the following, it is usually LEAST desirable for a conference leader to

   A. call the name of a person after asking a question
   B. summarize proceedings periodically
   C. make a practice of repeating questions
   D. ask a question without indicating who is to reply

7._____

8. Assume that, in a certain organization, a situation has developed in which there is little difference in status or authority between individuals.
Which of the following would be the *most likely* result with regard to communication in this organization?

   A. Both the accuracy and flow of communication will be improved.
   B. Both the accuracy and flow of communication will substantially decrease.
   C. Employees will seek more formal lines of communication.
   D. Neither the flow nor the accuracy of communication will be improved over the former hierarchical structure.

8._____

9. The main function of many agency administrative officers is "information management."
Information that is received by an administrative officer may be classified as active or passive, depending upon whether or not it requires the recipient to take some action.
Of the following, the item received which is *clearly* the MOST active information is

   A. an appointment of a new staff member
   B. a payment voucher for a new desk
   C. a press release concerning a past event
   D. the minutes of a staff meeting

9._____

10. Of the following, the one LEAST considered to be a communication barrier is

   A. group feedback   B. charged words
   C. selective perception   D. symbolic meanings

10._____

11. Management studies support the hypothesis that, in spite of the tendency of employees to censor the information communicated to their supervisor, subordinates are *more likely* to communicate problem-oriented information UPWARD when they have a

   A. long period of service in the organization
   B. high degree of trust in the supervisor
   C. high educational level
   D. low status on the organizational ladder

11._____

12. Electronic data processing equipment can produce more information faster than can be   12._____
generated by any other means. In view of this, the MOST important problem faced by
management at present is to

    A. keep computers fully occupied
    B. find enough computer personnel
    C. assimilate and properly evaluate the information
    D. obtain funds to establish appropriate information systems

13. A well-designed management information system *essentially* provides each executive   13._____
and manager the information he needs for

    A. determining computer time requirements
    B. planning and measuring results
    C. drawing a new organization chart
    D. developing a new office layout

14. It is generally agreed that management policies should be periodically reappraised and   14._____
restated in accordance with current conditions.
Of the following, the approach which would be MOST effective in determining whether a
policy should be revised is to

    A. conduct interviews with staff members at all levels in order to ascertain the rela-
tionship between the policy and actual practice
    B. make proposed revisions in the policy and apply it to current problems
    C. make up hypothetical situations using both the old policy and a revised version in
order to make comparisons
    D. call a meeting of top level staff in order to discuss ways of revising the policy

15. Your superior has asked you to notify division employees of an important change in one   15._____
of the operating procedures described in the division manual. Every employee presently
has a copy of this manual.
Which of the following is normally the MOST practical way to get the employees to
understand such a change?

    A. Notify each employee individually of the change and answer any questions he
might have
    B. Send a written notice to key personnel, directing them to inform the people under
them
    C. Call a general meeting, distribute a corrected page for the manual, and discuss the
change
    D. Send a memo to employees describing the change in general terms and asking
them to make the necessary corrections in their copies of the manual

16. Assume that the work in your department involves the use of many technical terms.   16._____
In such a situation, when you are answering inquiries from the general public, it would
usually be BEST to

    A. use simple language and avoid the technical terms
    B. employ the technical terms whenever possible
    C. bandy technical terms freely, but explain each term in parentheses
    D. apologize if you are forced to use a technical term

17. Suppose that you receive a telephone call from someone identifying himself as an employee in another city department who asks to be given information which your own department regards as confidential.
Which of the following is the BEST way of handling such a request?

    A. Give the information requested, since your caller has official standing
    B. Grant the request, provided the caller gives you a signed receipt
    C. Refuse the request, because you have no way of knowing whether the caller is really who he claims to be
    D. Explain that the information is confidential and inform the caller of the channels he must go through to have the information released to him

17.____

18. Studies show that office employees place high importance on the social and human aspects of the organization. What office employees like best about their jobs is the kind of people with whom they work. So strive hard to group people who are most likely to get along well together.
Based on this information, it is *most reasonable* to assume that office workers are MOST pleased to work in a group which

    A. is congenial   B. has high productivity
    C. allows individual creativity
    D. is unlike other groups

18.____

19. A certain supervisor does not compliment members of his staff when they come up with good ideas. He feels that coming up with good ideas is part of the job and does not merit special attention.
This supervisor's practice is

    A. *poor,* because recognition for good ideas is a good motivator
    B. *poor,* because the staff will suspect that the supervisor has no good ideas of his own
    C. *good,* because it is reasonable to assume that employees will tell their supervisor of ways to improve office practice
    D. *good,* because the other members of the staff are not made to seem inferior by comparison

19.____

20. Some employees of a department have sent an anonymous letter containing many complaints to the department head. Of the following, what is this *most likely* to show about the department?

    A. It is probably a good place to work.
    B. Communications are probably poor.
    C. The complaints are probably unjustified.
    D. These employees are probably untrustworthy.

20.____

21. Which of the following actions would usually be MOST appropriate for a supervisor to take *after* receiving an instruction sheet from his superior explaining a new procedure which is to be followed?

    A. Put the instruction sheet aside temporarily until he determines what is wrong with the old procedure
    B. Call his superior and ask whether the procedure is one he must implement immediately

21.____

C. Write a memorandum to the superior asking for more details
D. Try the new procedure and advise the superior of any problems or possible improvements

22. Of the following, which one is considered the PRIMARY advantage of using a committee to resolve a problem in an organization? 22.____

    A. No one person will be held accountable for the decision since a group of people was involved
    B. People with different backgrounds give attention to the problem
    C. The decision will take considerable time so there is unlikely to be a decision that will later be regretted
    D. One person cannot dominate the decision-making process

23. Employees in a certain office come to their supervisor with all their complaints about the office and the work. Almost every employee has had at least one minor complaint at some time. 23.____
The situation with respect to complaints in this office may BEST be described as *proba-bly*

    A. *good;* employees who complain care about their jobs and work hard
    B. *good;* grievances brought out into the open can be corrected
    C. *bad;* only serious complaints should be discussed
    D. *bad;* it indicates the staff does not have confidence in the administration

24. The administrator who allows his staff to suggest ways to do their work will *usually* find that 24.____

    A. this practice contributes to high productivity
    B. the administrator's ideas produce greater output
    C. clerical employees suggest inefficient work methods
    D. subordinate employees resent performing a management function

25. The MAIN purpose for a supervisor's questioning the employees at a conference he is holding is to 25.____

    A. stress those areas of information covered but not understood by the participants
    B. encourage participants to think through the problem under discussion
    C. catch those subordinates who are not paying attention
    D. permit the more knowledgeable participants to display their grasp of the problems being discussed

KEYS (CORRECT ANSWERS)

1.	D		11.	B
2.	A		12.	C
3.	C		13.	B
4.	D		14.	A
5.	B		15.	C
6.	B		16.	A
7.	C		17.	D
8.	D		18.	A
9.	A		19.	A
10.	A		20.	B

21.	D
22.	B
23.	B
24.	A
25.	B

TEST 2

DIRECTIONS: Each question or incomplete statement is followed by several suggested answers or completions. Select the one that BEST answers the question or completes the statement. *PRINT THE LETTER OF THE CORRECT ANSWER IN THE SPACE AT THE RIGHT.*

1. For a superior to use *consultative supervision* with his subordinates effectively, it is ESSENTIAL that he   1.____

    A. accept the fact that his formal authority will be weakened by the procedure
    B. admit that he does not know more than all his men together and that his ideas are not always best
    C. utilize a committee system so that the procedure is orderly
    D. make sure that all subordinates are consulted so that no one feels left out

2. The "grapevine" is an informal means of communication in an organization. The attitude of a supervisor with respect to the grapevine should be to   2.____

    A. ignore it since it deals mainly with rumors and sensational information
    B. regard it as a serious danger which should be eliminated
    C. accept it as a real line of communication which should be listened to
    D. utilize it for most purposes instead of the official line of communication

3. The supervisor of an office that must deal with the public should realize that planning in this type of work situation   3.____

    A. is *useless* because he does not know how many people will request service or what service they will request
    B. *must be done at a higher level* but that he should be ready to implement the results of such planning
    C. is *useful* primarily for those activities that are not concerned with public contact
    D. is *useful* for all the activities of the office, including those that relate to public contact

4. Assume that it is your job to receive incoming telephone calls. Those calls which you cannot handle yourself have to be transferred to the appropriate office.
If you receive an outside call for an extension line which is busy, the one of the following which you should do FIRST is to   4.____

    A. interrupt the person speaking on the extension and tell him a call is waiting
    B. tell the caller the line is busy and let him know every thirty seconds whether or not it is free
    C. leave the caller on "hold" until the extension is free
    D. tell the caller the line is busy and ask him if he wishes to wait

5. Your superior has subscribed to several publications directly related to your division's work, and he has asked you to see to it that the publications are circulated among the supervisory personnel in the division. There are eight supervisors involved.
The BEST method of insuring that all eight see these publications is to   5.____

    A. place the publication in the division's general reference library as soon as it arrives
    B. inform each supervisor whenever a publication arrives and remind all of them that they are responsible for reading it

    C.   prepare a standard slip that can be stapled to each publication, listing the eight supervisors and saying, "Please read, initial your name, and pass along"

    D.   send a memo to the eight supervisors saying that they may wish to purchase individual subscriptions in their own names if they are interested in seeing each issue

6.   Your superior has telephoned a number of key officials in your agency to ask whether they can meet at a certain time next month. He has found that they can all make it, and he has asked you to confirm the meeting.
Which of the following is the BEST way to confirm such a meeting?   6._____

    A.   Note the meeting on your superior's calendar
    B.   Post a notice of the meeting on the agency bulletin board
    C.   Call the officials on the day of the meeting to remind them of the meeting
    D.   Write a memo to each official involved, repeating the time and place of the meeting

7.   Assume that a new city regulation requires that certain kinds of private organizations file information forms with your department. You have been asked to write the short explanatory message that will be printed on the front cover of the pamphlet containing the forms and instructions.
Which of the following would be the MOST appropriate way of beginning this message?   7._____

    A.   Get the readers' attention by emphasizing immediately that there are legal penalties for organizations that fail to file before a certain date
    B.   Briefly state the nature of the enclosed forms and the types of organizations that must file
    C.   Say that your department is very sorry to have to put organizations to such an inconvenience
    D.   Quote the entire regulation adopted by the city, even if it is quite long and is expressed in complicated legal language

8.   Suppose that you have been told to make up the vacation schedule for the 18 employees in a particular unit. In order for the unit to operate effectively, only a few employees can be on vacation at the same time.
Which of the following is the MOST advisable approach in making up the schedule?   8._____

    A.   Draw up a schedule assigning vacations in alphabetical order
    B.   Find out when the supervisors want to take their vacations, and randomly assign whatever periods are left to the non-supervisory personnel
    C.   Assign the most desirable times to employees of longest standing and the least desirable times to the newest employees
    D.   Have all employees state their own preference, and then work out any conflicts in consultation with the people involved

9.   Assume that you have been asked to prepare job descriptions for various positions in your department.
Which of the following are the basic points that should be covered in a *job description*?   9._____

    A.   General duties and responsibilities of the position, with examples of day-to-day tasks
    B.   Comments on the performances of present employees

    C.   Estimates of the number of openings that may be available in each category during the coming year

    D.   Instructions for carrying out the specific tasks assigned to your department

10.   Of the following, the biggest DISADVANTAGE in allowing a free flow of communications in an agency is that such a free flow   10._____

    A.   *decreases* creativity
    B.   *increases* the use of the "grapevine"
    C.   *lengthens* the chain of command
    D.   *reduces* the executive's power to direct the flow of information

11.   A downward flow of authority in an organization is one example of _____ communication.   11._____

    A. horizontal   B. informal   C. circular   D. vertical

12.   Of the following, the one that would *most likely* block effective communication is   12._____

    A. concentration only on the issues at hand   B. lack of interest or commitment
    C. use of written reports   D. use of charts and graphs

13.   An ADVANTAGE of the *lecture* as a teaching tool is that it   13._____

    A. enables a person to present his ideas to a large number of people
    B. allows the audience to retain a maximum of the information given
    C. holds the attention of the audience for the longest time
    D. enables the audience member to easily recall the main points

14.   An ADVANTAGE of the *small-group* discussion as a teaching tool is that   14._____

    A. it always focuses attention on one person as the leader
    B. it places collective responsibility on the group as a whole
    C. its members gain experience by summarizing the ideas of others
    D. each member of the group acts as a member of a team

15.   The one of the following that is an ADVANTAGE of a *large-group* discussion, when compared to a small-group discussion, is that the large-group discussion   15._____

    A. moves along more quickly than a small-group discussion
    B. allows its participants to feel more at ease, and speak out more freely
    C. gives the whole group a chance to exchange ideas on a certain subject at the same occasion
    D. allows its members to feel a greater sense of personal responsibility

———

KEYS (CORRECT ANSWERS)

1.	D		6.	D
2.	C		7.	B
3.	D		8.	D
4.	D		9.	A
5.	C		10.	D

11.	D
12.	B
13.	A
14.	D
15.	C

EDUCATING AND INTERACTING WITH THE PUBLIC

These questions test for knowledge of techniques used to interact effectively with individual citizens and/or community groups, to educate or inform them about topics of concern, to publicize or clarify agency programs or policies, to negotiate conflicts or resolve complaints, and to represent one's agency or program in a manner in keeping with good public relations practices. Questions may also cover interacting with others in cooperative efforts of public outreach or service. There will be 15 questions in this subject area on the written test.

TEST TASK:
You will be presented with a variety of situations in which you must apply knowledge of how best to interact with other people.

SAMPLE QUESTION:
A person approaches you expressing anger about a recent action by your department. Which one of the following should be your first response to this person?

A. Interrupt to say you cannot discuss the situation until he calms down.
B. Say you are sorry that he has been negatively affected by your department's action.
C. Listen and express understanding that he has been upset by your department's action.
D. Give him an explanation of the reasons for your department's action.

The correct answer to this sample question is choice C

C. SOLUTION:

Choice A is not correct. It would be inappropriate to interrupt. In addition, saying that you cannot discuss the situation until the person calms down will likely aggravate him further.

Choice B is not correct. Apologizing for your department's action implies that the action was improper.

Choice C is the correct answer to this question. By listening and expressing understanding that your department's action has upset him, you demonstrate that you have heard and understand his feelings and point of view.

Choice D is not correct. While an explanation of the reasons for the action may be appropriate at a later time, at this moment the person is angry and would not be receptive to such an explanation.

EXAMINATION SECTION
TEST 1

DIRECTIONS: Each question or incomplete statement is followed by several suggested answers or completions. Select the one that BEST answers the question or completes the statement. *PRINT THE LETTER OF THE CORRECT ANSWER IN THE SPACE AT THE RIGHT.*

1. When conducting a needs assessment for the purpose of education planning, an agency's FIRST step is to identify or provide

    A.   a profile of population characteristics
    B.   barriers to participation
    C.   existing resources
    D.   profiles of competing resources

1.____

2. Research has demonstrated that of the following, the most effective medium for communicating with external publics is/are

    A.   video news releases
    B.   television
    C.   radio
    D.   newspapers

2.____

3. Basic ideas behind the effort to influence the attitudes and behaviors of a constituency include each of the following, EXCEPT the idea that

    A.   words, rather than actions or events, are most likely to motivate
    B.   demands for action are a usual response
    C.   self-interest usually figures heavily into public involvement
    D.   the reliability of change programs is difficult to assess

3.____

4. An agency representative is trying to craft a pithy message to constituents in order to encourage the use of agency program resources. Choosing an audience for such messages is easiest when the message

    A.   is project- or behavior-based
    B.   is combined with other messages
    C.   is abstract
    D.   has a broad appeal

4.____

5. Of the following factors, the most important to the success of an agency's external education or communication programs is the

    A.   amount of resources used to implement them
    B.   public's prior experiences with the agency
    C.   real value of the program to the public
    D.   commitment of the internal audience

5.____

6. A representative for a state agency is being interviewed by a reporter from a local news network. The representative is being asked to defend a program that is extremely unpopular in certain parts of the municipality. When a constituency is known to be opposed to a position, the most useful communication strategy is to present

6.____

A. only the arguments that are consistent with constituents' views
B. only the agency's side of the issue
C. both sides of the argument as clearly as possible
D. both sides of the argument, omitting key information about the opposing position

7. The most significant barriers to effective agency community relations include   7._____
      I.   widespread distrust of communication strategies
      II. the media's "watchdog" stance
      III. public apathy
      IV. statutory opposition

A. I only
B. I and II
C. II and III
D. III and IV

8. In conducting an education program, many agencies use workshops and seminars in a   8._____
classroom setting. Advantages of classroom-style teaching over other means of educating the public include each of the following, EXCEPT:

A. enabling an instructor to verify learning through testing and interaction with the tar-
   get audience
B. enabling hands-on practice and other participatory learning techniques
C. ability to reach an unlimited number of participants in a given length of time
D. ability to convey the latest, most up-to-date information

9. The _____ model of community relations is characterized by an attempt to persuade   9._____
the public to adopt the agency's point of view.

A. two-way symmetric
B. two-way asymmetric
C. public information
D. press agency/publicity

10. Important elements of an internal situation analysis include the   10._____
      I.   list of agency opponents
      II. communication audit
      III. updated organizational almanac
      IV. stakeholder analysis

A. I and II
B. I, II and III
C. II and III
D. I, II, III and IV

11. Government agency information efforts typically involve each of the following objectives,   11._____
EXCEPT to

A. implement changes in the policies of government agencies to align with public
   opinion
B. communicate the work of agencies
C. explain agency techniques in a way that invites input from citizens
D. provide citizen feedback to government administrators

12. Factors that are likely to influence the effectiveness of an educational campaign include the

    I.   level of homogeneity among intended participants
    II. number and types of media used
    III. receptivity of the intended participants
    IV. level of specificity in the message or behavior to be taught

    A. I and II
    B. I, II and III
    C. II and III
    D. I, II, III and IV

12.____

13. An agency representative is writing instructional objectives that will later help to measure the effectiveness of an educational program. Which of the following verbs, included in an objective, would be MOST helpful for the purpose of measuring effectiveness?

    A. Know
    B. Identify
    C. Learn
    D. Comprehend

13.____

14. A state education agency wants to encourage participation in a program that has just received a boost through new federal legislation. The program is intended to include participants from a wide variety of socioeconomic and other demographic characteristics. The agency wants to launch a broad-based program that will inform virtually every interested party in the state about the program's new circumstances. In attempting to deliver this message to such a wide-ranging constituency, the agency's best practice would be to

    A. broadcast the same message through as many different media channels as possible
    B. focus on one discrete segment of the public at a time
    C. craft a message whose appeal is as broad as the public itself
    D. let the program's achievements speak for themselves and rely on word-of-mouth

14.____

15. Advantages associated with using the World Wide Web as an educational tool include

    I.   an appeal to younger generations of the public
    II. visually-oriented, interactive learning
    III. learning that is not confined by space, time, or institutional association
    IV. a variety of methods for verifying use and learning

    A. I only
    B. I and II
    C. I, II and III
    D. I, II, III and IV

15.____

16. In agencies involved in health care, community relations is a critical function because it

    A. serves as an intermediary between the agency and consumers
    B. generates a clear mission statement for agency goals and priorities
    C. ensures patient privacy while satisfying the media's right to information
    D. helps marketing professionals determine the wants and needs of agency constituents

16.____

17. After an extensive campaign to promote its newest program to constituents, an agency learns that most of the audience did not understand the intended message. Most likely, the agency has

    A. chosen words that were intended to inform, rather than persuade
    B. not accurately interpreted what the audience really needed to know
    C. overestimated the ability of the audience to receive and process the message
    D. compensated for noise that may have interrupted the message

17.____

18. The necessary elements that lead to conviction and motivation in the minds of participants in an educational or information program include each of the following, EXCEPT the _____ of the message.

    A. acceptability
    B. intensity
    C. single-channel appeal
    D. pervasiveness

18.____

19. Printed materials are often at the core of educational programs provided by public agencies. The primary disadvantage associated with print is that it

    A. does not enable comprehensive treatment of a topic
    B. is generally unreliable in term of assessing results
    C. is often the most expensive medium available
    D. is constrained by time

19.____

20. Traditional thinking on public opinion holds that there is about _____ percent of the public who are pivotal to shifting the balance and momentum of opinion—they are concerned about an issue, but not fanatical, and interested enough to pay attention to a reasoned discussion.

    A. 2
    B. 10
    C. 33
    D. 51

20.____

21. One of the most useful guidelines for influencing attitude change among people is to

    A. invite the target audience to come to you, rather than approaching them
    B. use moral appeals as the primary approach
    C. use concrete images to enable people to see the results of behaviors or indifference
    D. offer tangible rewards to people for changes in behaviors

21.____

22. An agency is attempting to evaluate the effectiveness of its educational program. For this purpose, it wants to observe several focus groups discussing the same program. Which of the following would NOT be a guideline for the use of focus groups?

    A. Focus groups should only include those who have participated in the program.
    B. Be sure to accurately record the discussion.
    C. The same questions should be asked at each focus group meeting.
    D. It is often helpful to have a neutral, non-agency employee facilitate discussions.

22.____

23. Research consistently shows that _____ is the determinant most likely to make a news-paper editor run a news release.   23.____

    A. novelty
    B. prominence
    C. proximity
    D. conflict

24. Which of the following is NOT one of the major variables to take into account when con-sidering a population-needs assessment?   24.____

    A. State of program development
    B. Resources available
    C. Demographics
    D. Community attitudes

25. The first step in any communications audit is to   25.____

    A. develop a research instrument
    B. determine how the organization currently communicates
    C. hire a contractor
    D. determine which audience to assess

KEY (CORRECT ANSWERS)

1.	A		11.	A
2.	D		12.	D
3.	A		13.	B
4.	A		14.	B
5.	D		15.	C
6.	C		16.	A
7.	D		17.	B
8.	C		18.	C
9.	B		19.	B
10.	C		20.	B

21.	C
22.	A
23.	C
24.	C
25.	D

113

TEST 2

DIRECTIONS: Each question or incomplete statement is followed by several suggested answers or completions. Select the one that BEST answers the question or completes the statement. *PRINT THE LETTER OF THE CORRECT ANSWER IN THE SPACE AT THE RIGHT.*

1. A public relations practitioner at an agency has just composed a press release highlight-   1.____
    ing a program's recent accomplishments and success stories. In pitching such releases
    to print outlets, the practitioner should
        I.   e-mail, mail, or send them by messenger
        II.   address them to "editor" or "news director"
        III. have an assistant call all media contacts by telephone
        IV.   ask reporters or editors how they prefer to receive them

    A. I and II   B. I and IV   C. II, III and IV   D. III only

2. The "output goals" of an educational program are MOST likely to include   2.____

    A. specified ratings of services by participants on a standardized scale
    B. observable effects on a given community or clientele
    C. the number of instructional hours provided
    D. the number of participants served

3. An agency wants to evaluate satisfaction levels among program participants, and mails   3.____
    out questionnaires to everyone who has been enrolled in the last year. The primary prob-
    lem associated with this method of evaluative research is that it

    A. poses a significant inconvenience for respondents
    B. is inordinately expensive
    C. does not allow for follow-up or clarification questions
    D. usually involves a low response rate

4. A communications audit is an important tool for measuring   4.____

    A. the depth of penetration of a particular message or program
    B. the cost of the organization's information campaigns
    C. how key audiences perceive an organization
    D. the commitment of internal stakeholders

5. The "ABC's" of written learning objectives include each of the following, EXCEPT   5.____

    A. Audience   B. Behavior   C. Conditions   D. Delineation

6. When attempting to change the behaviors of constituents, it is important to keep in mind   6.____
    that
        I.   most people are skeptical of communications that try to get them to change
           their behaviors
        II.   in most cases, a person selects the media to which he exposes himself
        III. people tend to react defensively to messages or programs that rely on fear
           as a motivating factor
        IV.   programs should aim for the broadest appeal possible in order to include as
           many participants as possible

    A. I and II   B. I, II and III   C. II and III   D. I, II, III and IV

7. The "laws" of public opinion include the idea that it is 7.____

    A. useful for anticipating emergencies
    B. not sensitive to important events
    C. basically determined by self-interest
    D. sustainable through persistent appeals

8. Which of the following types of evaluations is used to measure public attitudes before 8.____
and after an information/educational program?

    A. retrieval study
    B. copy test
    C. quota sampling
    D. benchmark study

9. The primary source for internal communications is/are usually 9.____

    A. flow charts
    B. meetings
    C. voice mail
    D. printed publications

10. An agency representative is putting together informational materials—brochures and a 10.____
newsletter—outlining changes in one of the state's biggest benefits programs. In assembling print materials as a medium for delivering information to the public, the representative should keep in mind each of the following trends:

    I. For various reasons, the reading capabilities of the public are in general decline
    II. Without tables and graphs to help illustrate the changes, it is unlikely that the message will be delivered effectively
    III. Professionals and career-oriented people are highly receptive to information written in the form of a journal article or empirical study
    IV. People tend to be put off by print materials that use itemized and bulleted (•) lists.

    A. I and II   B. I, II and III   C. II and III   D. I, II, III and IV

11. Which of the following steps in a problem-oriented information campaign would typically 11.____
be implemented FIRST?

    A. Deciding on tactics
    B. Determining a communications strategy
    C. Evaluating the problem's impact
    D. Developing an organizational strategy

12. A common pitfall in conducting an educational program is to

    A. aim it at the wrong target audience
    B. overfund it
    C. leave it in the hands of people who are in the business of education, rather than those with expertise in the business of the organization
    D. ignore the possibility that some other organization is meeting the same educational need for the target audience

12.____

13. The key factors that affect the credibility of an agency's educational program include

    A. organization
    B. scope
    C. sophistication
    D. penetration

13.____

14. Research on public opinion consistently demonstrates that it is

    A. easy to move people toward a strong opinion on anything, as long as they are approached directly through their emotions
    B. easier to move people away from an opinion they currently hold than to have them form an opinion about something they have not previously cared about
    C. easy to move people toward a strong opinion on anything, as long as the message appeals to their reason and intellect
    D. difficult to move people toward a strong opinion on anything, no matter what the approach

14.____

15. In conducting an education program, many agencies use meetings and conferences to educate an audience about the organization and its programs. Advantages associated with this approach include
    I. a captive audience that is known to be interested in the topic
    II. ample opportunities for verifying learning
    III. cost-efficient meeting space
    IV. the ability to provide information on a wider variety of subjects

    A. I and II
    B. I, III and IV
    C. II and III
    D. I, II, III and IV

15.____

16. An agency is attempting to evaluate the effectiveness of its educational programs. For this purpose, it wants to observe several focus groups discussing particular programs. For this purpose, a focus group should never number more than _____ participants.

    A. 5   B. 10   C. 15   D. 20

16.____

17. A _____ speech is written so that several agency members can deliver it to different audiences with only minor variations.

    A. basic   B. printed   C. quota   D. pattern

17.____

18. Which of the following statements about public opinion is generally considered to be FALSE?   18.____

    A. Opinion is primarily reactive rather than proactive.
    B. People have more opinions about goals than about the means by which to achieve them.
    C. Facts tend to shift opinion in the accepted direction when opinion is not solidly structured.
    D. Public opinion is based more on information than desire.

19. An agency is trying to promote its educational program. As a general rule, the agency should NOT assume that   19.____

    A. people will only participate if they perceive an individual benefit
    B. promotions need to be aimed at small, discrete groups
    C. if the program is good, the audience will find out about it
    D. a variety of methods, including advertising, special events, and direct mail, should be considered

20. In planning a successful educational program, probably the first and most important question for an agency to ask is: 20.____

    A. What will be the content of the program?
    B. Who will be served by the program?
    C. When is the best time to schedule the program?
    D. Why is the program necessary?

21. Media kits are LEAST likely to contain   21.____

    A. fact sheets
    B. memoranda
    C. photographs with captions
    D. news releases

22. The use of pamphlets and booklets as media for communication with the public often involves the disadvantage that   22.____

    A. the messages contained within them are frequently nonspecific
    B. it is difficult to measure their effectiveness in delivering the message
    C. there are few opportunities for people to refer to them
    D. color reproduction is poor

23. The most important prerequisite of a good educational program is an   23.____

    A. abundance of resources to implement it
    B. individual staff unit formed for the purpose of program delivery
    C. accurate needs assessment
    D. uneducated constituency

24. After an education program has been delivered, an agency conducts a program evalua-   24.____
tion to determine whether its objectives have been met. General rules about how to conduct such an education program evaluation include each of the following, EXCEPT that it

    A. must be done immediately after the program has been implemented
    B. should be simple and easy to use
    C. should be designed so that tabulation of responses can take place quickly and
       inexpensively
    D. should solicit mostly subjective, open-ended responses if the audience was large

25. Using electronic media such as television as means of educating the public is typically   25.____
recommended ONLY for agencies that
    I. have a fairly simple message to begin with
    II. want to reach the masses, rather than a targeted audience
    III. have substantial financial resources
    IV. accept that they will not be able to measure the results of the campaign with
       much precision

    A. I and II
    B. I, II and III
    C. II and IV
    D. I, II, III and IV

KEY (CORRECT ANSWERS)

1.	B		11.	C
2.	C		12.	D
3.	D		13.	A
4.	C		14.	D
5.	D		15.	B
6.	B		16.	B
7.	C		17.	D
8.	D		18.	D
9.	D		19.	C
10.	A		20.	D

21.	B
22.	B
23.	C
24.	D
25.	D

EXAMINATION SECTION
TEST 1

DIRECTIONS: Each question or incomplete statement is followed by several suggested answers or completions. Select the one that BEST answers the question or completes the statement. *PRINT THE LETTER OF THE CORRECT ANSWER IN THE SPACE AT THE RIGHT.*

1. A management approach widely used today is based on the belief that decisions should be made and actions should be taken by managers closest to the organization's problems.
   This style of management is MOST appropriately called _____ management.

   A. scientific
   B. means-end
   C. decentralized
   D. internal process

1.____

2. As contrasted with tall organization structures with narrow spans of control, flat organization structures with wide spans of control MOST usually provide

   A. fast communication and information flows
   B. more levels in the organizational hierarchy
   C. fewer workers reporting to supervisors
   D. lower motivation because of tighter control standards

2.____

3. Use of the systems approach is MOST likely to lead to

   A. consideration of the impact on the whole organization of actions taken in any part of that organization
   B. the placing of restrictions on departmental authority
   C. use of mathematical models to suboptimize production
   D. consideration of the activities of each unit of an organization as a totality without regard to the remainder of the organization

3.____

4. An administrator, with overall responsibility for all administrative operations in a large operating agency, is considering organizing the agency's personnel office around either of the following two alternative concepts:
   Alternative I-   a corps of specialists for each branch of personnel subject matter, whose skills, counsel, or work products are coordinated only by the agency personnel officer
   Alternative II-   a crew of so-called *personnel generalists,* who individually work with particular segments of the organization but deal with all subspecialties of the personnel function
   The one of the following which MOST tends to be a DRAWBACK of Alternative I, as compared with Alternative II, is that

   A. training and employee relations work call for education, interests, and talents that differ from those required for classification and compensation work
   B. personnel office staff may develop only superficial familiarity with the specialized areas to which they have been assigned
   C. supervisors may fail to get continuing overall personnel advice on an integrated basis
   D. the personnel specialists are likely to become so interested in and identified with the operating view as to particular cases that they lose their professional objectivity and become merely advocates of what some supervisor wants

4.____

5. The matrix summary or decision matrix is a useful tool for making choices.   5.____
Its effectiveness is MOST dependent upon the user's ability to

    A. write a computer program (Fortran or Cobol)
    B. assign weights representing the relative importance of the objectives
    C. solve a set of two equations with two unknowns
    D. work with matrix algebra

6. An organizational form which is set up only on an *ad hoc* basis to meet specific goals is   6.____
said PRIMARILY to use

    A. clean break departmentation
    B. matrix or task force organization
    C. scalar specialization
    D. geographic or area-wide decentralization

7. The concept of job enlargement would LEAST properly be implemented by   7.____

    A. permitting workers to follow through on tasks or projects from start to finish
    B. delegating the maximum authority possible for decision-making to lower levels in the hierarchy
    C. maximizing the number of professional classes in the classification plan
    D. training employees to grow beyond whatever tasks they have been performing

8. As used in the area of administration, the principle of *unity of command* MOST specifi-   8.____
cally means that

    A. an individual should report to only one superior for any single activity
    B. individuals make better decisions than do committees
    C. in large organizations, chains of command are normally too long
    D. an individual should not supervise over five subordinates

9. The methods of operations research, statistical decision-making, and linear program-   9.____
ming have been referred to as the tool kit of the manager.
Utilization of these tools is LEAST useful in the performance of which of the following
functions?

    A. Elimination of the need for using judgment when making decisions
    B. Facilitation of decision-making without the need for sub-optimization
    C. Quantifying problems for management study
    D. Research and analysis of management operations

10. When acting in their respective managerial capacities, the chief executive officer and the   10.____
office supervisor both perform the fundamental functions of management. Of the following differences between the two, the one which is generally considered to be the LEAST
significant is the

    A. breadth of the objectives
    B. complexity of measuring actual efficiency of performance
    C. number of decisions made
    D. organizational relationships affected by actions taken

11. The ability of operations researchers to solve complicated problems rests on their use of   11.____
models.
These models can BEST be described as

    A. mathematical statements of the problem
    B. physical constructs that simulate a work layout
    C. toy-like representations of employees in work environments
    D. role-playing simulations

12. Of the following, it is MOST likely to be proper for the agency head to allow the agency   12.____
personnel officer to make final selection of appointees from certified eligible lists where
there are

    A. *small* numbers of employees to be hired in newly-developed professional fields
    B. *large* numbers of persons to be hired for key managerial positions
    C. *large* numbers of persons to be hired in very routine occupations where the individual discretion of operating officials is not vital
    D. *small* numbers of persons to be hired in highly specialized professional occupations which are vital to the agency's operations

13. Of the following, an operating agency personnel office is LEAST likely to be able to exert   13.____
strong influence or control within the operating agency by

    A. interpreting to the operating agency head what is intended by the directives and rules emanating from the central personnel agency
    B. establishing the key objectives of those line divisions of the operating agency employing large numbers of staff and operating under the management-by-objectives approach
    C. formulating and proposing to the agency head the internal policies and procedures on personnel matters required within the operating agency
    D. exercising certain discretionary authority in the application of the agency head's general personnel policies to actual specific situations

14. PERT is a recently developed system used *primarily* to   14.____

    A. evaluate the quality of applicants' backgrounds
    B. analyze and control the timing aspects of a major project
    C. control the total expenditure of agency funds within a monthly or quarterly time period
    D. analyze and control the differential effect on costs of purchasing in different quantities

15. Assume that an operating agency has among its vacant positions two positions, each of   15.____
which encompasses mixed duties. Both require appointees to have considerable education and experience, but these requirements are essential only for the more difficult duties of these positions. In the place of these positions, an administrator creates two new positions, one in which the higher duties are concentrated and the other with the lesser functions requiring only minimum preparation.
Of the following, it is generally MOST appropriate to characterize the administrator's action as a(n)

A. *undesirable* example of deliberate downgrading of standards and requirements
B. *undesirable* manipulation of the classification system for non-merit purposes
C. *desirable* broadening of the definition of a class of positions
D. *desirable* example of job redesign

16. Of the following, the LEAST important stumbling block to the development of personnel mobility among governmental jurisdictions is the   16.____

A. limitations on lateral entry above junior levels in many jurisdictions
B. continued collection of filing fees for civil service tests by many governmental jurisdictions
C. absence of reciprocal exchange of retirement benefit eligibility between governments
D. disparities in salary scales between governments

17. Of the following, the MAJOR disadvantage of a personnel system that features the *selection out* (forced retirement) of those who have been passed over a number of times for promotion is that such a system   17.____

A. wastes manpower which is perfectly competent at one level but unable to rise above that level
B. wastes funds by requiring review boards
C. leads to excessive recruiting of newcomers from outside the system
D. may not be utilized in *closed* career systems with low maximum age limits for entrance

18. Of the following, the fields in which operating agency personnel offices generally exercise the MOST stringent controls over first line supervisors in the agency are   18.____

A. methods analysis and work simplification
B. selection and position classification
C. vestibule training and Gantt chart
D. suggestion systems and staff development

19. Of the following, computers are normally MOST effective in handling   19.____

A. large masses of data requiring simple processing
B. small amounts of data requiring constantly changing complex processing
C. data for which reported values are often subject to inaccuracies
D. large amounts of data requiring continual programming and reprocessing

20. Contingency planning, which has long been used by the military and is assuming increasing importance in other organizations, may BEST be described as a process which utilizes   20.____

A. alternative plans based on varying assumptions
B. *crash programs* by organizations departmentalized along process lines
C. plans which mandate substitution of equipment for manpower at predetermined operational levels
D. plans that individually and accurately predict future events

21. In the management of inventory, two kinds of costs normally determine when to order   21.____
and in what amounts. The one of the following choices which includes BOTH of these
kinds of costs is _____ costs and _____ costs.

    A. carrying; storage   B. personnel; order
    C. computer; order   D. personnel; computer

22. At top management levels, the one of the following which is generally the MOST impor-   22.____
tant executive skill is skill in

    A. budgeting procedures
    B. a technical discipline
    C. controlling actions in accordance with previously approved plans
    D. seeing the organization as a whole

23. Of the following, the BEST way to facilitate the successful operation of a committee is to   23.____
set guidelines establishing its

    A. budget exclusive of personnel costs
    B. location
    C. schedule of meetings or conferences
    D. scope or purpose

24. Executive training programs that single out particular managers and groom them for pro-   24.____
motion create the so-called organizational *crown princes.*
Of the following, the MOST serious problem that arises in connection with this
practice is that

    A. the managers chosen for promotion seldom turn out to be the best managers
       since the future potential of persons cannot be predicted
    B. not enough effort is made to remove organizational obstacles in the way of their
       development and achievement
    C. the resentment of the managers not selected for the program has an adverse
       effect on the motivation of those managers not selected
    D. performance appraisal and review are not carried out systematically enough

25. Of the following, the LEAST likely result of the use of the concept of job enlargement is   25.____
that

    A. coordination will be simplified
    B. the individual's job will become less challenging
    C. worker satisfaction will increase
    D. fewer people will have to give attention to each piece of work

KEY (CORRECT ANSWERS)

1.	C		11.	A
2.	A		12.	C
3.	A		13.	B
4.	C		14.	B
5.	B		15.	D
6.	B		16.	B
7.	C		17.	A
8.	A		18.	B
9.	A		19.	A
10.	C		20.	A

21.	A
22.	D
23.	D
24.	C
25.	B

TEST 2

DIRECTIONS: Each question or incomplete statement is followed by several suggested answers or completions. Select the one that BEST answers the question or completes the statement. *PRINT THE LETTER OF THE CORRECT ANSWER IN THE SPACE AT THE RIGHT.*

1. The one of the following which is MOST likely to be emphasized in the use of the brain-storming technique is the

    A. early consideration of cost factors of all ideas which may be suggested
    B. avoidance of impractical suggestions
    C. separation of the generation of ideas from their evaluation
    D. appraisal of suggestions concurrently with their initial presentation

1.____

2. Of the following, the BEST method for assessing managerial performance is generally to

    A. compare the manager's accomplishments against clear, specific, agreed-upon goals
    B. compare the manager's traits with those of his peers on a predetermined objective scale
    C. measure the manager's behavior against a listing of itemized personal traits
    D. measure the manager's success according to the enumeration of the *satisfaction* principle

2.____

3. As compared with recruitment from outside, selection from within the service must generally show GREATER concern for the

    A. prestige in which the public service as a whole is held by the public
    B. morale of the candidate group comprising the recruitment field
    C. cost of examining per candidate
    D. benefits of the use of standardized and validated tests

3.____

4. Performance budgeting focuses PRIMARY attention upon which one of the following? The

    A. things to be acquired, such as supplies and equipment
    B. general character and relative importance of the work to be done or the service to be rendered
    C. list of personnel to be employed, by specific title
    D. separation of employee performance evaluations from employee compensation

4.____

5. Of the following, the FIRST step in the installation and operation of a performance budgeting system generally should be the

    A. identification of program costs in relationship to the accounting system and operating structure
    B. identification of the specific end results of past programs in other jurisdictions
    C. identification of work programs that are meaningful for management purposes
    D. establishment of organizational structures each containing only one work program

5.____

6. Of the following, the MOST important purpose of a system of quarterly allotments of appropriated funds generally is to enable the

    6._____

    A. head of the judicial branch to determine the legality of agency requests for budget increases
    B. operating agencies of government to upgrade the quality of their services without increasing costs
    C. head of the executive branch to control the rate at which the operating agencies obligate and expend funds
    D. operating agencies of government to avoid payment for services which have not been properly rendered by employees

7. In the preparation of the agency's budget, the agency's central budget office has two responsibilities: program review and management improvement.
Which one of the following questions concerning an operating agency's program is MOST closely related to the agency budget officer's program review responsibility?

    7._____

    A. Can expenditures for supplies, materials, or equipment be reduced?
    B. Will improved work methods contribute to a more effective program?
    C. What is the relative importance of this program as compared with other programs?
    D. Will a realignment of responsibilities contribute to a higher level of program performance?

8. Of the following, the method of evaluating relative rates of return normally and generally thought to be MOST useful in evaluating government operations is _____ analysis.

    8._____

    A. cost-benefit
    B. budget variance
    C. investment capital
    D. budget planning program

9. The one of the following assumptions that is LEAST likely to be made by a democratic or permissive type of leader is that

    9._____

    A. commitment to goals is seldom a result of monetary rewards alone
    B. people can learn not only to accept, but also to seek, responsibility
    C. the average person prefers security over advancement
    D. creativity may be found in most segments of the population

10. In attempting to motivate subordinates, a manager should PRINCIPALLY be aware of the fact that

    10._____

    A. the psychological qualities of people, in general, are easily predictable
    B. fear, as a traditional form of motivation, has lost much of its former power to motivate people in our modern industrial society
    C. fear is still the most potent force in motivating the behavior of subordinates in the public service
    D. the worker has very little control over the quality and quantity of his output

11. Assume that the following figures represent the number of work-units that were produced   11._____
during a week by each of sixteen employees in a division:

12	16	13	18
21	12	16	13
16	13	17	21
13	15	18	20

If all of the employees of the division who produced thirteen work-units during the
week had instead produced fifteen work-units during that same week, then for that
week, the

    A.   mean, median, and mode would all change
    B.   mean and mode would change, but the median would remain the same
    C.   mode and median would change, but the mean would remain the same
    D.   mode, mean, and median would all still remain unchanged in value

12. An important law in motivation theory is called the *law of effect.* This law says that behav-   12._____
ior which satisfies a person's needs tends to be repeated; behavior which does not satisfy a person's needs tends to be eliminated. The one of the following which is the BEST
interpretation of this law is that

    A.   productivity depends on personality traits
    B.   diversity of goals leads to instability of motivation
    C.   the greater the satisfaction, the more likely it is that the behavior will be reinforced
    D.   extrinsic satisfaction is more important than intrinsic reward

13. Of the following, the MOST acceptable reason an administrator can give for taking advice   13._____
from other employees in the organization only when he asks for it is that he wants to

    A.   encourage creativity and high morale
    B.   keep dysfunctional pressures and inconsistent recommendations to a minimum
    C.   show his superiors and peers who is in charge
    D.   show his subordinates who is in charge

14. A complete picture of the communication channels in an organization can BEST be   14._____
revealed by

    A.   observing the planned paperwork system
    B.   recording the highly intermittent patterns of communication
    C.   plotting the entire flow of information over a period of time
    D.   monitoring the *grapevine*

Questions 15-16.

DIRECTIONS: Answer Questions 15 and 16 SOLELY on the basis of the passage below.

Management by objectives (MBO) may be defined as the process by which the superior and the subordinate managers of an organization jointly define its common goals, define each individual's major areas of responsibility in terms of the results expected of him and use these measures as guides for operating the unit and assessing the contribution of each of its members.

The MBO approach requires that after organizational goals are established and communicated, targets must be set for each individual position which are congruent with organizational goals. Periodic performance reviews and a final review using the objectives set as criteria are also basic to this approach.

Recent studies have shown that MBO programs are influenced by attitudes and perceptions of the boss, the company, the reward-punishment system, and the program itself. In addition, the manner in which the MBO program is carried out can influence the success of the program. A study done in the late sixties indicates that the best results are obtained when the manager sets goals which deal with significant problem areas in the organizational unit, or with the subordinate's personal deficiencies. These goals must be clear with regard to what is expected of the subordinate. The frequency of feedback is also important in the success of a management-by-Objectives program. Generally, the greater the amount of feedback, the more successful the MBO program.

15.   According to the above passage, the expected output for individual employees should be determined   15.____

    A.   after a number of reviews of work performance
    B.   after common organizational goals are defined
    C.   before common organizational goals are defined
    D.   on the basis of an employee's personal qualities

16.   According to the above passage, the management-by-objectives approach requires   16.____

    A.   less feedback than other types of management programs
    B.   little review of on-the-job performance after the initial setting of goals
    C.   general conformance between individual goals and organizational goals
    D.   the setting of goals which deal with minor problem areas in the organization

Questions 17-19.

DIRECTIONS: Answer Questions 17 to 19 SOLELY on the basis of the passage below.

During the last decade, a great deal of interest has been generated around the phenomenon of organizational development, or the process of developing human resources through conscious organisation effort. Organizational development (OD) stresses improving interpersonal relationships and organizational skills, such as communication, to a much greater degree than individual training ever did.

The kind of training that an organization should emphasize depends upon the present and future structure of the organization. If future organizations are to be unstable, shifting coalitions, then individual skills and abilities, particularly those emphasizing innovativeness, creativity, flexibility, and the latest technological knowledge, are crucial, and individual training is most appropriate.

But if there is to be little change in organizational structure, then the main thrust of training should be group-oriented or organizational development. This approach seems better designed for overcoming hierarchical barriers, for developing a degree of interpersonal relationships which make communication along the chain of command possible, and for retaining a modicum of innovation and/or flexibility.

17. According to the above passage, group-oriented training is MOST useful in   17.____

    A. developing a communications system that will facilitate understanding through the chain of command
    B. highly flexible and mobile organizations
    C. preventing the crossing of hierarchical barriers within an organization
    D. saving energy otherwise wasted on developing methods of dealing with rigid hierarchies

18. The one of the following conclusions which can be drawn MOST appropriately from the   18.____
above passage is that

    A. behavioral research supports the use of organizational development training methods rather than individualized training
    B. it is easier to provide individualized training in specific skills than to set up sensitivity training programs
    C. organizational development eliminates innovative or flexible activity
    D. the nature of an organization greatly influences which training methods will be most effective

19. According to the above passage, the one of the following which is LEAST important for   19.____
large-scale organizations geared to rapid and abrupt change is

    A. current technological information
    B. development of a high degree of interpersonal relationships
    C. development of individual skills and abilities
    D. emphasis on creativity

Questions 20-25.

DIRECTIONS: Each of Questions 20 through 25 consists of a statement which contains one word that is incorrectly used because it is not in keeping with the meaning that the quotation is evidently intended to convey. Determine which word is INCORRECTLY used. Select from the choices lettered A, B, C, and D the word which, when substituted for the incorrectly used word, would BEST help to convey the meaning of the statement.

20. One of the considerations likely to affect the currency of classification, particularly in professional and managerial occupations, is the impact of the incumbent's capacities on the job. Some work is highly susceptible to change as the result of the special talents or interests of the classifier. Organization should never be so rigid as not to capitalize on the innovative or unusual proclivities of its key employees. While a machine operator may not be able, even subtly, to change the character or level of his job, the design engineer, the attorney, or the organization and methods analyst might readily do so. Reliance on his judgment and the scope of his assignments may both grow as the result of his skill, insight, and capacity.

    20.____

    A. unlikely   B. incumbent   C. directly   D. scope

21. The supply of services by the state is not governed by market price. The aim is to supply such services to all who need them and to treat all consumers equally. This objective especially compels the civil servant to maintain a role of strict impartiality, based on the principle of equality of individual citizens vis-a-vis their government. However, there is a clear difference between being neutral and being impartial. If the requirement is construed to mean that all civil servants should be political eunuchs, devoid of the drive and motivation essential to dynamic administration, then the concept of impartiality is being seriously utilized. Modern governments should not be stopped from demanding that their hirelings have not only the technical but the emotional qualifications necessary for wholehearted effort.

    21.____

    A. determined   B. rule   C. stable   D. misapplied

22. The manager was barely listening. Recently, at the divisional level, several new fronts of troubles had erupted, including a requirement to increase production yet hold down operating costs and somehow raise quality standards. Though the three objectives were basically obsolete, top departmental management was insisting on the simultaneous attainment of them, an insistence not helping the manager's ulcer, an old enemy within. Thus, the manager could not find time for interest in individuals-only in statistics which regiments of individuals, like unconsidered Army privates, added up to.

    22.____

    A. quantity   B. battalion   C. incompatible   D. quiet

23. When a large volume of data flows directly between operators and first-line supervisors, senior executives tend to be out of the mainstream of work. Summary reports can increase their remoteness. An executive needs to know the volume, quality, and cost of completed work, and exceptional problems. In addition, he may desire information on key operating conditions. Summary reports on these matters are, therefore, essential features of a communications network and make delegation without loss of control possible.

    23.____

    A. unimportant   B. quantity
    C. offset   D. incomplete

24. Of major significance in management is harmony between the overall objectives of the organization and the managerial objectives within that organization. In addition, harmony among goals of managers is impossible; they should not be at cross-purposes. Each manager's goal should supplement and assist the goals of his colleagues. Likewise, the objectives of individuals or nonmanagement members should be harmonized with those of the manager. When this is accomplished, genuine teamwork is the result, and human relations are aided materially. The integration of managers' and individuals' goals aids in achieving greater work satisfaction at all levels.

24.____

    A. competition   B. dominate
    C. incremental   D. vital

25. Change constantly challenges the manager. Some of this change is evolutionary, some revolutionary, some recognizable, some nonrecognizable. Both forces within an enterprise and forces outside the enterprise cause managers to act and react in initiating changes in their immediate working environment. Change invalidates existing operations. Goals are not being accomplished in the best manner, problems develop, and frequently because of the lack of time, only patched-up solutions are followed. The result is that the mode of management is profound in nature and temporary in effectiveness. A complete overhaul of managerial operations should take place. It appears quite likely that we are just beginning to see the real effects of change in our society; the pace probably will accelerate in ways that few really understand or know how to handle.

25.____

    A. confirms   B. decline
    C. instituting   D. superficial

KEY (CORRECT ANSWERS)

1.	C	11.	B
2.	A	12.	C
3.	B	13.	B
4.	B	14.	C
5.	C	15.	B
6.	C	16.	C
7.	C	17.	A
8.	A	18.	D
9.	C	19.	B
10.	B	20.	B

21.	D
22.	C
23.	C
24.	D
25.	D

EXAMINATION SECTION
TEST 1

DIRECTIONS: Each question or incomplete statement is followed by several suggested answers or completions. Select the one that BEST answers the question or completes the statement. *PRINT THE LETTER OF THE CORRECT ANSWER IN THE SPACE AT THE RIGHT.*

1. Assume that a manager is preparing a list of reasons to justify making a major change in methods and procedures in his agency.
Which of the following reasons would be LEAST appropriate on such a list?

    A. Improve the means for satisfying needs and wants of agency personnel
    B. Increase efficiency
    C. Intensify competition and stimulate loyalty to separate work groups
    D. Contribute to the individual and group satisfaction of agency personnel

1.____

2. Many managers recognize the benefits of decentralization but are concerned about the danger of over-relaxation of control as a result of increased delegation.
Of the following, the MOST appropriate means of establishing proper control under decentralization is for the manager to

    A. establish detailed standards for all phases of operation
    B. shift his attention from operating details to appraisal of results
    C. keep himself informed by decreasing the time span covered by reports
    D. make unilateral decisions on difficult situations that arise in decentralized locations

2.____

3. In some agencies, the counsel to the agency head is given the right to bypass the chain of command and issue orders directly to the staff concerning matters that involve certain specific processes and practices.
This situation MOST NEARLY illustrates the principle of

    A. the acceptance theory of authority
    B. multiple-linear authority
    C. splintered authority
    D. functional authority

3.____

4. Assume that a manager is writing a brief report to his superior outlining the advantages of matrix organization. Of the following, it would be INCORRECT to state that

    A. in matrix organization, a project is emphasized by designating one individual as the focal point for all matters pertaining to it
    B. utilization of manpower can be flexible in matrix organization because a reservoir of specialists is maintained in the line operations
    C. the usual line staff arrangement is generally reversed in matrix organization
    D. in matrix organization, responsiveness to project needs is generally faster due to establishing needed communication lines and decision points

4.____

5. It is commonly understood that communication is an important part of the administrative process.
Which of the following is NOT a valid principle of the communication process in administration?

    A. The channels of communication should be spontaneous.
    B. The lines of communication should be as direct and as short as possible.
    C. Communications should be authenticated.
    D. The persons serving in communications centers should be competent.

    5.____

6. The PRIMARY purpose of the quantitative approach in management is to

    A. identify better alternatives for management decision-making
    B. substitute data for judgment
    C. match opinions to data
    D. match data to opinions

    6.____

7. If an executive wants to make a strong case for running his agency as a flat type of structure, he should point out that the PRIMARY advantage of doing so is to

    A. provide less experience in decision-making for agency personnel
    B. facilitate frequent contact between each superior and his immediate subordinates
    C. improve communication and unify attitudes
    D. improve communication and diversify attitudes

    7.____

8. In deciding how detailed his delegation of authority to a subordinate should be, a manager should follow the general principle that

    A. delegation of authority is more detailed at the top of the organizational structure
    B. detailed delegation of authority is associated with detailed work assignments
    C. delegation of authority should be in sufficient detail to prevent overlapping assignments
    D. detailed delegation of authority is associated with broad work assignments

    8.____

9. In recent years, newer and more fluid types of organizational forms have been developed. One of these is a type of free-form organization.
Another name for this type of organization is the

    A. project organization
    C. naturalistic structure
    B. semimix organization
    D. semipermanent structure

    9.____

10. Which of the following is the MAJOR objective of operational or management systems audits?

    A. Determining the number of personnel needed
    B. Recommending opportunities for improving operating and management practices
    C. Detecting fraud
    D. Determining organization problems

    10.____

11. Assume that a manager observes that conflict exists between his agency and another operating agency of government.
Which of the following statements is the LEAST probable cause of this conflict?

    A. Incompatibility between the agencies' goals but similarity in their resource allocations
    B. Compatibility between agencies' goals and resources
    C. Status differences between agency personnel
    D. Differences in perceptions of each other's policies

11.____

12. Of the following, a MAJOR purpose of brainstorming as a problem-solving technique is to

    A. develop the ability to concentrate
    B. encourage creative thinking
    C. evaluate employees' ideas
    D. develop critical ability

12.____

13. The one of the following requirements which is LEAST likely to accompany regular delegation of work from a manager to a subordinate is a(n)

    A. need to review the organization's workload
    B. indication of what work the subordinate is to do
    C. need to grant authority to the subordinate
    D. obligation for the subordinate who accepts the work to try to complete it

13.____

14. Of the following, the one factor which is generally considered LEAST essential to successful committee operation is

    A. stating a clear definition of the authority and scope of the committee
    B. selecting the committee chairman carefully
    C. limiting the size of the committee to four persons
    D. limiting the subject matter to that which can be handled in group discussion

14.____

15. In using the program evaluation and review technique, the *critical path* is the path that

    A. requires the shortest time
    B. requires the longest time
    C. focuses most attention on social constraints
    D. focuses most attention on repetitious jobs

15.____

16. Which one of the following is LEAST characteristic of the management-by-objectives approach?

    A. The scope within which the employee may exercise decision-making is broadened
    B. The employee starts with a self-appraisal of his performances, abilities, and potential
    C. Emphasis is placed on activities performed; activities orientation is maximized
    D. Each employee participates in determining his own objectives

16.____

17. The function of management which puts into effect the decisions, plans, and programs that have previously been worked out for achieving the goals of the group is MOST appropriately called

    A. scheduling   B. classifying
    C. budgeting   D. directing

17.____

18. In the establishment of a plan to improve office productive efficiency, which of the following guidelines is LEAST helpful in setting sound work standards?

    A. Employees must accept the plan's objectives.
    B. Current production averages must be promulgated as work standards for a group.
    C. The work flow must generally be fairly constant.
    D. The operation of the plan must be expressed in terms understandable to the worker.

18.____

19. The one of the following activities which, generally speaking, is of *relatively* MAJOR importance at the lower-management level and of *somewhat* LESSER importance at higher-management levels is

    A. actuating   B. forecasting
    C. organizing   D. planning

19.____

20. Three styles of leadership exist: democratic, authoritarian, and laissez-faire.
Of the following work situations, the one in which a democratic approach would normally be the MOST effective is when the work is

    A. routine and moderately complex
    B. repetitious and simple
    C. complex and not routine
    D. simple and not routine

20.____

21. Governmental and business organizations *generally* encounter the GREATEST difficulties in developing tangible measures of which one of the following?

    A. The level of expenditures
    B. Contributions to social welfare
    C. Retention rates
    D. Causes of labor unrest

21.____

22. Of the following, a *management-by-objectives* program is BEST described as

    A. a new comprehensive plan of organization
    B. introduction of budgets and financial controls
    C. introduction of long–range planning
    D. development of future goals with supporting and related progress reviews

22.____

23. Research and analysis is probably the most widely used technique for selecting alterna-   23.____
tives when major planning decisions are involved.
Of the following, a VALUABLE characteristic of research and analysis is that this technique

    A.   places the problem in a meaningful conceptual framework
    B.   involves practical application of the various alternatives
    C.   accurately analyzes all important tangibles
    D.   is much less expensive than other problem–solving methods

24. If a manager were assigned the task of using a systems approach to designing a new   24.____
work unit, which of the following should he consider FIRST in carrying out his design?

    A.   Networks
    B.   Work flows and information processes
    C.   Linkages and relationships
    D.   Decision points and control loops

25. The MAIN distinction between Theory X and Theory Y approaches to organization, in   25.____
accordance with Douglas McGregor's view, is that Theory Y

    A.   considers that work is natural to people; Theory X assumes that people are lazy
and avoid work
    B.   leads to a tall, narrow organization structure, while Theory X leads to one that is
flat
    C.   organizations motivate people with money; Theory X organizations motivate peo-
ple with good working conditions
    D.   represents authoritarian management, while Theory X management is participa-
tive

———

KEY (CORRECT ANSWERS)

1.	C		11.	B
2.	B		12.	B
3.	D		13.	A
4.	C		14.	C
5.	A		15.	B
6.	A		16.	C
7.	C		17.	D
8.	B		18.	B
9.	A		19.	A
10.	B		20.	C

21. B
22. D
23. A
24. B
25. A

———

TEST 2

DIRECTIONS: Each question or incomplete statement is followed by several suggested answers or completions. Select the one that BEST answers the question or completes the statement. *PRINT THE LETTER OF THE CORRECT ANSWER IN THE SPACE AT THE RIGHT.*

1. Of the following, the stage in decision-making which is usually MOST difficult is

   A. stating the alternatives
   B. predicting the possible outcome of each alternative
   C. evaluating the relative merits of each alternative
   D. minimizing the undesirable aspects of the alternative selected

   1._____

2. In a department where a clerk is reporting both to a senior clerk in charge of the mail room and also to a supervising clerk in charge of the duplicating section, there may be a breakdown of the management principle called

   A. horizontal specialization   B. job enrichment
   C. unity of command   D. Graicunas' Law

   2._____

3. Of the following, the failure by line managers to accept and appreciate the benefits and limitations of a new program or system VERY frequently can be traced to the

   A. budgetary problems involved
   B. resultant need to reduce staff
   C. lack of controls it engenders
   D. failure of top management to support its implementation

   3._____

4. Although there is general agreement that *management by objectives* has made a major contribution to modern management of large organizations, criticisms of the system during the past few years have resulted in

   A. mounting pressure for relaxation of management goals
   B. renewed concern with human values and the manager's personal needs
   C. over-mechanistic application of the perceptions of the behavioral scientists
   D. disillusionment with *management by objectives* on the part of a majority of managers

   4._____

5. Of the following, which is usually considered to be a MAJOR obstacle to the systematic analysis of potential problems by managers?

   A. Managers have a tendency to think that all the implications of some proposed step cannot be fully understood.
   B. Rewards rarely go to those managers who are most successful at resolving current problems in management.
   C. There is a common conviction of managers that their goals are difficult to achieve.
   D. Managers are far more concerned about correcting today's problems than with preventing tomorrow's.

   5._____

6. Which of the following should generally have the MOST influence on the selection of supervisors?   6.____

    A. Experience within the work unit where the vacancies exist
    B. Amount of money needed to effect the promotion
    C. Personal preferences of the administration
    D. Evaluation of capacity to exercise supervisory responsibilities

7. In questioning a potential administrator for selection purposes, the one of the following practices which is MOST desirable is to   7.____

    A. encourage the job applicant to give primarily *yes* or *no* replies
    B. get the applicant to talk freely and in detail about his background
    C. let the job applicant speak most of the time
    D. probe the applicant's attitudes, motivation, and willingness to accept responsibility

8. In implementing the managerial function of training subordinates, it is USEFUL to know that a widely agreed–upon definition of human learning is that learning   8.____

    A. is a relatively permanent change in behavior that results from reinforced practice or experience
    B. involves an improvement, but not necessarily a change in behavior
    C. involves a change in behavior, but not necessarily an improvement
    D. is a temporary change in behavior which must be subject to practice or experience

9. If a manager were thinking about using a committee of subordinates to solve an operating problem, which of the following would generally NOT be an advantage of such use of the committee approach?   9.____

    A. Improved coordination   B. Low cost
    C. Increased motivation   D. Integrated judgment

10. Which one of the following management approaches MOST often uses model–building techniques to solve management problems?   10.____
    _____ approach

    A. Behavioral   B. Fiscal
    C. Quantitative   D. Process

11. Of the following, the MOST serious risk in using budgets as a tool for management control is the   11.____

    A. probable neglect of other good management practices
    B. likelihood of guesswork because of the need to plan far in advance
    C. possibility of undue emphasis on factors that are easiest to measure
    D. danger of making qualitative rather than quantitative assessments of performance

12. In government budgeting, the problem of relating financial transactions to the fiscal year   12.____
    in which they are budgeted is BEST met by

    A. determining the cash balance by comparing how much money has been received
       and how much has been paid out
    B. applying net revenue to the fiscal year in which they are collected as offset by rele-
       vant expenses
    C. adopting a system whereby appropriations are entered when they are received
       and expenditures are entered when they are paid out
    D. entering expenditures on the books when the obligation to make the expenditure is
       made

13. If the agency's bookkeeping system records income when it is received and expenditures   13.____
    when the money is paid out, this sytem is USUALLY known as a _____ system.

    A. cash   B. flow–payment
    C. deferred   D. fiscal year income

14. An audit, as the term applies to budget execution, is MOST NEARLY a   14.____

    A. procedure based on the budget estimates
    B. control exercised by the executive on the legislature in the establishment of pro-
       gram priorities
    C. check on the legality of expenditures and is based on the appropriations act
    D. requirement which must be met before funds can be spent

15. In government budgeting, there is a procedure known as *allotment.*   15.____
    Of the following statements which relate to allotment, select the one that is MOST gen-
    erally considered to be correct.
    Allotment

    A. increases the practice of budget units coming back to the legislative branch for
       supplemental appropriations
    B. is simply an example of red tape
    C. eliminates the requirement of timing of expenditures
    D. is designed to prevent waste

16. In government budgeting, the establishment of the schedules of allotments is MOST   16.____
    generally the responsibility of the

    A. budget unit and the legislature
    B. budget unit and the executive
    C. budget unit *only*
    D. executive and the legislature

141

17. Of the following statements relating to preparation of an organization's budget request, which is the MOST generally valid precaution?   17.____

    A. Give specific instructions on the format of budget requests and required supporting data
    B. Because of the complexity of preparing a budget request, avoid argumentation to support the requests
    C. Put requests in whatever format is desirable
    D. Consider that final approval will be given to initial estimates

18. Of the following statements which relate to the budget process in a well-organized government, select the one that is MOST NEARLY correct.   18.____

    A. The budget cycle is the step-by-step process which is repeated each and every fiscal year.
    B. Securing approval of the budget does not take place within the budget cycle.
    C. The development of a new budget and putting it into effect is a two-step process known as the budget cycle.
    D. The fiscal period, usually a fiscal year, has no relation to the budget cycle.

19. If a manager were asked what PPBS stands for, he would be RIGHT if he said   19.____

    A. public planning budgeting system
    B. planning programming budgeting system
    C. planning projections budgeting system
    D. programming procedures budgeting system

Questions 20–21.

DIRECTIONS: Answer Questions 20 and 21 on the basis of the following information.

Sample Budget

Refuse Collection	Amount
Personal Services	$ 30,000
Contractual Services	5,000
Supplies and Materials	5,000
Capital Outlay	10,000
	$ 50,000

Residential Collections		
Dwellings–1 pickup per week		1,000
Tons of refuse collected per year		375
Cost of collections per ton	$	8
Cost per dwelling pickup per year	$	3
Total annual cost	$	3,000

20. The sample budget shown is a simplified example of a _____ budget.　　　20._____

    A. factorial　　　　　　　　　　　B. performance
    C. qualitative　　　　　　　　　　D. rational

21. The budget shown in the sample differs CHIEFLY from line-item and program budgets in　　21._____
that it includes

    A. objects of expenditure but not activities or functions
    B. only activities, functions, and control
    C. activities and functions but not objects of expenditures
    D. levels of service

Question 22.

DIRECTIONS: Answer Question 22 on the basis of the following information.

Sample Budget

Environmental Safety
    Air Pollution Protection

Personal Services	$20,000,000	
Contractual Services	4,000,000	
Supplies and Materials	4,000,000	
Capital Outlay	2,000,000	
Total Air Pollution Protection		$ 30,000,000

Water Pollution Protection

Personal Services	$23,000,000	
Supplies and Materials	4,500,000	
Capital Outlay	20,500,000	
Total Water Pollution Protection		$ 48,000,000
Total Environmental Safety		$ 78,000,000

22. Based on the above budget, which is the MOST valid statement?　　　22._____

    A. Environmental Safety, Air Pollution Protection, and Water Pollution Protection could
all be considered program elements.
    B. The object listings included water pollution protection and capital outlay.
    C. Examples of the program element listings in the above are personal services and
supplies and materials.
    D. Contractual Services and Environmental Safety were the program element listings.

23. Which of the following is NOT an advantage of a program budget over a line-item bud-　　23._____
get?
A program budget

    A. allows us to set up priority lists in deciding what activities we will spend our money
on
    B. gives us more control over expenditures than a line-item budget
    C. is more informative in that we know the broad purposes of spending money
    D. enables us to see if one program is getting much less money than the others

24. If a manager were trying to explain the fundamental difference between traditional   24._____
accounting theory and practice and the newer practice of managerial accounting, he
would be MOST accurate if he said that

   A. traditional accounting practice focused on providing information for persons out-
      side organizations, while managerial accounting focuses on providing information
      for people inside organizations
   B. traditional accounting practice focused on providing information for persons inside
      organizations while managerial accounting focuses on providing information for
      persons outside organizations
   C. managerial accounting is exclusively concerned with historical facts while tradi-
      tional accounting stresses future projections exclusively
   D. traditional accounting practice is more budget-focused than managerial account-
      ing

25. Which of the following formulas is used to determine the number of days required to pro-   25._____
cess work?

   A. $\dfrac{\text{Employees x Daily Output}}{\text{Volume}}$ = Days to Process Work

   B. $\dfrac{\text{Volume x Daily Output}}{\text{Employees}}$ = Days to Process Work

   C. $\dfrac{\text{Volume}}{\text{Employees x Daily Output}}$ = Days to Process Work

   D. $\dfrac{\text{Employees x Volume}}{\text{Daily Output}}$ = Days to Process Work

—————

KEY (CORRECT ANSWERS)

1.	C		11.	C
2.	C		12.	D
3.	D		13.	A
4.	B		14.	C
5.	D		15.	D
6.	D		16.	C
7.	D		17.	A
8.	A		18.	A
9.	B		19.	B
10.	C		20.	B

21.	D
22.	A
23.	B
24.	A
25.	C

TEST 3

DIRECTIONS: Each question or incomplete statement is followed by several suggested answers or completions. Select the one that BEST answers the question or completes the statement. *PRINT THE LETTER OF THE CORRECT ANSWER IN THE SPACE AT THE RIGHT.*

1. Electronic data processing equipment can produce more information faster than can be generated by any other means.
   In view of this, the MOST important problem faced by management at present is to

   A. keep computers fully occupied
   B. find enough computer personnel
   C. assimilate and properly evaluate the information
   D. obtain funds to establish appropriate information systems

   1.____

2. A well-designed management information system ESSENTIALLY provides each executive and manager the information he needs for

   A. determining computer time requirements
   B. planning and measuring results
   C. drawing a new organization chart
   D. developing a new office layout

   2.____

3. It is generally agreed that management policies should be periodically reappraised and restated in accordance with current conditions.
   Of the following, the approach which would be MOST effective in determining whether a policy should be revised is to

   A. conduct interviews with staff members at all levels in order to ascertain the relationship between the policy and actual practice
   B. make proposed revisions in the policy and apply it to current problems
   C. make up hypothetical situations using both the old policy and a revised version in order to make comparisons
   D. call a meeting of top level staff in order to discuss ways of revising the policy

   3.____

4. Every manager has many occasions to lead a conference or participate in a conference of some sort.
   Of the following statements that pertain to conferences and conference leadership, which is generally considered to be MOST valid?

   A. Since World War II, the trend has been toward fewer shared decisions and more conferences.
   B. The most important part of a conference leader's job is to direct discussion.
   C. In providing opportunities for group interaction, management should avoid consideration of its past management philosophy.
   D. A good administrator cannot lead a good conference if he is a poor public speaker.

   4.____

5. Of the following, it is usually LEAST desirable for a conference leader to

   A. turn the question to the person who asked it
   B. summarize proceedings periodically
   C. make a practice of not repeating questions
   D. ask a question without indicating who is to reply

   5.____

6. The behavioral school of management thought bases its beliefs on certain assumptions.   6.____
   Which of the following is NOT a belief of this school of thought?

   A. People tend to seek and accept responsibility.
   B. Most people can be creative in solving problems.
   C. People prefer security above all else.
   D. Commitment is the most important factor in motivating people.

7. The one of the following objectives which would be LEAST appropriate as a major goal of   7.____
   research in the field of human resources management is to

   A. predict future conditions, events, and manpower needs
   B. evaluate established policies, programs, and practices
   C. evaluate proposed policies, programs, and practices
   D. identify deficient organizational units and apply suitable penalties

8. Of the following general interviewing methods or techniques, the one that is USUALLY   8.____
   considered to be effective in counseling, grievances, and appraisal interviews is the
   _____ interview.

   A. directed   B. non-directed
   C. panel   D. patterned

9. The ESSENTIAL first phase of decision-making is   9.____

   A. finding alternative solutions
   B. making a diagnosis of the problem
   C. selecting the plan to follow
   D. analyzing and comparing alternative solutions

10. Assume that, in a certain organization, a situation has developed in which there is little   10.____
    difference in status or authority between individuals.
    Which of the following would be the MOST likely result with regard to communication in
    this organization?

    A. Both the accuracy and flow of communication will be improved.
    B. Both the accuracy and flow of communication will substantially decrease.
    C. Employees will seek more formal lines of communication.
    D. Neither the flow nor the accuracy of communication will be improved over the
       former hierarchical structure.

11. The main function of many agency administrative offices is *information management.*   11.____
    Information that is received by an administrative officer may be classified as active or
    passive, depending upon whether or not it requires the recipient to take some action.
    Of the following, the item received which is clearly the MOST active information is

    A. an appointment of a new staff member
    B. a payment voucher for a new desk
    C. a press release concerning a past city event
    D. the minutes of a staff meeting

12. Which one of the following sets BEST describes the general order in which to teach an operation to a new employee?

    A. Prepare, present, tryout, follow-up
    B. Prepare, test, tryout, re-test
    C. Present, test, tryout, follow-up
    D. Test, present, follow-up, re-test

12.____

13. Of the following, public employees may be separated from public service

    A. for the same reasons which are generally acceptable for discharging employees in private industry
    B. only under the most trying circumstances
    C. under procedures that are neither formalized nor subject to review
    D. solely in extreme cases involving offenses of gravest character

13.____

14. Of the following, the one LEAST considered to be a communication barrier is

    A. group feedback
    B. charged words
    C. selective perception
    D. symbolic meanings

14.____

15. Of the following ways for a manager to handle his appointments, the BEST way, according to experts in administration, generally is to

    A. schedule his own appointments and inform his secretary not to reserve his time without his approval
    B. encourage everyone to make appointments through his secretary and tell her when he makes his own appointments
    C. see no one who has not made a previous appointment
    D. permit anyone to see him without an appointment

15.____

16. Assume that a manager decides to examine closely one of five units under his supervision to uncover problems common to all five.
His research technique is MOST closely related to the method called

    A. experimentation
    B. simulation
    C. linear analysis
    D. sampling

16.____

17. If one views the process of management as a dynamic process, which one of the following functions is NOT a legitimate part of that process?

    A. Communication
    B. Decision-making
    C. Organizational slack
    D. Motivation

17.____

18. Which of the following would be the BEST statement of a budget-oriented purpose for a government administrator? To

    A. provide 200 hours of instruction in basic reading for 3500 adult illiterates at a cost of $1 million in the next fiscal year
    B. inform the public of adult educational programs
    C. facilitate the transfer to a city agency of certain functions of a federally-funded program which is being phased out
    D. improve the reading skills of the adult citizens in the city

18.____

19. Modern management philosophy and practices are changing to accommodate the   19.____
    expectations and motivations of organization personnel.
    Which of the following terms INCORRECTLY describes these newer managerial
    approaches?

    A. Rational management   B. Participative management
    C. Decentralization   D. Democratic supervision

20. Management studies support the hypothesis that, in spite of the tendency of employees   20.____
    to censor the information communicated to their supervisor, subordinates are MORE
    likely to communicate problem-oriented information upward when they have

    A. a long period of service in the organization
    B. a high degree of trust in the supervisor
    C. a high educational level
    D. low status on the organizational ladder

KEY (CORRECT ANSWERS)

1.	C		11.	A
2.	B		12.	A
3.	A		13.	A
4.	B		14.	A
5.	A		15.	B
6.	C		16.	D
7.	D		17.	C
8.	B		18.	A
9.	B		19.	A
10.	D		20.	B

SUPERVISION, ADMINISTRATION, MANAGEMENT AND ORGANIZATION
EXAMINATION SECTION
TEST 1

DIRECTIONS: Each question or incomplete statement is followed by several suggested answers or completions. Select the one that BEST answers the question or completes the statement. *PRINT THE LETTER OF THE CORRECT ANSWER IN THE SPACE AT THE RIGHT.*

1. In coaching a subordinate on the nature of decision–making, an executive would be right   1._____
    if he stated that the one of the following which is *generally* the BEST definition of deci-
    sion-making is:

    A. Choosing between alternatives
    B. Making diagnoses of feasible ends
    C. Making diagnoses of feasible means
    D. Comparing alternatives

2. Of the following, which one would be LEAST valid as a purpose of an organizational pol-   2._____
    icy statement? To

    A. keep personnel from performing improper actions and functions on routine matters
    B. prevent the mishandling of non-routine matters
    C. provide management personnel with a tool that precludes the need for their use of
        judgment
    D. provide standard decisions and approaches in handling problems of a recurrent
        nature

3. Much has been written criticizing bureaucratic organizations. Current thinking on the   3._____
    subject is GENERALLY that

    A. bureaucracy is on the way out
    B. bureaucracy, though not perfect, is unlikely to be replaced
    C. bureaucratic organizations are most effective in dealing with constant change
    D. bureaucratic organizations are most effective when dealing with sophisticated cus-
        tomers or clients

4. The development of alternate plans as a major step in planning will normally result in the   4._____
    planner having several possible courses of action available. GENERALLY, this is

    A. *desirable,* since such development helps to determine the most suitable alternative
        and to provide for the unexpected
    B. *desirable,* since such development makes the use of planning premises and con-
        straints unnecessary
    C. *undesirable,* since the planners should formulate only one way of achieving given
        goals at a given time
    D. *undesirable,* since such action restricts efforts to modify the planning to take
        advantage of opportunities

5. The technique of departmentation by task force includes the assigning of a team or task   5.____
force to a definite project or block of work which extends from the beginning to the
completing of a wanted and definite type and quantity of work. Of the following, the
MOST important factor aiding the successful use of this technique *normally* is

    A. having the task force relatively large, at least one hundred members
    B. having a definite project termination date established
    C. telling each task force member what his next assignment will be only after the cur-
       rent project ends
    D. utilizing it only for projects that are regularly recurring

6. With respect to communication in small group settings such as may occur in business,   6.____
government and the military, it is GENERALLY true that people *usually* derive more satisfaction and are usually more productive under conditions which

    A. permit communication only with superiors
    B. permit the minimum intragroup communication possible
    C. are generally restricted by management
    D. allow open communication among all group members

7. If an executive were asked to list some outstanding features of decentralization, which   7.____
one of the following would NOT be such a feature? Decentralization

    A. provides decision-making experience for lower level managers
    B. promotes uniformity of policy
    C. is a relatively new concept in management
    D. is similar to the belief in encouragement of free enterprise

8. Modern management experts have emphasized the importance of the informal organiza-   8.____
tion in motivating employees to increase productivity. Of the following, the characteristic
which would have the MOST direct influence on employee motivation is the tendency of
members of the informal organization to

    A. resist change
    B. establish their own norms
    C. have similar outside interests
    D. set substantially higher goals than those of management

9. According to leading management experts, the decision-making process contains sepa-   9.____
rate and distinct steps that must be taken in an orderly sequence. Of the following
arrangements, which one is in CORRECT order?

    A. I. Search for alternatives II.diagnosis III. comparison IV. choice
    B. I.Diagnosis II. comparison III. search for alternatives IV. choice
    C. I. Diagnosis II. search for alternatives III. comparison IV. choice
    D. I.Diagnosis II.search for alternatives III. choice IV. comparison

10. Of the following, the growth of professionalism in large organizations can PRIMARILY   10.____
be expected to result in

    A. greater equalization of power
    B. increased authoritarianism
    C. greater organizational disloyalty
    D. increased promotion opportunities

11. Assume an executive carries out his responsibilities to his staff according to what is now known about managerial leadership. Which of the following statements would MOST accurately reflect his assumptions about proper management?   11._____

   A. Efficiency in operations results from allowing the human element to participate in a minimal way.
   B. Efficient operation results from balancing work considerations with personnel considerations.
   C. Efficient operation results from a workforce committed to its self interest.
   D. Efficient operation results from staff relationships that produce a friendly work climate.

12. Assume that an executive is called upon to conduct a management audit. To do this properly, he would have to take certain steps in a specific sequence. Of the following steps, which step should this manager take FIRST?   12._____

   A. Managerial performance must be surveyed.
   B. A method of reporting must be established.
   C. Management auditing procedures and documentation must be developed.
   D. Criteria for the audit must be considered.

13. If a manager is required to conduct a scientific investigation of an organizational problem, the FIRST step he should take is to   13._____

   A. state his assumptions about the problem
   B. carry out a search for background information
   C. choose the right approach to investigate the validity of his assumptions
   D. define and state the problem

14. An executive would be *right* to assert that the principle of delegation states that decisions should be made PRIMARILY   14._____

   A. by persons in an executive capacity qualified to make them
   B. by persons in a non-executive capacity
   C. at as low an organization level of authority as practicable
   D. by the next lower level of authority

15. Of the following, which one is NOT regarded by management authorities as a FUNDAMENTAL characteristic of an *ideal* bureaucracy?   15._____

   A. Division of labor and specialization
   B. An established hierarchy
   C. Decentralization of authority
   D. A set of operating rules and regulations

16. As the number of subordinates in a manager's span of control increases, the ACTUAL number of possible relationships   16._____

   A. increases disproportionately to the number of subordinates
   B. increases in equal number to the number of subordinates
   C. reaches a stable level
   D. will first increase then slowly decrease

17. An executive's approach to controlling the activities of his subordinates concentrated on ends rather than means, and was diagnostic rather than punitive. This manager may MOST properly be characterized as using the managerial technique of management-by-

    A. exception   B. objectives   C. crisis   D. default

17.____

18. In conducting a training session on the administrative control process, which of the following statements would be LEAST calid for an executive to make? Controlling

    A. requires checking upon assignments to see what is being done
    B. involves comparing what is being done to what ought to be done
    C. requires corrective action when what is being done does not meet expectations
    D. occurs after all the other managerial processes have been performed

18.____

19. The "brainstorming" technique for creative solutions of management problems MOST generally consists of

    A. bringing staff together in an exchange of a quantity of free wheeling ideas
    B. isolating individual staff members to encourage thought
    C. developing improved office procedures
    D. preparation of written reports on complex problems

19.____

20. Computer systems hardware MOST often operates in relation to which one of the following steps in solving a data-processing problem?

    A. Determining the problem
    B. Defining and stating the problem
    C. Implementing the programmed solution
    D. Completing the documentation of every unexplored solution

20.____

21. There is a tendency in management to upgrade objectives. This trend is generally regarded as

    A. *desirable;* the urge to improve is demonstrated by adopting objectives that have been adjusted to provide improved service
    B. *undesirable;* the typical manager searches for problems which obstruct his objectives
    C. *desirable;* it is common for a manager to find that the details of an immediate operation have occupied so much of his time that he has lost sight of the basic overall objective
    D. *undesirable;* efforts are wasted when they are expended on a mass of uncertain objectives, since the primary need of most organizations is a single target or several major ones

21.____

22. Of the following, it is generally LEAST effective for an executive to delegate authority where working conditions involve

    A. rules establishing normal operating procedures
    B. consistent methods of operation
    C. rapidly changing work standards
    D. complex technology

22.____

23. If an executive was explaining the difficulty of making decisions under *risk* conditions, he would be MOST accurate if he said that such decisions would be difficult to make when the decision maker has

    A. limited information and experience and can expect many outcomes for each action
    B. much information and experience and can expect many outcomes for each action
    C. much information and experience and can expect few outcomes for each action
    D. limited information and experience and can expect few outcomes for each action

23.____

24. If an executive were asked to list some outstanding features of centralized organization, which one of the following would be INCORRECT? Centralized organization

    A. lessens risks of errors by unskilled subordinates
    B. utilizes the skills of specialized experts at a central location
    C. produces uniformity of policy and non-uniformity of action
    D. enables closer control of operations than a decentralized set-up

24.____

25. It is possible for an organization's management to test whether or not the organization has a sound structure. Of the following, which one is NOT a test of soundness in an organization's structure? The

    A. ability to replace key personnel with minimum loss of effectiveness
    B. ability of information and decisions to flow more freely through the *grapevine* than through formal channels
    C. presence of definite objectives for each unit in the organizational system
    D. provision for orderly organizational growth with the ability to handle change as the need arises

25.____

KEY(CORRECT ANSWERS)

1.	A		11.	B
2.	C		12.	D
3.	B		13.	D
4.	A		14.	C
5.	B		15.	C
6.	D		16.	A
7.	B		17.	B
8.	B		18.	D
9.	C		19.	A
10.	A		20.	C

21.	A
22.	C
23.	A
24.	C
25.	B

TEST 2

DIRECTIONS: Each question or incomplete statement is followed by several suggested answers or completions. Select the one that BEST answers the question or completes the statement. *PRINT THE LETTER OF THE CORRECT ANSWER IN THE SPACE AT THE RIGHT.*

1. Management experts generally believe that computer-based management information systems (MIS) have greater potential for improving the process of management than any other development in recent decades. The one of the following which MOST accurately describes the objectives of MIS is to

    1.____

    A.   provide information for decision-making on planning, initiating, and controlling the operations of the various units of the organization
    B.   establish mechanization of routine functions such as clerical records, payroll, inventory and accounts receivable in order to promote economy and efficiency
    C.   computerize decision-making on planning, initiative, organizing and controlling the operations of an organization
    D.   provide accurate facts and figures on the various programs of the organization to be used for purposes of planing and research

2. The one of the following which is the BEST application on the *management-by-exception* principle is that this principle

    2.____

    A.   stimulates communication and aids in management of crisis situations, thus reducing the frequency of decision-making
    B.   saves time and reserves top-management decisions only for crisis situations, thus reducing the frequency of decision-making
    C.   stimulates communication, saves time and reduces the frequency of decision-making
    D.   is limited to crisis-management situations

3. It is *generally* recognized that each organization is dependent upon the availability of qualified personnel. Of the following, the MOST important factor affecting the availability of qualified people to each organization is

    3.____

    A.   innovations in technology and science
    B.   the general decline in the educational levels of our population
    C.   the rise of sentiment against racial discrimination
    D.   pressure by organized community groups

4. A *fundamental* responsibility of all managers is to decide what physical facilities and equipment are needed to help attain basic goals. Good planning for the purchase and use of equipment is seldom easy to do and is *complicated* MOST by the fact that

    4.____

    A.   organizations rarely have stable sources of supply
    B.   nearly all managers tend to be better at personnel planning than at equipment planning
    C.   decisions concerning physical resources are made too often on a *crash basis* rather than under carefully prepared policies
    D.   legal rulings relative to depreciation fluctuate very frequently

5. In attempting to reconcile managerial objectives and an individual employee's goals, it is generally LEAST desirable for management to

    A. recognize the capacity of the individual to contribute toward realization of managerial goals
    B. encourage self-development of the employee to exceed minimum job performance
    C. consider an individual employee's work separately from other employees
    D. demonstrate that an employee advances only to the extent that he contributes directly to the accomplishment of stated goals

5.____

6. As a management tool for discovering individual training needs a job analysis would generally be of LEAST assistance in determining

    A. the performance requirements of individual jobs
    B. actual employee performance on the job
    C. acceptable standards of performance
    D. training needs for individual jobs

6.____

7. One of the major concerns of organizational managers today is how the spread of automation will affect them and the status of their positions. Realistically speaking, one can say that the MOST likely effect of our newer forms of highly automated technology on managers will be to

    A. make most top-level positions superfluous or obsolete
    B. reduce the importance of managerial work in general
    C. replace the work of managers with the work of technicians
    D. increase the importance of and demand for top managerial personnel

7.____

8. Which one of the following is LEAST likely to be an area or cause of trouble in the use of staff people (e.g., assistants to the administrator)?

    A. Misunderstanding of the role the staff people are supposed to play, as a result of vagueness of definition of their duties and authority
    B. Tendency of staff personnel almost always to be older than line personnel at comparable salary levels with whom they must deal
    C. Selection of staff personnel who fail to have simultaneously both competence in their specialties and skill in staff work
    D. The staff person fails to understand mixed staff and operating duties

8.____

9. The one of the following which is the BEST measure of decentralization in an agency is the

    A. amount of checking required on decisions made at lower levels in the chain of command
    B. amount of checking required on decisions made at lower levels of the chain of command and the number of functions affected thereby
    C. number of functions affected by decisions made at higher levels
    D. number of functions affected by middle echelon decision-making

9.____

10. Which of the following is generally NOT a valid statement with respect to the supervisory   10.____
    process?

    A. General supervision is more effective than close supervision.
    B. Employee-centered supervisors lead more effectively than do production-cen-
        tered supervisors.
    C. Employee satisfaction is directly related to productivity.
    D. Low-producing supervisors use techniques that are different from high-producing
        supervisors

11. The one of the following which is the MOST essential element for proper evaluation of   11.____
    the performance of subordinate supervisors is a

    A. careful definition of each supervisor's specific job responsibilities and of his
        progress in meeting mutually agreed upon work goals
    B. system of rewards and penalties based on each supervisor's progress in meeting
        clearly defined performance standards
    C. definition of personality traits, such as industry, initiative, dependability and cooper-
        ativeness, required for effective job performance
    D. breakdown of each supervisor's job into separate components and a rating of his
        performance on each individual task

12. The one of the following which is the PRINCIPAL advantage of specialization for the   12.____
    operating efficiency of a public service agency is that specialization

    A. reduces the amount of red tape in coordinating the activities of mutually dependent
        departments
    B. simplifies the problem of developing adequate job controls
    C. provides employees with a clear understanding of the relationship of their activities
        to the overall objectives of the agency
    D. reduces destructive competition for power between departments

13. Of the following, the group which *generally* benefits MOST from supervisory training pro-   13.____
    grams in public service agencies are those supervisors who have

    A. accumulated a long period of total service to the agency
    B. responsibility for a large number of subordinate personnel
    C. been in the supervisory ranks for a long period of time
    D. a high level of formalized academic training

14. A list of conditions which encourages good morale inside a work group would NOT   14.____
    include a

    A. high rate of agreement among group members on values and objectives
    B. tight control system to minimize the risk of individual error
    C. good possibility that joint action will accomplish goals
    D. past history of successful group accomplishment

15. Of the following, the MOST important factor to be considered in selecting a training strat-   15.____
    egy or program is the

    A. requirements of the job to be performed by the trainees
    B. educational level or prior training of the trainees
    C. size of the training group
    D. quality and competence of available training specialists

16. Of the following, the one which is considered to be LEAST characteristic of the higher   16.____
    ranks of management is

    A. that higher levels of management benefit from modern technology
    B. that success is measured by the extent to which objectives are achieved
    C. the number of subordinates that directly report to an executive
    D. the deemphasis of individual and specialized performance

17. Assume that an executive is preparing a training syllabus to be used in training members   17.____
    of his staff. Which of the following would NOT be a valid principle of the learning process
    for this manager to keep in mind in the preparation of the training syllabus?

    A. When a person has thoroughly learned a task, it takes a lot of effort to create a little
       more improvement
    B. In complicated learning situations, there is a period in which an additional period of
       practice produces an equal amount of improvement in learning
    C. The less a person knows about the task, the slower the initial progress
    D. The more the person knows about the task, the slower the initial progress

18. Of the following, which statement BEST illustrates when collective bargaining agree-   18.____
    ments are working well?

    A. Executives strongly support subordinate managers.
    B. The management rights clause in the contract is clear and enforced.
    C. Contract provisions are competently interpreted.
    D. The provisions of the agrement are properly interpreted, communicated and
       observed.

19. An executive who wishes to encourage subordinates to communicate freely with him   19.____
    about a job-related problem should FIRST

    A. state his own position on the problem before listening to the subordinates' ideas
    B. invite subordinates to give their own opinions on the problem
    C. ask subordinates for their reactions to his own ideas about the problem
    D. guard the confidentiality of management information about the problem

20. The ability to deal constructively with intra-organizational conflict is an essential attribute   20.____
    of the successful manager. The one of the following types of conflict which would be
    LEAST difficult to handle constructively is a situation in which there is

    A. agreement on objectives, but disagreement as to the probable results of adopting
       the various alternatives
    B. agreement on objectives, disagreement on alternative courses of action, and rela-
       tive certainty as to the outcome of one of the alternatives
    C. disagreement on objectives and on alternative courses of action, but relative cer-
       tainty as to the outcome of the alternatives
    D. disagreement on objectives and on alternative courses of action, but uncertainty as
       to the outcome of the alternatives

21. Which of the following statements is LEAST accurate in describing formal job evaluation and wage and salary classification plans? 21.____

    A. Parties that disagree on wage matters can examine an established system rather than unsupported opinions.
    B. The use of such plans tends to overlook the effect of age and seniority of employees on job values in the plan
    C. Such plans can eliminate salary controversies in organizations designing and using them properly
    D. These plans are not particularly useful in checking on executive compensation

22. In carrying out disciplinary action, the MOST important procedure for all managers to follow is to 22.____

    A. sell all levels of management on the need for discipline from the organization's viewpoint
    B. follow up on a disciplinary action and not assume that the action has been effective
    C. convince all executives that proper discipline is a legitimate tool for their use
    D. convince all executives that they need to display confidence in the organization's rules

Questions 23–25.

DIRECTIONS: Questions 23 through 25 are based on the following situation. Richard Ford, a top administrator, is responsible for output in his organization. Because productivity had been lagging for two periods in a row, Ford decided to establish a committee of his subordinate managers to investigate the reasons for the poor performance and to make recommendations for improvements. After two meetings, the committee came to the conclusions and made the recommendations that follow:

    Output forecasts had been handed down from the top without prior consultation with middle management and first level supervision. Lines of authority and responsibility had been unclear. The planning and control process should be decentralized.
    After receiving the committee's recommendations, Ford proceeded to take the following actions:
    Ford decided he would retain final authority to establish quotas but would delegate to the middle managers the responsibility for meeting quotas.
    After receiving Ford's decision, the middle managers proceeded to delegate to the first-line supervisors the authority to establish their own quotas. The middle managers eventually received and combined the first-line supervisors' quotas so that these conformed with Ford's.

23. Ford's decision to delegate responsibility for meeting quotas to the middle managers is INCONSISTENT with sound management principles because of which one of the following? 23.____

    A. Ford shouldn't have involved himself in the first place.
    B. Middle managers do not have the necessary skills.
    C. Quotas should be established by the chief executive.
    D. Responsibility should not be delegated.

24. The principle of coextensiveness of responsibility and authority bears on Ford's decision.   24._____
    In this case, it IMPLIES that

    A. authority should exceed responsibility
    B. authority should be delegated to match the degree of responsibility
    C. both authority and responsibility should be retained and not delegated
    D. responsibility should be delegated but authority should be retained

25. The middle managers' decision to delegate to the first-line supervisors the authority to   25._____
    establish quotas was INCORRECTLY reasoned because

    A. delegation and control must go together
    B. first-line supervisors are in no position to establish quotas
    C. one cannot delegate authority that one does not possess
    D. the meeting of quotas should not be delegated

_____

KEY(CORRECT ANSWERS)

1.	A	11.	A
2.	C	12.	B
3.	A	13.	D
4.	C	14.	B
5.	C	15.	A
6.	B	16.	C
7.	D	17.	D
8.	B	18.	D
9.	B	19.	B
10.	C	20.	B

21.	C
22.	B
23.	D
24.	B
25.	C

_____

TEST 3

DIRECTIONS: Each question or incomplete statement is followed by several suggested answers or completions. Select the one that BEST answers the question or completes the statement. *PRINT THE LETTER OF THE CORRECT ANSWER IN THE SPACE AT THE RIGHT.*

1. A danger which exists in any organization as complex as that required for administration   1.____
   of a large public agency, is that each department comes to believe that it exists for its
   own sake. The one of the following which has been attempted in some organizations as a
   cure for this condition is to

   A. build up the departmental esprit de corps
   B. expand the functions and jurisdictions of the various departments so that better
      integration is possible
   C. develop a body of specialists in the various subject matter fields which cut across
      departmental lines
   D. delegate authority to the lowest possible echelon
   E. systematically transfer administrative personnel from one department to another

2. At best, the organization chart is ordinarily and necessarily an idealized picture of the   2.____
   intent of top management, a reflection of hopes and aims rather than a photograph of the
   operating facts within the organization.
   The one of the following which is the basic reason for this is that the organization chart

   A. does not show the flow of work within the organization
   B. speaks in terms of positions rather than of live employees
   C. frequently contains unresolved internal ambiguities
   D. is a record of past organization or of proposed future organization and never a pho-
      tograph of the living organization
   E. does not label the jurisdiction assigned to each component unit

3. The drag of inadequacy is always downward. The need in administration is always for the   3.____
   reverse; for a department head to project his thinking to the city level, for the unit chief to
   try to see the problems of the department.
   The inability of a city administration to recruit administrators who can satisfy this need
   usually results in departments characterized by

   A. disorganization   B. poor supervision
   C. circumscribed viewpoints   D. poor public relations
   E. a lack of programs

4. When, as a result of a shift in public sentiment, the elective officers of a city are   4.____
   changed, is it desirable for career administrators to shift ground without performing any
   illegal or dishonest act in order to conform to the policies of the new elective officers?

   A. *No;* the opinions and beliefs of the career officials are the result of long experience
      in administration and are more reliable than those of politicians.
   B. *Yes;* only in this way can citizens, political officials and career administrators alike
      have confidence in the performance of their respective functions.
   C. *No;* a top career official who is so spineless as to change his views or procedures
      as a result of public opinion is of little value to the public service.
   D. *Yes;* legal or illegal, it is necessary that a city employee carry out the orders of his
      superior officers
   E. *No;* shifting ground with every change in administration will preclude the use of a
      constant overall policy

5. Participation in developing plans which will affect levels in the organization in addition to his own, will contribute to an individual's understanding of the entire system. When possible, this should be encouraged.
This policy is, in general,

    A. *desirable;* the maintenance of any organization depends upon individual understanding
    B. *undesirable;* employees should participate only in thise activities which affect their own level, otherwise conflicts in authority may arise
    C. *desirable;* an employee's will to contribute to the maintenance of an organization depends to a great extent on the level which he occupies
    D. *undesirable;* employees can be trained more efficiently and economically in an organized training program than by participating in plan development
    E. *desirable;* it will enable the employee to make intelligent suggestions for adjustment of the plan in the future

5.____

6. Constant study should be made of the information contained in reports to isolate those elements of experience which are static, those which are variable and repetitive, and those which are variable and due to chance
Knowledge of those elements of experience in his organization which are static or constant will enable the operating official to

    A. fix responsibility for their supervision at a lower level
    B. revise the procedure in order to make the elements variable
    C. arrange for follow-up and periodic adjustment
    D. bring related data together
    E. provide a frame of reference within which detailed standards for measurement can be installed

6.____

7. A chief staff officer, serving as one of the immediate advisors to the department head, has demonstrated a special capacity for achieving internal agreements and for sound judgment. As a result he has been used more and more as a source of counsel and assistance by the department head. Other staff officers and line officials as well have discovered that it is wise for them to check with this colleague in advance on all problematical matters handed up to the department head. Developments such as this are

    A. *undesirable;* they disrupt the normal lines for flow of work in an organization
    B. *desirable;* they allow an organization to make the most of its strength wherever such strength resides
    C. *undesirable;* they tend to undermine the authority of the department head and put it in the hands of a staff officer who does not have the responsibility
    D. *desirable;* they tend to resolve internal ambiguities in organization
    E. *undesirable;* they make for bad morale by causing *cutthroat* competition

7.____

8. A common difference among executives is that some are not content unless they are out in front in everything that concerns their organization, while others prefer to run things by pulling strings, by putting others out in front and by stepping into the breach only when necessary.
Generally speaking, an advantage this latter method of operation has over the former is that it

8.____

A. results in a higher level of morale over a sustained period of time
B. gets results by exhortation and direct stimulus
C. makes it unnecessary to calculate integrated moves
D. makes the personality of the executive felt further down the line
E. results in the executive getting the reputation for being a good fellow

9. Administrators frequently have to get facts by interviewing people. Although the interview is a legitimate fact gathering technique, it has definite limitations which should not be overlooked. The one of the following which is an important limitation is that

9.____

A. people who are initerviewed frequently answer questions with guesses rather than admit their ignorance
B. it is a poor way to discover the general attitude and thinking of supervisors interviewed
C. people sometimes hesitate to give information during an interview which they will submit in written form
D. it is a poor way to discover how well employees understand departmental policies
E. the material obtained from the interview can usually be obtained at lower cost from existing records

10. It is desirable and advantageous to leave a maximum measure of planning responsibility to operating agencies or units, rather than to remove the responsibility to a central planning staff agency.
Adoption of the former policy (decentralized planning) would lead to

10.____

A. *less effective planning;* operating personnel do not have the time to make long-term plans
B. *more effective planning;* operating units are usually better equipped technically than any staff agency and consequently are in a better position to set up valid plans
C. *less effective planning;* a central planning agency has a more objective point of view than any operating agency can achieve
D. *more effective planning;* plans are conceived in terms of the existing situation and their exeuction is carried out with the will to succeed
E. *less effective planning;* there is little or no opportunity to check deviation from plans in the proposed set-up

Questions 11–15.

DIRECTIONS: The following sections appeared in a report on the work production of two bureaus of a department. Base your answers to questions 11 through 15 on this information. Throughout the report, assume that each month has 4 weeks.

Each of the two bureaus maintains a chronological file. In Bureau A, every 9 months on the average, this material fills a standard legal size file cabinet sufficient for 12,000 work units. In Bureau B, the same type of cabinet is filled in 18 months. Each bureau maintains three complete years of information plus a current file. When the current file cabinet is filled, the cabinet containing the oldest material is emptied, the contents disposed of and the cabinet used for current material. The similarity of these operations makes it possible to consolidate these files with little effort.

Study of the practice of using typists as filing clerks for periods when there is no typing work showed: (1) Bureau A has for the past 6 months completed a total of 1500 filing work units a week using on the average 100 man-hours of trained file clerk time and 20 man-hours of typist time; (2) Bureau B has in the same period completed a total of 2000 filing work units a week using on the average 125 man-hours of trained file clerk time and 60 hours of typist time. This includes all work in chronological files. Assuming that all clerks work at the same speed and that all typists work at the same speed, this indicates that work other than filing should be found for typists or that they should be given some training in the filing procedures used... It should be noted that Bureau A has not been producing the 1,600 units of technical (not filing) work per 30 day period required by Schedule K, but is at present 200 units behind. The Bureau should be allowed 3 working days to get on schedule.

11. What percentage (approximate) of the total number of filing work units completed in both units consists of the work involved in the maintenance of the chronological files?   11.____

    A. 5%   B. 10%   C. 15%   D. 20%   E. 25%

12. If the two chronological files are consolidated, the number of months which should be allowed for filling a cabinet is   12.____

    A. 2   B. 4   C. 6   D. 8   E. 14

13. The MAXIMUM number of file cabinets which can be released for other uses as a result of the consolidation recommended is   13.____

    A. 0   B. 1   C. 2   D. 3
    E. not determinable on the basis of the data given

14. If all the filing work for both units is consolidated without diminution in the amount to be done and all filing work is done by trained file clerks, the number of clerks required (35–hour work week) is   14.____

    A. 4   B. 5   C. 6   D. 7   E. 8

15. In order to comply with the recommendation with respect to Schedule K, the present work production of Bureau A must be increased by   15.____

    A. 50%   B. 100%   C. 150%   D. 200%
    E. an amount which is not determinable

16. A certain training program during World War II resulted in the training of thousands of supervisors in industry. The methods of this program were later successfully applied in various governmental agencies. The program was based upon the assumption that there is an irreducible minimum of three supervisory skills. The ONE of these skills among the following is   16.____

    A. to know how to perform the job at hand well
    B. to be able to deal personally with workers, especially face to face
    C. to be able to imbue workers with the will to perform the job well
    D. to know the kind of work that is done by one's unit and the policies and procedures of one's agency
    E. the *know-how* of administrative and supervisory processes

17. A comment made by an employee about a training course was, *We never have any idea how we are getting along in that course.* The fundamental error in training methods to which this criticism points is   17.____

A. insufficient student participation
B. failure to develop a feeling of need or active want for the material being presented
C. the training sessions may be too long
D. no attempt may have been made to connect the new material with what was already known
E. no goals have been set for the students

18. Assume that you are attending a departmental conference on efficiency ratings at which it is proposed that a man-to-man rating scale be introduced. You should point out that, of the following, the CHIEF weakness of the man-to-man rating scale is that   18.____

A. it involves abstract numbers rather than concrete employee characteristics
B. judges are unable to select their own standards for comparison
C. the standard for comparison shifts from man to man for each person rated
D. not every person rated is given the opportunity to serve as a standard for comparison
E. standards for comparison will vary from judge to judge

19. Assume that you are conferring with a supervisor who has assigned to his subordinates efficiency ratings which you believe to be generally too low. The supervisor argues that his ratings are generally low because his subordinates are generally inferior. Of the following, the evidence MOST relevant to the point at issue can be secured by comparing efficiency ratings assigned by the supervisor   19.____

A. with ratings assigned by other supervisors in the same agency
B. this year with ratings assigned by him in previous years
C. to men recently transferred to his unit with ratings previously earned by these men
D. with the general city average of ratings assigned by all supervisors to all employees
E. with the relative order of merit of his employees as determined independently by promotion test marks

20. The one of the following which is NOT among the most common of the compensable factors used in wage evaluation studies is   20.____

A. initiative and ingenuity required   B. physical demand
C. responsibility for the safety of others   D. working conditions
E. presence of avoidable hazards

21. If independent functions are separated, there is an immediate gain in conserving special skills. If we are to make optimum use of the abilities of our employees, these skills must be conserved.
Assuming the correctness of this statement, it follows that   21.____

A. if we are not making optimum use of employee abilities, independent functions have not been separated
B. we are making optimum use of employee abilities if we conserve special skills
C. we are making optimum use of employee abilities if independent functions have been separated
D. we are not making optimum use of employee abilities if we do not conserve special skills
E. if special skills are being conserved, independent functions need not be separated

22. A reorganization of the bureau to provide for a stenographic pool instead of individual unit stenographers will result in more stenographic help being available to each unit when it is required, and consequently will result in greater productivity for each unit. An analysis of the space requirements shows that setting up a stenographic pool will require a minimum of 400 square feet of good space. In order to obtain this space, it will be necessary to reduce the space available for technical personnel, resulting in lesser productivity for each unit.

22.____

On the basis of the above discussion, it can be stated that, in order to obtain greater productivity for each unit,

    A. a stenographic pool should be set up
    B. further analysis of the space requirement should be made
    C. it is not certain as to whether or not a stenographic pool should be set up
    D. the space available for each technician should be increased in order to compensate for the absence of a stenographic pool
    E. a stenographic pool should not be set up

23. The adoption of a single consolidated form will mean that most of the form will not be used in any one operation. This would create waste and confusion.

23.____

This conclusion is based upon the unstated hypothesis that

    A. if waste and confusion are to be avoided, a single consolidated form should be used
    B. if a single consolidated form is constructed, most of it can be used in each operation
    C. if waste and confusion are to be avoided, most of the form employed should be used
    D. most of a single consolidated form is not used
    E. a single consolidated form should not be used

KEY(CORRECT ANSWERS)

1.	E		11.	C
2.	B		12.	C
3.	C		13.	B
4.	B		14.	D
5.	E		15.	E
6.	A		16.	B
7.	B		17.	E
8.	A		18.	E
9.	A		19.	C
10.	D		20.	E

21. D
22. C
23. C

EXAMINATION SECTION
TEST 1

DIRECTIONS: Each question or incomplete statement is followed by several suggested
answers or completions. Select the one that BEST answers the question or
completes the statement. *PRINT THE LETTER OF THE CORRECT ANSWER
IN THE SPACE AT THE RIGHT.*

1. An executive assigns A, the head of a staff unit, to devise plans for reducing the delay in   1.____
submittal of reports by a local agency headed by C. The reports are under the supervision of C's subordinate line official B with whom A is to deal directly. In his investigation,
A finds: (1) the reasons for the delay; and (2) poor practices which have either been overlooked or condoned by line official B.
Of the following courses of action A could take, the BEST one would be to

   A.   develop recommendations with line official B with regard to reducing the delay and
correcting the poor practices and then report fully to his own executive
   B.   discuss the findings with C in an attempt to correct the situation before making any
formal report on the poor practices
   C.   report both findings to his executive, attaching the explanation offered by C
   D.   report to his executive on the first finding and discuss the second in a friendly way
with line official B
   E.   report the first finding to his executive, ignoring the second until his opinion is
requested

2. Drafts of a proposed policy, prepared by a staff committee, are circulated to ten members   2.____
of the field staff of the organization by route slips with a request for comments within two
weeks. Two members of the field staff make extensive comments, four offer editorial suggestions and the remainder make minor favorable comments. Shortly after, it found that
the statement needs considerable revision by the field staff.
Of the following possible reasons for the original failure of the field staff to identify difficulties, the MOST likely is that the

   A.   field staff did not take sufficient time to review the material
   B.   field staff had not been advised of the type of contribution expected
   C.   low morale of the field staff prevented their showing interest
   D.   policy statement was too advanced for the staff
   E.   staff committee was not sufficiently representative

3. Operator participation in management improvement work is LEAST likely to   3.____

   A.   assure the use of best available management technique
   B.   overcome the stigma of the outside expert
   C.   place responsibility for improvement in the person who knows the job best
   D.   simplify installation
   E.   take advantage of the desire of most operators to seek self-improvement

4. In general, the morale of workers in an agency is MOST frequently and MOST signifi-   4.____
cantly affected by the

A. agency policies of organizational structure and operational procedures
B. distance of the employee's job from his home community
C. fringe benefits
D. number of opportunities for advancement
E. relationship with supervisors

5. Of the following, the PRIMARY function of a work distribution chart is to   5._____

    A. analyze the soundness of existing divisions of labor
    B. eliminate unnecessary clerical detail
    C. establish better supervisory techniques
    D. simplify work methods
    E. weed out core functions

6. In analyzing a process chart, which one of the following should be asked FIRST?   6._____

    A. How   B. When   C. Where   D. Who   E. Why

7. Which one of the following is NOT an advantage of the interview method of collecting   7._____
data?
It

    A. enables interviewer to judge the person interviewed on such matters as general
       attitude, knowledge, etc.
    B. helps build up personal relations for later installation of changes
    C. is a flexible method that can be adjusted to changing circumstances
    D. permits the obtaining of *off the record* information
    E. produces more accurate information than other methods

8. Which one of the following may be defined as *a regularly recurring appraisal of the man-*   8._____
ner in which all elements of agency management are being carried out?

    A. Functional survey   B. Operations audit
    C. Organization survey   D. Over-all survey
    E. Reconnaissance survey

9. An analysis of the flow of work in a department should begin with the _____ work.   9._____

    A. major routine   B. minor routine
    C. supervisory   D. technical
    E. unusual

10. Which method would MOST likely be used to get first-hand information on complaints   10._____
from the public?

    A. Study of correspondence
    B. Study of work volume
    C. Tracing specific transactions through a series of steps
    D. Tracing use of forms
    E. Worker desk audit

11. People will generally produce the MOST if   11._____

    A. management exercises close supervision over the work
    B. there is strict discipline in the group

C. they are happy in their work
D. they feel involved in their work
E. they follow *the one best way*

12. The normal analysis of which chart listed below is MOST closely related to organizational analysis? _____ chart.

    12.____

A. Layout
B. Operation
C. Process
D. Work count
E. Work distribution

13. The work count would be LEAST helpful in accomplishing which one of the following?

    13.____

A. Demonstrating personnel needs
B. Improving the sequence of steps
C. Measuring the value of a step
D. Spotting bottlenecks
E. Stimulating interest in work

14. Which of the following seems LEAST useful as a guide in interviewing an employee in a procedure and methods survey?

    14.____

A. Explaining who you are and the purpose of your visit
B. Having a general plan of what you intend to get from the interview
C. Listening carefully and not interrupting
D. Trying out his reactions to your ideas for improvements
E. Trying to analyze his reasons for saying what he says

15. Which one of the following is an advantage of the questionnaire method of gathering facts as compared with the interview method?

    15.____

A. Different people may interpret the questions differently.
B. Less *off the record* information is given.
C. More time may be taken in order to give exact answers.
D. Personal relationships with the people involved are not established.
E. There is less need for follow-up.

16. Which one of the following is generally NOT an advantage of the personal observation method of gathering facts?
It

    16.____

A. enables staff to use *off the record* information if personally observed
B. helps in developing valid recommendations
C. helps the person making the observation acquire *know how* valuable for later installation and follow-up
D. is economical in time and money
E. may turn up other problems in need of solution

17. Which of the following would MOST often be the best way to minimize resistance to change?

    17.____

A. Break the news about the change gently to the people affected.
B. Increase the salary of the people affected by the change.

C. Let the people concerned participate in arriving at the decision to change.
D. Notify all people concerned with the change, both orally and in writing.
E. Stress the advantages of the new system.

18. The functional organization chart

18.____

A. does not require periodic revision
B. includes a description of the duties of each organization segment
C. includes positions and titles for each organization segment
D. is the simplest type of organization chart
E. is used primarily by newly established agencies

19. The principle of span of control has frequently been said to be in conflict with the

19.____

A. principle of unity of command
B. principle that authority should be commensurate with responsibility
C. principle that like functions should be grouped into one unit
D. principle that the number of levels between the top of an organization and the bottom should be small
E. scalar principle

20. If an executive delegates to his subordinates authority to handle problems of a routine nature for which standard solutions have been established, he may expect that

20.____

A. fewer complaints will be received
B. he has made it more difficult for his subordinates to solve these problems
C. he has opened the way for confusion in his organization
D. there will be a lack of consistency in the methods applied to the solution of these problems
E. these routine problems will be handled efficiently and he will have more time for other non-routine work

21. Which of the following would MOST likely be achieved by a change in the basic organization structure from the *process* or *functional* type to the *purpose* or *product* type?

21.____

A. Easier recruitment of personnel in a tight labor market
B. Fixing responsibility at a lower level in the organization
C. Greater centralization
D. Greater economy
E. Greater professional development

22. Usually the MOST difficult problem in connection with a major reorganization is

22.____

A. adopting a pay plan to fit the new structure
B. bringing the organization manual up-to-date
C. determining the new organization structure
D. gaining acceptance of the new plan by the higher level employees
E. gaining acceptance of the new plan by the lower level employees

23. Which of the following statements MOST accurately describes the work of the chiefs of MOST staff divisions in departments?
Chiefs

23.____

A. focus more on getting the job done than on how it is done
B. are mostly interested in short-range results
C. nearly always advise but rarely if ever command or control
D. usually command or control but rarely advise
E. provide service to the rest of the organization and/or assist the chief executive in planning and controlling operations

24. In determining the type of organization structure of an enterprise, the one factor that might be given relatively greater weight in a small organization than in a larger organization of the same nature is the   24.____

    A. geographical location of the enterprise
    B. individual capabilities of incumbents
    C. method of financing to be employed
    D. size of the area served
    E. type of activity engaged in

25. Functional foremanship differs MOST markedly from generally accepted principles of administration in that it advocates   25.____

    A. an unlimited span of control
    B. less delegation of responsibility
    C. more than one supervisor for an employee
    D. nonfunctional organization
    E. substitution of execution for planning

KEY (CORRECT ANSWERS)

1. A		11. D
2. B		12. E
3. A		13. B
4. E		14. D
5. A		15. C
6. E		16. D
7. E		17. C
8. B		18. B
9. A		19. D
10. A		20. E

21. B
22. D
23. E
24. B
25. C

TEST 2

DIRECTIONS: Each question or incomplete statement is followed by several suggested answers or completions. Select the one that BEST answers the question or completes the statement. *PRINT THE LETTER OF THE CORRECT ANSWER IN THE SPACE AT THE RIGHT*

1. Decentralization of the authority to make decisions is a necessary result of increased complexity in an organization, but for the sake of efficiency and coordination of operations, such decentralization must be planned carefully.
   A good general rule is that

   A. any decision should be made at the lowest possible point in the organization where all the information and competence necessary for a sound decision are available
   B. any decision should be made at the highest possible point in the organization, thus guaranteeing the best decision
   C. any decision should be made at the lowest possible point in the organization, but always approved by management
   D. any decision should be made by management and referred to the proper subordinate for comment
   E. no decision should be made by any individual in the organization without approval by a superior

   1.____

2. One drawback of converting a conventional consecutive filing system to a terminal digit filing system for a large installation is that

   A. conversion would be expensive in time and manpower
   B. conversion would prevent the proper use of recognized numeric classification systems, such as the Dewey decimal, in classifying files material
   C. responsibility for proper filing cannot be pinpointed in the terminal digit system
   D. the terminal digit system requires considerably more space than a normal filing system
   E. the terminal digit system requires long, specialized training on the part of files personnel

   2.____

3. The basic filing system that would ordinarily be employed in a large administrative headquarters unit is the _____ file system.

   A. alphabetic   B. chronological
   C. mnemonic   D. retention
   E. subject classification

   3.____

4. A records center is of benefit in a records management program primarily because

   A. all the records of the organization are kept in one place
   B. inactive records can be stored economically in less expensive storage areas
   C. it provides a place where useless records can be housed at little or no cost to the organization
   D. obsolete filing and storage equipment can be utilized out of view of the public
   E. records analysts can examine an organization's files without affecting the unit's operation or upsetting the supervisors

   4.____

174

5. In examining a number of different forms to see whether any could be combined or elimi-   5.____
nated, which of the following would one be MOST likely to use?

    A. Forms analysis sheet of recurring data
    B. Forms control log
    C. Forms design and approval request
    D. Forms design and guide sheet
    E. Numerical file

6. The MOST important reason for control of *bootleg* forms is that   6.____

    A. they are more expensive than authorized forms
    B. they are usually poorly designed
    C. they can lead to unnecessary procedures
    D. they cannot be reordered as easily as authorized forms
    E. violation of rules and regulations should not be allowed

7. With a box design of a form, the caption title or question to be answered should be   7.____
located in the _____ of the box.

    A. center at the bottom   B. center at the top
    C. lower left corner   D. lower right corner
    E. upper left corner

8. A two-part snapout form would be MOST properly justified if   8.____

    A. it is a cleaner operation
    B. it is prepared ten times a week
    C. it saves time in preparation
    D. it is to be filled out by hand rather than by typewriter
    E. proper registration is critical

9. When deciding whether or not to approve a request for a new form, which reference is   9.____
normally MOST pertinent?

    A. Alphabetical Forms File
    B. Functional Forms File
    C. Numerical Forms File
    D. Project completion report
    E. Records retention data

10. Which of the following statements BEST explains the significance of the famed Haw-   10.____
thorne Plant experiments? They showed that

    A. a large span of control leads to more production than a small span of control
    B. morale has no relationship to production
    C. personnel counseling is of relatively little importance in a going organization
    D. the special attention received by a group in an experimental situation has a greater
       impact on production than changes in working conditions
    E. there is a direct relationship between the amount of illumination and production

11. Which of the following would most often NOT result from a highly efficient management   11.____
control system?

A. Facilitation of delegation
B. Highlighting of problem areas
C. Increase in willingness of people to experiment or to take calculated risks
D. Provision of an objective test of new ideas or new methods and procedures
E. Provision of information useful for revising objectives, programs, and operations

12. The PERT system is a   12._____

    A. method for laying out office space on a modular basis utilizing prefabricated parti-
       tions
    B. method of motivating personnel to be continuously alert and to improve their
       appearance
    C. method of program planning and control using a network or flow plan
    D. plan for expanding reporting techniques
    E. simplified method of cost accounting

13. The term *management control* is MOST frequently used to mean   13._____

    A. an objective and unemotional approach by management
    B. coordinating the efforts of all parts of the organization
    C. evaluation of results in relation to plan
    D. giving clear, precise orders to subordinates
    E. keeping unions from making managerial decisions

14. Which one of the following factors has the MOST bearing on the frequency with which a   14._____
control report should be made?

    A. Degree of specialization of the work
    B. Degree of variability in activities
    C. Expense of the report
    D. Number of levels of supervision
    E. Number of personnel involved

15. The value of statistical records is MAINLY dependent upon the   15._____

    A. method of presenting the material
    B. number of items used
    C. range of cases sampled
    D. reliability of the information used
    E. time devoted to compiling the material

16. When a supervisor delegates an assignment, he should   16._____

    A. delegate his responsibility for the assignment
    B. make certain that the assignment is properly performed
    C. participate in the beginning and final stages of the assignment
    D. retain all authority needed to complete the assignment
    E. oversee all stages of the assignment

17. Assume that the department in which you are employed has never given official sanction to a mid-afternoon coffee break. Some bureaus have it and others do not. In the latter case, some individuals merely absent themselves for about 15 minutes at 3 P.M. while others remain on the job despite the fatigue which seems to be common among all employees in this department at that time.
The course of action which you should recommend, if possible, is to

    A. arrange a schedule of mid-afternoon coffee breaks for all employees
    B. forbid all employees to take a mid-afternoon coffee break
    C. permit each bureau to decide for itself whether or not it will have a coffee break
    D. require all employees who wish a coffee break to take a shorter lunch period
    E. arrange a poll to discover the consensus of the department

17.____

18. The one of the following which is LEAST important in the management of a suggestion program is

    A. giving awards which are of sufficient value to encourage competition
    B. securing full support from the department's officers and executives
    C. publicizing the program and the awards given
    D. holding special conferences to analyze and evaluate some of the suggestions needed
    E. providing suggestion boxes in numerous locations

18.____

19. The one of the following which is MOST likely to decrease morale is

    A. insistence on strict adherence to safety rules
    B. making each employee responsible for the tidiness of his work area
    C. overlooking evidence of hostility between groups of employees
    D. strong, aggressive leadership
    E. allocating work on the basis of personal knowledge of the abilities and interests of the members of the department

19.____

20. Assume that a certain office procedure has been standard practice for many years. When a new employee asks why this particular procedure is followed, the supervisor should FIRST

    A. explain that everyone does it that way
    B. explain the reason for the procedure
    C. inform him that it has always been done that way in that particular office
    D. tell him to try it for a while before asking questions
    E. tell him he has never thought about it that way

20.____

21. Several employees complain informally to their supervisor regarding some new procedures which have been instituted. The supervisor should IMMEDIATELY

    A. explain that management is responsible
    B. state frankly that he had nothing to do with it
    C. refer the matter to the methods analyst
    D. tell the employees to submit their complaint as a formal grievance
    E. investigate the complaint

21.____

22. A new employee asks his supervisor *how he is doing*. Actually, he is not doing well in   22.____
some phases of the job, but it is felt that he will learn in time.
The BEST response for the supervisor to make is:

    A. Some things you are doing well, and in others I am sure you will improve
    B. Wait until the end of your probationary period when we will discuss this matter
    C. You are not doing too well
    D. You are doing very well
    E. I'll be able to tell you when I go over your record

23. The PRINCIPAL aim of a supervisor is to   23.____

    A. act as liaison between employee and management
    B. get the work done
    C. keep up morale
    D. train his subordinates
    E. become chief of the department

24. When the work of two bureaus must be coordinated, direct contact between the subordi-   24.____
nates in each bureau who are working on the problem is

    A. *bad,* because it violates the chain of command
    B. *bad,* because they do not have authority to make decisions
    C. *good,* because it enables quicker results
    D. *good,* because it relieves their superiors of any responsibility
    E. *bad,* because they may work at cross purposes

25. Of the following, the organization defect which can be ascertained MOST readily merely   25.____
by analyzing an accurate and well-drawn organization chart is

    A. ineffectiveness of an activity
    B. improper span of control
    C. inappropriate assignment of functions
    D. poor supervision
    E. unlawful delegation of authority

KEY (CORRECT ANSWERS)

1.	A	11.	C
2.	A	12.	C
3.	E	13.	C
4.	B	14.	B
5.	A	15.	D
6.	C	16.	B
7.	E	17.	A
8.	E	18.	E
9.	B	19.	C
10.	D	20.	B

21.	E
22.	A
23.	B
24.	C
25.	B

PRINCIPLES AND PRACTICES OF ADMINISTRATION, SUPERVISION & MANAGEMENT

TABLE OF CONTENTS

PRINCIPLES AND PRACTICES OF ADMINISTRATION, SUPERVISION & MANAGEMENT

Most people are inclined to think of administration as something that only a few persons are responsible for in a large organization. Perhaps this is true if you are thinking of Administration with a capital *A*, but administration with a lower case a is a responsibility of supervisors at all levels each working day.

All of us feel we are pretty good supervisors and that we do a good job of administering the workings of our agency. By and large, this is true, but every so often it is good to check up on ourselves. Checklists appear from time to time in various publications which psychologists say, tell whether or not a person will make a good wife, husband, doctor, lawyer, or supervisor.

The following questions are an excellent checklist to test yourself as a supervisor and administrator.

Remember, Administration gives direction and points the way but administration carries the ideas to fruition. Each is dependent on the other for its success. Remember, too, that no unit is too small for these departmental functions to be carried out. These statements apply equally as well to the Chief Librarian as to the Department Head with but one or two persons to supervise.

GENERAL ADMINISTRATION - General Responsibilities of Supervisors

1. Have I prepared written statements of functions, activities, and duties for my organizational unit?

2. Have I prepared procedural guides for operating activities?

3. Have I established clearly in writing, lines of authority and responsibility for my organizational unit?

4. Do I make recommendations for improvements in organization, policies, administrative and operating routines and procedures, including simplification of work and elimination of non-essential operations?

5. Have I designated and trained an understudy to function in my absence?

6. Do I supervise and train personnel within the unit to effectively perform their assignments?

7. Do I assign personnel and distribute work on such a basis as to carry out the organizational unit's assignment or mission in the most effective and efficient manner?

8. Have I established administrative controls by:

   a. Fixing responsibility and accountability on all supervisors under my direction for the proper performance of their functions and duties.

b. Preparing and submitting periodic work load and progress reports covering the operations of the unit to my immediate superior.

c. Analysis and evaluation of such reports received from subordinate units.

d. Submission of significant developments and problems arising within the organizational unit to my immediate superior.

e. Conducting conferences, inspections, etc., as to the status and efficiency of unit operations.

9. Do I maintain an adequate and competent working force?

10. Have I fostered good employee-department relations, seeing that established rules, regulations, and instructions are being carried out properly?

11. Do I collaborate and consult with other organizational units performing related functions to insure harmonious and efficient working relationships?

12. Do I maintain liaison through prescribed channels with city departments and other governmental agencies concerned with the activities of the unit?

13. Do I maintain contact with and keep abreast of the latest developments and techniques of administration (professional societies, groups, periodicals, etc.) as to their applicability to the activities of the unit?

14. Do I communicate with superiors and subordinates through prescribed organizational channels?

15. Do I notify superiors and subordinates in instances where bypassing is necessary as soon thereafter as practicable?

16. Do I keep my superior informed of significant developments and problems?

SEVEN BASIC FUNCTIONS OF THE SUPERVISOR

1. <u>PLANNING</u>
   This means working out goals and means to obtain goals. <u>What</u> needs to be done, <u>who</u> will do it, <u>how</u>, <u>when</u>, and <u>where</u> it is to be done.

   <u>SEVEN STEPS IN PLANNING</u>

   1. Define job or problem clearly.
   2. Consider priority of job.
   3. Consider time-limit - starting and completing.
   4. Consider minimum distraction to, or interference with, other activities.
   5. Consider and provide for contingencies - possible emergencies.
   6. Break job down into components.
   7. Consider the 5 W's and H:

WHY	...	is it necessary to do the job? (Is the purpose clearly defined?)
WHAT	...	needs to be done to accomplish the defined purpose?
	...	is needed to do the job? (money, materials, etc.)
WHO	...	is needed to do the job?
	...	will have responsibilities?
WHERE	...	is the work to be done?
WHEN	...	is the job to begin and end? (schedules, etc.)
HOW	...	is the job to be done? (methods, controls, records, etc.)

2. ORGANIZING

This means dividing up the work, establishing clear lines of responsibility and authority and coordinating efforts to get the job done.

3. STAFFING

The whole personnel function of bringing in and training staff, getting the right man and fitting him to the right job - the job to which he is best suited.

In the normal situation, the supervisor's responsibility regarding staffing normally includes providing accurate job descriptions, that is, duties of the jobs, requirements, education and experience, skills, physical, etc.; assigning the work for maximum use of skills; and proper utilization of the probationary period to weed out unsatisfactory employees.

4. DIRECTING

Providing the necessary leadership to the group supervised. Important work gets done to the supervisor's satisfaction.

5. COORDINATING

The all-important duty of inter-relating the various parts of the work.

The supervisor is also responsible for controlling the coordinated activities. This means measuring performance according to a time schedule and setting quotas to see that the goals previously set are being reached. Reports from workers should be analyzed, evaluated, and made part of all future plans.

6. REPORTING

This means proper and effective communication to your superiors, subordinates, and your peers (in definition of the job of the supervisor). Reports should be read and information contained therein should be used not be filed away and forgotten. Reports should be written in such a way that the desired action recommended by the report is forthcoming.

7. BUDGETING

This means controlling current costs and forecasting future costs. This forecast is based on past experience, future plans and programs, as well as current costs.

You will note that these seven functions can fall under three topics:

Planning	)	
Organizing	)	Make a Plan
Staffing	)	
Directing	)	Get things done
Controlling	)	

Reporting   )
Budgeting   )   Watch it work

PLANNING TO MEET MANAGEMENT GOALS

I. <u>WHAT IS PLANNING</u>?
A. Thinking a job through before new work is done to determine the best way to do it
B. A method of doing something
C. Ways and means for achieving set goals
D. A means of enabling a supervisor to deliver with a minimum of effort, all details involved in coordinating his work

II. <u>WHO SHOULD MAKE PLANS</u>?
Everybody!
All levels of supervision must plan work. (Top management, heads of divisions or bureaus, first line supervisors, and individual employees.) The higher the level, the more planning required.

III. <u>WHAT ARE THE RESULTS OF POOR PLANNING</u>?
A. Failure to meet deadline
B. Low employee morale
C. Lack of job coordination
D. Overtime is frequently necessary
E. Excessive cost, waste of material and manhours

IV. <u>PRINCIPLES OF PLANNING</u>
A. Getting a clear picture of your objectives. What exactly are you trying to accomplish?
B. Plan the whole job, then the parts, in proper sequence.
C. Delegate the planning of details to those responsible for executing them.
D. Make your plan flexible.
E. Coordinate your plan with the plans of others so that the work may be processed with a minimum of delay.
F. Sell your plan before you execute it.
G. Sell your plan to your superior, subordinate, in order to gain maximum participation and coordination.
H. Your plan should take precedence. Use knowledge and skills that others have brought to a similar job.
I. Your plan should take account of future contingencies; allow for future expansion.
J. Plans should include minor details. Leave nothing to chance that can be anticipated.
K. Your plan should be simple and provide standards and controls. Establish quality and quantity standards and set a standard method of doing the job. The controls will indicate whether the job is proceeding according to plan.
L. Consider possible bottlenecks, breakdowns, or other difficulties that are likely to arise.

V. Q. WHAT ARE THE *YARDSTICKS* BY WHICH PLANNING SHOULD BE MEASURED?
A. Any plan should:
- Clearly state a definite course of action to be followed and goal to be achieved, with consideration for emergencies.
- Be realistic and practical.

- State what's to be done, when it's to be done, where, how, and by whom.
- Establish the most efficient sequence of operating steps so that more is accomplished in less time, with the least effort, and with the best quality results.
- Assure meeting deliveries without delays.
- Establish the standard by which performance is to be judged.

Q. WHAT KINDS OF PLANS DOES EFFECTIVE SUPERVISION REQUIRE?
A. Plans should cover such factors as:
- Manpower - right number of properly trained employees on the job.
- Materials - adequate supply of the right materials and supplies.
- Machines - full utilization of machines and equipment, with proper maintenance.
- Methods - most efficient handling of operations.
- Deliveries - making deliveries on time.
- Tools - sufficient well-conditioned tools
- Layout - most effective use of space.
- Reports - maintaining proper records and reports.
- Supervision - planning work for employees and organizing supervisor's own time.

I. MANAGEMENT

Question: *What do we mean by management?*

Answer: *Getting work done through others.*

Management could also be defined as planning, directing, and controlling the operations of a bureau or division so that all factors will function properly and all persons cooperate efficiently for a common objective.

II. MANAGEMENT PRINCIPLES

1. There should be a hierarchy - wherein authority and responsibility run upward and downward through several levels - with a broad base at the bottom and a single head at the top.

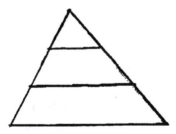

2. Each and every unit or person in the organization should be answerable ultimately to the manager at the apex. In other words, *The buck stops here!*

3. Every necessary function involved in the bureau's objectives is assigned to a unit in that bureau.

4. Responsibilities assigned to a unit are specifically clear-cut and understood.

5. Consistent methods of organizational structure should be applied at each level of the organization.

6. Each member of the bureau from top to bottom knows:
   to whom he reports
   who reports to him.

7. No member of one bureau reports to more than one supervisor.
   No dual functions

8. Responsibility for a function is matched by authority necessary to perform that function.
   Weight of authority

9. Individuals or units reporting to a supervisor do not exceed the number which can be feasibly and effectively coordinated and directed.
   Concept of *span of control*

10. Channels of command (management) are not violated by staff units, although there should be staff services to facilitate and coordinate management functions.

11. Authority and responsibility should be decentralized to units and individuals who are responsible for the actual performance of operations.
    Welfare - down to Welfare Centers
    Hospitals - down to local hospitals

12. Management should exercise control through attention to policy problems of exceptional importance, rather than through review of routine actions of subordinates.

13. Organizations should never be permitted to grow so elaborate as to hinder work accomplishments.
    Empire building

II. ORGANIZATION STRUCTURE
   Types of Organizations.
   The purest form is a leader and a few followers, such as:

```
                          ┌─── Supervisor ───┐
   ───────────────────────────────────────────────────────
   ┌─ Worker ─┐      ┌─ Worker ─┐      ┌─ Worker ─┐      ┌─ Worker ─┐
```

(Refer to organization chart) from supervisor to workers.

The line of authority is direct,
The workers know exactly where they stand in relation to their boss, to whom they report for instructions and direction.

Unfortunately, in our present complex society, few organizations are similar to this example of a pure line organization. In this era of specialization, other people are often needed in the simplest of organizations. These specialists are known as staff. The sole purpose for their existence (staff) is to assist, advise, suggest, help or counsel line organizations. Staff has no authority to direct line people - nor do they give them direct instructions.

```
                    ┌─────────────┐
                    │ SUPERVISOR  │
                    └─────────────┘
                           │
   ┌────────────┬──────────┴─────────┬────────────┐
┌───────────┐ ┌────────────┐ ┌─────────────┐ ┌─────────┐
│ Personnel │ │ Accounting │ │ Inspection  │ │ Legal   │
└───────────┘ └────────────┘ └─────────────┘ └─────────┘
 ┌────────┐    ┌────────┐     ┌────────┐      ┌────────┐
 │ Worker │    │ Worker │     │ Worker │      │ Worker │
 └────────┘    └────────┘     └────────┘      └────────┘
```

Line Functions

1. Directs

2. Orders

3. Responsibility for carrying out activities from beginning to end

4. Follows chain of command

5. Is identified with what it does

6. Decides when and how to use staff advice

7. Line executes

Staff Functions

1. Advises

2. Persuades and sells

3. Staff studies, reports, recommends but does not carry out

4. May advise across department lines

5. May find its ideas identified with others

6. Has to persuade line to want its advice

7. Staff - Conducts studies and research. Provides advice and instructions in technical matters. Serves as technical specialist to render specific services

Types and Functions of Organization Charts.
An organization chart is a picture of the arrangement and inter-relationship of the subdivisions of an organization.

1. Types of Charts:
    a. Structural - basic relationships only
    b. Functional - includes functions or duties
    c. Personnel - positions, salaries, status, etc.
    d. Process Chart - work performed
    e. Gantt Chart - actual performance against planned
    f. Flow Chart - flow and distribution of work

2. Functions of Charts:
    a. Assist in management planning and control
    b. Indicate duplication of functions
    c. Indicate incorrect stressing of functions
    d. Indicate neglect of important functions
    e. Correct unclear authority
    f. Establish proper span of control

3. Limitations of Charts:
    a. Seldom maintained on current basis

b. Chart is oversimplified
c. Human factors cannot adequately be charted

4. Organization Charts should be:
   a. Simple
   b. Symmetrical
   c. Indicate authority
   d. Line and staff relationship differentiated
   e. Chart should be dated and bear signature of approving officer
   f. Chart should be displayed, not hidden

ORGANIZATION

There are four basic principles of organization:

1. Unity of command
2. Span of control
3. Uniformity of assignment
4. Assignment of responsibility and delegation of authority

Unity of Command

Unity of command means that each person in the organization should receive orders from one, and only one, supervisor. When a person has to take orders from two or more people, (a) the orders may be in conflict and the employee is upset because he does not know which he should obey, or, (b) different orders may reach him at the same time and he does not know which he should carry out first.

Equally as bad as having two bosses is the situation where the supervisor is by-passed. Let us suppose you are a supervisor whose boss by-passes you (deals directly with people reporting to you). To the worker, it is the same as having two bosses; but to you, the supervisor, it is equally serious. By-passing on the part of your boss will undermine your authority, and the people under you will begin looking to your boss for decisions and even for routine orders.

You can prevent by-passing by telling the people you supervise that if anyone tries to give them orders, they should direct that person to you.

Span of Control

Span of control on a given level involves:

a. The number of people being supervised
b. The distance
c. The time involved in supervising the people. (One supervisor cannot supervise too many workers effectively.)

Span of control means that a supervisor has the right number (not too many and not too few) of subordinates that he can supervise well.

Uniformity of Assignment

In assigning work, you as the supervisor should assign to each person jobs that are similar in nature. An employee who is assigned too many different types of jobs will waste time in going from one kind of work to another. It takes time for him to get to top production in one kind of task and, before he does so, he has to start on another.

When you assign work to people, remember that:

a. Job duties should be definite. Make it clear from the beginning <u>what</u> they are to do, <u>how</u> they are to do it, and <u>why</u> they are to do it. Let them know how much they are expected to do and how well they are expected to do it.

b. Check your assignments to be certain that there are no workers with too many unrelated duties, and that no two people have been given overlapping responsibilities. Your aim should be to have every task assigned to a specific person with the work fairly distributed and with each person doing his part.

<u>Assignment of Responsibility and Delegation of Authority</u>

A supervisor cannot delegate his final responsibility for the work of his department. The experienced supervisor knows that he gets his work done through people. He can't do it all himself. So he must assign the work and the responsibility for the work to his employees. Then they must be given the authority to carry out their responsibilities.

By assigning responsibility and delegating authority to carry out the responsibility, the supervisor builds in his workers initiative, resourcefulness, enthusiasm, and interest in their work. He is treating them as responsible adults. They can find satisfaction in their work, and they will respect the supervisor and be loyal to the supervisor.

PRINCIPLES OF ORGANIZATION

1. <u>Definition</u>
   Organization is the method of dividing up the work to provide the best channels for coordinated effort to get the agency's mission accomplished.

2. <u>Purpose of Organization</u>
   a. To enable each employee within the organization to clearly know his responsibilities and relationships to his fellow employees and to organizational units.
   b. To avoid conflicts of authority and overlapping of jurisdiction.
   c. To ensure teamwork.

3. <u>Basic Considerations in Organizational Planning</u>
   a. The basic plans and objectives of the agency should be determined, and the organizational structure should be adapted to carry out effectively such plans and objectives.
   b. The organization should be built around the major functions of the agency and not individuals or groups of individuals.
   c. The organization should be sufficiently flexible to meet new and changing conditions which may be brought about from within or outside the department.
   d. The organizational structure should be as simple as possible and the number of organizational units kept at a minimum.
   e. The number of levels of authority should be kept at a minimum. Each additional management level lengthens the chain of authority and responsibility and increases the time for instructions to be distributed to operating levels and for decisions to be obtained from higher authority.

f. The form of organization should permit each executive to exercise maximum initiative within the limits of delegated authority.

4. Bases for Organization
   a. Purpose (Examples: education, police, sanitation)
   b. Process (Examples: accounting, legal, purchasing)
   c. Clientele (Examples: welfare, parks, veteran)
   d. Geographic (Examples: borough offices, precincts, libraries)

5. Assignments of Functions
   a. Every function of the agency should be assigned to a specific organizational unit. Under normal circumstances, no single function should be assigned to more than one organizational unit.
   b. There should be no overlapping, duplication, or conflict between organizational elements.
   c. Line functions should be separated from staff functions, and proper emphasis should be placed on staff activities.
   d. Functions which are closely related or similar should normally be assigned to a single organizational unit.
   e. Functions should be properly distributed to promote balance, and to avoid overemphasis of less important functions and underemphasis of more essential functions.

6. Delegation of Authority and Responsibility
   a. Responsibilities assigned to a specific individual or organizational unit should carry corresponding authority, and all statements of authority or limitations thereof should be as specific as possible.
   b. Authority and responsibility for action should be decentralized to organizational units and individuals responsible for actual performance to the greatest extent possible, without relaxing necessary control over policy or the standardization of procedures. Delegation of authority will be consistent with decentralization of responsibility but such delegation will not divest an executive in higher authority of his overall responsibility.
   c. The heads of organizational units should concern themselves with important matters and should delegate to the maximum extent details and routines performed in the ordinary course of business.
   d. All responsibilities, authorities, and relationships should be stated in simple language to avoid misinterpretation.
   e. Each individual or organizational unit charged with a specific responsibility will be held responsible for results.

7. Employee Relationships
   a. The employees reporting to one executive should not exceed the number which can be effectively directed and coordinated. The number will depend largely upon the scope and extent of the responsibilities of the subordinates.
   b. No person should report to more than one supervisor. Every supervisor should know who reports to him, and every employee should know to whom he reports. Channels of authority and responsibility should not be violated by staff units.
   c. Relationships between organizational units within the agency and with outside organizations and associations should be clearly stated and thoroughly understood to avoid misunderstanding.

DELEGATING

1. <u>What is Delegating?</u>
   Delegating is assigning a job to an employee, giving him the authority to get that job done, and giving him the responsibility for seeing to it that the job is done.

   a. <u>What to Delegate</u>
      (1) Routine details
      (2) Jobs which may be necessary and take a lot of time, but do not have to be done by the supervisor personally (preparing reports, attending meetings, etc.)
      (3) Routine decision-making (making decisions which do not require the supervisor's personal attention)

   b. <u>What Not to Delegate</u>
      (1) Job details which are *executive functions* (setting goals, organizing employees into a good team, analyzing results so as to plan for the future)
      (2) Disciplinary power (handling grievances, preparing service ratings, reprimands, etc.)
      (3) Decision-making which involves large numbers of employees or other bureaus and departments
      (4) Final and complete responsibility for the job done by the unit being supervised

   c. <u>Why Delegate?</u>
      (1) To strengthen the organization by developing a greater number of skilled employees
      (2) To improve the employee's performance by giving him the chance to learn more about the job, handle some responsibility, and become more interested in getting the job done
      (3) To improve a supervisor's performance by relieving him of routine jobs and giving him more time for *executive functions* (planning, organizing, controlling, etc.) which cannot be delegated

2. <u>To Whom to Delegate</u>
   People with abilities not being used. Selection should be based on ability, not on favoritism.

REPORTS

<u>Definition</u>

A report is an orderly presentation of factual information directed to a specific reader for a specific purpose.

<u>Purpose</u>

The general purpose of a report is to bring to the reader useful and factual information about a condition or a problem. Some specific purposes of a report may be:

1. To enable the reader to appraise the efficiency or effectiveness of a person or an operation
2. To provide a basis for establishing standards
3. To reflect the results of expenditures of time, effort, and money
4. To provide a basis for developing or altering programs

<u>Types</u>
1. Information Report - Contains facts arranged in sequence
2. Summary (Examination) Report - Contains facts plus an analysis or discussion of the significance of the facts. Analysis may give advantages and disadvantages or give qualitative and quantitative comparisons
3. Recommendation Report - Contains facts, analysis, and conclusion logically drawn from the facts and analysis, plus a recommendation based upon the facts, analysis, and conclusions

<u>Factors to Consider Before Writing Report</u>

1. <u>Why</u> write the report - The purpose of the report should be clearly defined.
2. <u>Who</u> will read the report - What level of language should be used? Will the reader understand professional or technical language?
3. <u>What</u> should be said - What does the reader need or want to know about the subject?
4. <u>How</u> should it be said - Should the subject be presented tactfully? Convincingly? In a stimulating manner?

<u>Preparatory Steps</u>

1. Assemble the facts - Find out who, why, what, where, when, and how.
2. Organize the facts - Eliminate unnecessary information.
3. Prepare an outline - Check for orderliness, logical sequence.
4. Prepare a draft - Check for correctness, clearness, completeness, conciseness, and tone.
5. Prepare it in final form - Check for grammar, punctuation, appearance.

<u>Outline For a Recommendation Report</u>
Is the report:

1. Correct in information, grammar, and tone?
2. Clear?
3. Complete?
4. Concise?
5. Timely?
6. Worth its cost?

Will the report accomplish its purpose?

MANAGEMENT CONTROLS

1. <u>Control</u>
What is control? What is controlled? Who controls?

The essence of control is action which adjusts operations to predetermined standards, and its basis is information in the hands of managers. Control is checking to determine whether plans are being observed and suitable progress toward stated objectives is being made, and action is taken, if necessary, to correct deviations.

We have a ready-made model for this concept of control in the automatic systems which are widely used for process control in the chemical and petroleum industries. A process control system works this way. Suppose, for example, it is desired to maintain a constant rate of flow of oil through a pipe at a predetermined or set-point value. A signal, whose strength represents the rate of flow, can be produced in a measuring device and transmitted to a control mechanism. The control mechanism, when it detects any deviation of the actual from the set-point signal, will reposition the value regulating flow rate.

2. Basis For Control

A process control mechanism thus acts to adjust operations to predetermined standards and does so on the basis of information it receives. In a parallel way, information reaching a manager gives him the opportunity for corrective action and is his basis for control. He cannot exercise control without such information, and he cannot do a complete job of managing without controlling.

3. Policy

What is policy?

Policy is simply a statement of an organization's intention to act in certain ways when specified types of circumstances arise. It represents a general decision, predetermined and expressed as a principle or rule, establishing a normal pattern of conduct for dealing with given types of business events - usually recurrent. A statement is therefore useful in economizing the time of managers and in assisting them to discharge their responsibilities equitably and consistently.

Policy is not a means of control, but policy does generate the need for control.

Adherence to policies is not guaranteed nor can it be taken on faith. It has to be verified. Without verification, there is no basis for control. Policy and procedures, although closely related and interdependent to a certain extent, are not synonymous. A policy may be adopted, for example, to maintain a materials inventory not to exceed one million dollars. A procedure for inventory control would interpret that policy and convert it into methods for keeping within that limit, with consideration, too, of possible but foreseeable expedient deviation.

4. Procedure

What is procedure?

A procedure specifically prescribes:

a. What work is to be performed by the various participants
b. Who are the respective participants
c. When and where the various steps in the different processes are to be performed
d. The sequence of operations that will insure uniform handling of recurring transactions
e. The *paper* that is involved, its origin, transition, and disposition

Necessary appurtenances to a procedure are:

a. Detailed organizational chart

---

    b. Flow charts
    c. Exhibits of forms, all presented in close proximity to the text of the procedure

5. **Basis of Control - Information in the Hands of Managers**
If the basis of control is information in the hands of managers, then <u>reporting</u> is elevated to a level of very considerable importance.

Types of reporting may include:

    a. Special reports and routine reports
    b. Written, oral, and graphic reports
    c. Staff meetings
    d. Conferences
    e. Television screens
    f. Non-receipt of information, as where management is by exception
    g. Any other means whereby information is transmitted to a manager as a basis for control action

FRAMEWORK OF MANAGEMENT

<u>Elements</u>
1. <u>Policy</u> - It has to be verified, controlled.

2. <u>Organization</u> - is part of the giving of an assignment. The organizational chart gives to each individual in his title, a first approximation of the nature of his assignment and orients him as being accountable to a certain individual. Organization is not in a true sense a means of control. Control is checking to ascertain whether the assignment is executed as intended and acting on the basis of that information.

3. <u>Budgets</u> - perform three functions:

    a. They present the objectives, plans, and programs of the organization in financial terms.
    b. They report the progress of actual performance against these predetermined objectives, plans, and programs.
    c. Like organizational charts, delegations of authority, procedures and job descriptions, they define the assignments which have flowed from the Chief Executive. Budgets are a means of control in the respect that they report progress of actual performance against the program. They provide information which enables managers to take action directed toward bringing actual results into conformity with the program.

4. <u>Internal Check</u> - provides in practice for the principle that the same person should not have responsibility for all phases of a transaction. This makes it clearly an aspect of organization rather than of control. Internal Check is static, or built-in.

5. <u>Plans, Programs, Objectives</u>
People must know what they are trying to do. <u>Objectives</u> fulfill this need. Without them, people may work industriously and yet, working aimlessly, accomplish little.

Plans and Programs complement Objectives, since they propose how and according to what time schedule the objectives are to be reached.

6. Delegations of Authority

Among the ways we have for supplementing the titles and lines of authority of an organizational chart are delegations of authority. Delegations of authority clarify the extent of authority of individuals and in that way serve to define assignments. That they are not means of control is apparent from the very fact that wherever there has been a delegation of authority, the need for control increases. This could hardly be expected to happen if delegations of authority were themselves means of control.

Manager's Responsibility

Control becomes necessary whenever a manager delegates authority to a subordinate because he cannot delegate and then simply sit back and forget all about it. A manager's accountability to his own superior has not diminished one whit as a result of delegating part of his authority to a subordinate. The manager must exercise control over actions taken under the authority so delegated. That means checking serves as a basis for possible corrective action.

Objectives, plans, programs, organizational charts, and other elements of the managerial system are not fruitfully regarded as either controls or means of control. They are pre-established standards or models of performance to which operations are adjusted by the exercise of management control. These standards or models of performance are dynamic in character for they are constantly altered, modified, or revised. Policies, organizational set-up, procedures, delegations, etc. are constantly altered but, like objectives and plans, they remain in force until they are either abandoned or revised. All of the elements (or standards or models of performance), objectives, plans and prpgrams, policies, organization, etc. can be regarded as a *framework of management*.

Control Techniques

Examples of control techniques:
1. Compare against established standards
2. Compare with a similar operation
3. Compare with past operations
4. Compare with predictions of accomplishment

Where Forecasts Fit

Control is after-the-fact while forecasts are before. Forecasts and projections are important for setting objectives and formulating plans.

Information for aiming and planning does not have to before-the-fact. It may be an after-the-fact analysis proving that a certain policy has been impolitic in its effect on the relation of the company or department with customer, employee, taxpayer, or stockholder; or that a certain plan is no longer practical, or that a certain procedure is unworkable.

The prescription here certainly would not be in control (in these cases, control would simply bring operations into conformity with obsolete standards) but the establishment of new standards, a new policy, a new plan, and a new procedure to be controlled too.

Information is, of course, the basis for all communication in addition to furnishing evidence to management of the need for reconstructing the framework of management.

PROBLEM SOLVING

The accepted concept in modern management for problem solving is the utilization of the following steps:

1. Identify the problem
2. Gather data
3. List possible solutions
4. Test possible solutions
5. Select the best solution
6. Put the solution into actual practice

Occasions might arise where you would have to apply the second step of gathering data before completing the first step.

You might also find that it will be necessary to work on several steps at the same time.

1. Identify the Problem

Your first step is to define as precisely as possible the problem to be solved. While this may sound easy, it is often the most difficult part of the process.

It has been said of problem solving that you are halfway to the solution when you can write out a clear statement of the problem itself.

Our job now is to get below the surface manifestations of the trouble and pinpoint the problem. This is usually accomplished by a logical analysis, by going from the general to the particular; from the obvious to the not-so-obvious cause.
Let us say that production is behind schedule. WHY? Absenteeism is high. Now, is absenteeism the basic problem to be tackled, or is it merely a symptom of low morale among the workforce? Under these circumstances, you may decide that production is not the problem; the problem is *employee morale*.

In trying to define the problem, remember there is seldom one simple reason why production is lagging, or reports are late, etc.

Analysis usually leads to the discovery that an apparent problem is really made up of several subproblems which must be attacked separately.

Another way is to limit the problem, and thereby ease the task of finding a solution, and concentrate on the elements which are within the scope of your control.

When you have gone this far, write out a tentative statement of the problem to be solved.

2. Gather Data

In the second step, you must set out to collect all the information that might have a bearing on the problem. Do not settle for an assumption when reasonable fact and figures are available.

If you merely go through the motions of problem-solving, you will probably shortcut the information-gathering step. Therefore, do not stack the evidence by confining your research to your own preconceived ideas.

As you collect facts, organize them in some form that helps you make sense of them and spot possible relationships between them. For example: Plotting cost per unit figures on a graph can be more meaningful than a long column of figures.

Evaluate each item as you go along. Is the source material: absolutely reliable, probably reliable, or not to be trusted.

One of the best methods for gathering data is to go out and look the situation over carefully. Talk to the people on the job who are most affected by this problem.

Always keep in mind that a primary source is usually better than a secondary source of information.

3. List Possible Solutions

This is the creative thinking step of problem solving. This is a good time to bring into play whatever techniques of group dynamics the agency or bureau might have developed for a joint attack on problems.

Now the important thing for you to do is: Keep an open mind. Let your imagination roam freely over the facts you have collected. Jot down every possible solution that occurs to you. Resist the temptation to evaluate various proposals as you go along. List seemingly absurd ideas along with more plausible ones. The more possibilities you list during this step, the less risk you will run of settling for merely a workable, rather than the best, solution.

Keep studying the data as long as there seems to be any chance of deriving additional - ideas, solutions, explanations, or patterns from it.

4. Test Possible Solutions

Now you begin to evaluate the possible solutions. Take pains to be objective. Up to this point, you have suspended judgment but you might be tempted to select a solution you secretly favored all along and proclaim it as the best of the lot.

The secret of objectivity in this phase is to test the possible solutions separately, measuring each against a common yardstick. To make this yardstick try to enumerate as many specific criteria as you can think of. Criteria are best phrased as questions which you ask of each possible solution. They can be drawn from these general categories:

Suitability   -   Will this solution do the job?
                    Will it solve the problem completely or partially?

Is it a permanent or a stopgap solution?

| Feasibility | - | Will this plan work in actual practice?
Can we afford this approach?
How much will it cost? |

| Acceptability | - | Will the boss go along with the changes required in the plan?
Are we trying to drive a tack with a sledge hammer? |

5. <u>Select the Best Solution</u>

This is the area of executive decision.

Occasionally, one clearly superior solution will stand out at the conclusion of the testing process. But often it is not that simple. You may find that no one solution has come through all the tests with flying colors.

You may also find that a proposal, which flunked miserably on one of the essential tests, racked up a very high score on others.

The best solution frequently will turn out to be a combination.

Try to arrange a marriage that will bring together the strong points of one possible solution with the particular virtues of another. The more skill and imagination that you apply, the greater is the likelihood that you will come out with a solution that is not merely adequate and workable, but is the best possible under the circumstances.

6. <u>Put the Solution Into Actual Practice</u>
As every executive knows, a plan which works perfectly on paper may develop all sorts of bugs when put into actual practice.

Problem-solving does not stop with selecting the solution which looks best in theory. The next step is to put the chosen solution into action and watch the results. The results may point towards modifications.

If the problem disappears when you put your solution into effect, you know you have the right solution.

If it does not disappear, even after you have adjusted your plan to cover unforeseen difficulties that turned up in practice, work your way back through the problem-solving solutions.

Would one of them have worked better?
Did you overlook some vital piece of data which would have given you a different slant on the whole situation? Did you apply all necessary criteria in testing solutions? If no light dawns after this much rechecking, it is a pretty good bet that you defined the problem incorrectly in the first place.

You came up with the wrong solution because you tackled the wrong problem.

Thus, step six may become step one of a new problem-solving cycle.

COMMUNICATION

1. <u>What is Communication</u>?
    We communicate through writing, speaking, action or inaction. In speaking to people face-to-face, there is opportunity to judge reactions and to adjust the message. This makes the supervisory chain one of the most, and in many instances the most, important channels of communication.

    In an organization, communication means keeping employees informed about the organization's objectives, policies, problems, and progress. Communication is the free interchange of information, ideas, and desirable attitudes between and among employees and between employees and management.

2. <u>Why is Communication Needed</u>?
    a. People have certain social needs
    b. Good communication is essential in meeting those social needs
    c. While people have similar basic needs, at the same time they differ from each other
    d. Communication must be adapted to these individual differences

    An employee cannot do his best work unless he knows why he is doing it. If he has the feeling that he is being kept in the dark about what is going on, his enthusiasm and productivity suffer.

    Effective communication is needed in an organization so that employees will understand what the organization is trying to accomplish; and how the work of one unit contributes to or affects the work of other units in the organization and other organizations.

3. <u>How is Communication Achieved?</u>
    Communication flows downward, upward, sideways.

    a. Communication may come from top management down to employees. This is <u>downward communication</u>.

        Some means of downward communication are:
        (1) Training (orientation, job instruction, supervision, public relations, etc.)
        (2) Conferences
        (3) Staff meetings
        (4) Policy statements
        (5) Bulletins
        (6) Newsletters
        (7) Memoranda
        (8) Circulation of important letters

        In downward communication, it is important that employees be informed in advance of changes that will affect them.

    b. Communications should also be developed so that the ideas, suggestions, and knowledge of employees will flow <u>upward</u> to top management.

Some means of upward communication are:
(1)   Personal discussion conferences
(2)   Committees
(3)   Memoranda
(4)   Employees suggestion program
(5)   Questionnaires to be filled in giving comments and suggestions about proposed actions that will affect field operations

Upward communication requires that management be willing to listen, to accept, and to make changes when good ideas are present. Upward communication succeeds when there is no fear of punishment for speaking out or lack of interest at the top. Employees will share their knowledge and ideas with management when interest is shown and recognition is given.

c.   The *advantages* of downward communication:
   (1)   It enables the passing down of orders, policies, and plans necessary to the continued operation of the station.
   (2)   By making information available, it diminishes the fears and suspicions which result from misinformation and misunderstanding.
   (3)   It fosters the pride people want to have in their work when they are told of good work.
   (4)   It improves the morale and stature of the individual to be *in the know.*
   (5)   It helps employees to understand, accept, and cooperate with changes when they know about them in advance.

d.   The *advantages* of upward communication:
   (1)   It enables the passing upward of information, attitudes, and feelings.
   (2)   It makes it easier to find out how ready people are to receive downward communication.
   (3)   It reveals the degree to which the downward communication is understood and accepted.
   (4)   It helps to satisfy the basic *social* needs.
   (5)   It stimulates employees to participate in the operation of their organization.
   (6)   It encourages employees to contribute ideas for improving the efficiency and economy of operations.
   (7)   It helps to solve problem situations before they reach the explosion point.

4.   Why Does Communication Fail?
   a.   The technical difficulties of conveying information clearly
   b.   The emotional content of communication which prevents complete transmission
   c.   The fact that there is a difference between what management needs to say, what it wants to say, and what it does say
   d.   The fact that there is a difference between what employees would like to say, what they think is profitable or safe to say, and what they do say

5.   How to Improve Communication.
   As a supervisor, you are a key figure in communication. To improve as a communicator, you should:
   a.   Know - Knowing your subordinates will help you to recognize and work with individual differences.

b.   Like - If you like those who work for you and those for whom you work, this will foster the kind of friendly, warm, work atmosphere that will facilitate communication.

c.   Trust - Showing a sincere desire to communicate will help to develop the mutual trust and confidence which are essential to the free flow of communication.

d.   Tell - Tell your subordinates and superiors *what's doing.* Tell your subordinates *why* as well as *how.*

e.   Listen - By listening, you help others to talk and you create good listeners. Don't forget that listening implies action.

f.   Stimulate - Communication has to be stimulated and encouraged. Be receptive to ideas and suggestions and motivate your people so that each member of the team identifies himself with the job at hand.

g.   Consult - The most effective way of consulting is to let your people participate, insofar as possible, in developing determinations which affect them or their work.

6.   How to Determine Whether You are Getting Across.
   a.   Check to see that communication is received and understood
   b.   Judge this understanding by actions rather than words
   c.   Adapt or vary communication, when necessary
   d.   Remember that good communication cannot cure all problems

7.   The Key Attitude.
   Try to see things from the other person's point of view. By doing this, you help to develop the permissive atmosphere and the shared confidence and understanding which are essential to effective two-way communication.

   Communication is a two-way process.
   a.   The basic purpose of any communication is to get action.
   b.   The only way to get action is through acceptance.
   c.   In order to get acceptance, communication must be humanly satisfying as well as technically efficient.

HOW ORDERS AND INSTRUCTIONS SHOULD BE GIVEN

Characteristics of Good Orders and Instructions

1.   Clear
   Orders should be definite as to
      - What is to be done
      - Who is to do it
      - When it is to be done
      - Where it is to be done
      - How it is to be done

2.   Concise
   Avoid wordiness. Orders should be brief and to the point.

3.   Timely
   Instructions and orders should be sent out at the proper time and not too long in advance of expected performance.

4. <u>Possibility of Performance</u>
   Orders should be feasible:
   a. Investigate before giving orders
   b. Consult those who are to carry out instructions before formulating and issuing them

5. <u>Properly Directed</u>
   Give the orders to the people concerned. Do not send orders to people who are not concerned. People who continually receive instructions that are not applicable to them get in the habit of neglecting instructions generally.

6. <u>Reviewed Before Issuance</u>
   Orders should be reviewed before issuance:
   a. Test them by putting yourself in the position of the recipient
   b. If they involve new procedures, have the persons who are to do the work review them for suggestions

7. <u>Reviewed After Issuance</u>
   Persons who receive orders should be allowed to raise questions and to point out unforeseen consequences of orders.

8. <u>Coordinated</u>
   Orders should be coordinated so that work runs smoothly.

9. <u>Courteous</u>
   Make a request rather than a demand. There is no need to continually call attention to the fact that you are the boss.

10. <u>Recognizable as an Order</u>
    Be sure that the order is recognizable as such.

11. <u>Complete</u>
    Be sure recipient has knowledge and experience sufficient to carry out order. Give illustrations and examples.

A DEPARTMENTAL PERSONNEL OFFICE IS RESPONSIBLE
<u>FOR THE FOLLOWING FUNCTIONS</u>

1. Policy
2. Personnel Programs
3. Recruitment and Placement
4. Position Classification
5. Salary and Wage Administration
6. Employee Performance Standards and Evaluation
7. Employee Relations
8. Disciplinary Actions and Separations
9. Health and Safety
10. Staff Training and Development
11. Personnel Records, Procedures, and Reports
12. Employee Services
13. Personnel Research

SUPERVISION

Leadership

All leadership is based essentially on authority. This comes from two sources: it is received from higher management or it is earned by the supervisor through his methods of supervision. Although effective leadership has always depended upon the leader's using his authority in such a way as to appeal successfully to the motives of the people supervised, the conditions for making this appeal are continually changing. The key to today's problem of leadership is flexibility and resourcefulness on the part of the leader in meeting changes in conditions as they occur.

Three basic approaches to leadership are generally recognized:

1. The Authoritarian Approach
   a. The methods and techniques used in this approach emphasize the *I* in leadership and depend primarily on the formal authority of the leader. This authority is sometimes exercised in a hardboiled manner and sometimes in a benevolent manner, but in either case the dominating role of the leader is reflected in the thinking, planning, and deci-sions of the group.
   b. Group results are to a large degree dependent on close supervision by the leader. Usually, the individuals in the group will not show a high degree of initiative or accep-tance of responsibility and their capacity to grow and develop probably will not be fully utilized. The group may react with resentment or submission, depending upon the manner and skill of the leader in using his authority
   c. This approach develops as a natural outgrowth of the authority that goes with the leader's job and his feeling of sole responsibility for getting the job done. It is relatively easy to use and does not require much resourcefulness.
   d. The use of this approach is effective in times of emergencies, in meeting close dead-lines as a final resort, in settling some issues, in disciplinary matters, and with depen-dent individuals and groups.

2. The Laissez-Faire or *Let 'em Alone* Approach
   a. This approach generally is characterized by an avoidance of leadership responsibility by the leader. The activities of the group depend largely on the choice of its members rather than the leader.
   b. Group results probably will be poor. Generally, there will be disagreements over petty things, bickering, and confusion. Except for a few aggressive people, individuals will not show much initiative and growth and development will be retarded. There may be a tendency for informal leaders to take over leadership of the group.
   c. This approach frequently results from the leader's dislike of responsibility, from his lack of confidence, from failure of other methods to work, from disappointment or criticism. It is usually the easiest of the three to use and requires both understanding and resourcefulness on the part of the leader.
   d. This approach is occasionally useful and effective, particularly in forcing dependent individuals or groups to rely on themselves, to give someone a chance to save face by clearing his own difficulties, or when action should be delayed temporarily for good cause.

3. <u>The Democratic Approach</u>

    a. The methods and techniques used in this approach emphasize the *we* in leadership and build up the responsibility of the group to attain its objectives. Reliance is placed largely on the earned authority of the leader.

    b. Group results are likely to be good because most of the job motives of the people will be satisfied. Cooperation and teamwork, initiative, acceptance of responsibility, and the individual's capacity for growth probably will show a high degree of development.

    c. This approach grows out of a desire or necessity of the leader to find ways to appeal effectively to the motivation of his group. It is the best approach to build up inside the person a strong desire to cooperate and apply himself to the job.
    It is the most difficult to develop, and requires both understanding and resourcefulness on the part of the leader.

    d. The value of this approach increases over a long period where sustained efficiency and development of people are important. It may not be fully effective in all situations, however, particularly when there is not sufficient time to use it properly or where quick decisions must be made.

All three approaches are used by most leaders and have a place in supervising people. The extent of their use varies with individual leaders, with some using one approach predominantly. The leader who uses these three approaches, and varies their use with time and circumstance, is probably the most effective. Leadership which is used predominantly with a democratic approach requires more resourcefulness on the part of the leader but offers the greatest possibilities in terms of teamwork and cooperation.

The one best way of developing democratic leadership is to provide a real sense of participation on the part of the group, since this satisfies most of the chief job motives. Although there are many ways of providing participation, consulting as frequently as possible with individuals and groups on things that affect them seems to offer the most in building cooperation and responsibility. Consultation takes different forms, but it is most constructive when people feel they are actually helping in finding the answers to the problems on the job.

There are some requirements of leaders in respect to human relations which should be considered in their selection and development. Generally, the leader should be interested in working with other people, emotionally stable, self-confident, and sensitive to the reactions of others. In addition, his viewpoint should be one of getting the job done through people who work cooperatively in response to his leadership. He should have a knowledge of individual and group behavior, but, most important of all, he should work to combine all of these requirements into a definite, practical skill in leadership.

<u>Nine Points of Contrast Between *Boss* and *Leader*</u>

1. The boss drives his men; the leader coaches them.
2. The boss depends on authority; the leader on good will.
3. The boss inspires fear; the leader inspires enthusiasm.
4. The boss says J; the leader says *We*.
5. The boss says *Get here on time;* the leader gets there ahead of time.
6. The boss fixes the blame for the breakdown; the leader fixes the breakdown.
7. The boss knows how it is done; the leader shows how.
8. The boss makes work a drudgery; the leader makes work a game.
9. The boss says *Go*; the leader says *Let's go*.

EMPLOYEE MORALE

Employee morale is the way employees feel about each other, the organization or unit in which they work, and the work they perform.

Some Ways to Develop and Maintain Good Employee Morale

1. Give adequate credit and praise when due.
2. Recognize importance of all jobs and equalize load with proper assignments, always giving consideration to personality differences and abilities.
3. Welcome suggestions and do not have an *all-wise* attitude. Request employees' assistance in solving problems and use assistants when conducting group meetings on certain subjects.
4. Properly assign responsibilities and give adequate authority for fulfillment of such assignments.
5. Keep employees informed about matters that affect them.
6. Criticize and reprimand employees privately.
7. Be accessible and willing to listen.
8. Be fair.
9. Be alert to detect training possibilities so that you will not miss an opportunity to help each employee do a better job, and if possible with less effort on his part.
10. Set a good example.
11. Apply the golden rule.

Some Indicators of Good Morale
1. Good quality of work
2. Good quantity
3. Good attitude of employees
4. Good discipline
5. Teamwork
6. Good attendance
7. Employee participation

MOTIVATION

Drives

A *drive,* stated simply, is a desire or force which causes a person to do or say certain things. These are some of the most usual drives and some of their identifying characteristics recognizable in people motivated by such drives:

1. Security (desire to provide for the future)
   Always on time for work
   Works for the same employer for many years
   Never takes unnecessary chances Seldom resists doing what he is told

2. Recognition (desire to be rewarded for accomplishment)
   Likes to be asked for his opinion
   Becomes very disturbed when he makes a mistake
   Does things to attract attention

Likes to see his name in print

3. <u>Position</u> (desire to hold certain status in relation to others)
   Boasts about important people he knows
   Wants to be known as a key man
   Likes titles
   Demands respect
   Belongs to clubs, for prestige

4. <u>Accomplishment</u> (desire to get things done)
   Complains when things are held up
   Likes to do things that have tangible results
   Never lies down on the job
   Is proud of turning out good work

5. <u>Companionship</u> (desire to associate with other people)
   Likes to work with others
   Tells stories and jokes
   Indulges in horseplay
   Finds excuses to talk to others on the job

6. <u>Possession</u> (desire to collect and hoard objects)
   Likes to collect things
   Puts his name on things belonging to him
   Insists on the same work location

Supervisors may find that identifying the drives of employees is a helpful step toward motivating them to self-improvement and better job performance. For example: An employee's job performance is below average. His supervisor, having previously determined that the employee is motivated by a drive for security, suggests that taking training courses will help the employee to improve, advance, and earn more money. Since earning more money can be a step toward greater security, the employee's drive for security would motivate him to take the training suggested by the supervisor. In essence, this is the process of charting an employee's future course by using his motivating drives to positive advantage.

EMPLOYEE PARTICIPATION

<u>What is Participation?</u>

Employee participation is the employee's giving freely of his time, skill and knowledge to an extent which cannot be obtained by demand.

<u>Why is it Important</u>?

The supervisor's responsibility is to get the job done through people. A good supervisor gets the job done through people who work willingly and well. The participation of employees is important because:

1. Employees develop a greater sense of responsibility when they share in working out operating plans and goals.
2. Participation provides greater opportunity and stimulation for employees to learn, and to develop their ability.

3. Participation sometimes provides better solutions to problems because such solutions may combine the experience and knowledge of interested employees who want the solutions to work.
4. An employee or group may offer a solution which the supervisor might hesitate to make for fear of demanding too much.
5. Since the group wants to make the solution work, they exert *pressure* in a constructive way on each other.
6. Participation usually results in reducing the need for close supervision.

How May Supervisors Obtain It?

Participation is encouraged when employees feel that they share some responsibility for the work and that their ideas are sincerely wanted and valued. Some ways of obtaining employee participation are:

1. Conduct orientation programs for new employees to inform them about the organization and their rights and responsibilities as employees.
2. Explain the aims and objectives of the agency. On a continuing basis, be sure that the employees know what these aims and objectives are.
3. Share job successes and responsibilities and give credit for success.
4. Consult with employees, both as individuals and in groups, about things that affect them.
5. Encourage suggestions for job improvements. Help employees to develop good suggestions. The suggestions can bring them recognition. The city's suggestion program offers additional encouragement through cash awards.

The supervisor who encourages employee participation is not surrendering his authority. He must still make decisions and initiate action, and he must continue to be ultimately responsible for the work of those he supervises. But, through employee participation, he is helping his group to develop greater ability and a sense of responsibility while getting the job done faster and better.

STEPS IN HANDLING A GRIEVANCE

1. Get the facts
   a. Listen sympathetically.
   b. Let him talk himself out.
   c. Get his story straight.
   d. Get his point of view.
   e. Don't argue with him.
   f. Give him plenty of time.
   g. Conduct the interview privately.
   h. Don't try to shift the blame or pass the buck.

2. Consider the facts
   a. Consider the employee's viewpoint.
   b. How will the decision affect similar cases.
   c. Consider each decision as a possible precedent.
   d. Avoid snap judgments - don't jump to conclusions.

3. <u>Make or get a decision</u>
   a. Frame an effective counter-proposal.
   b. Make sure it is fair to all.
   c. Have confidence in your judgment.
   d. Be sure you can substantiate your decision.

4. <u>Notify the employee of your decision</u>
   Be sure he is told; try to convince him that the decision is fair and just.

5. <u>Take action when needed and if within your authority</u>
   Otherwise, tell employee that the matter will be called to the attention of the proper person or that nothing can be done, and why it cannot.

6. <u>Follow through</u> to see that the desired result is achieved.

7. <u>Record key facts</u> concerning the complaint and the action taken.

8. <u>Leave the way open to him to appeal your decision</u> to a higher authority.

9. <u>Report all grievances to your superior</u>, whether they are appealed or not.

DISCIPLINE

Discipline is training that develops self-control, orderly conduct, and efficiency.

To discipline does not necessarily mean to punish.

To discipline does mean to train, to regulate, and to govern conduct.

<u>The Disciplinary Interview</u>

Most employees sincerely want to do what is expected of them. In other words, they are self-disciplined. Some employees, however, fail to observe established rules and standards, and disciplinary action by the supervisor is required.

The primary purpose of disciplinary action is to improve conduct without creating dissatisfaction, bitterness, or resentment in the process.

Constructive disciplinary action is more concerned with causes and explanations of breaches of conduct than with punishment. The disciplinary interview is held to get at the causes of apparent misbehavior and to motivate better performance in the future.

It is important that the interview be kept on as impersonal a basis as possible. If the supervisor lets the interview descend to the plane of an argument, it loses its effectiveness.

<u>Planning the Interview</u>

Get all pertinent facts concerning the situation so that you can talk in specific terms to the employee.

Review the employee's record, appraisal ratings, etc.

Consider what you know about the temperament of the employee. Consider your attitude toward the employee. Remember that the primary requisite of disciplinary action is fairness.

Don't enter upon the interview when angry.

Schedule the interview for a place which is private and out of hearing of others.

Conducting the Interview

1. Make an effort to establish accord.

2. Question the employee about the apparent breach of discipline. Be sure that the question is not so worded as to be itself an accusation.

3. Give the employee a chance to tell his side of the story. Give him ample opportunity to talk.

4. Use understanding-listening except where it is necessary to ask a question or to point out some details of which the employee may not be aware. If the employee misrepresents facts, make a plain, accurate statement of the facts, but don't argue and don't engage in personal controversy.

5. Listen and try to understand the reasons for the employee's (mis)conduct. First of all, don't assume that there has been a breach of discipline. Evaluate the employee's reasons for his conduct in the light of his opinions and feelings concerning the consistency and reasonableness of the standards which he was expected to follow. Has the supervisor done his part in explaining the reasons for the rules? Was the employee's behavior unintentional or deliberate? Does he think he had real reasons for his actions? What new facts is he telling? Do the facts justify his actions? What causes, other than those mentioned, could have stimulated the behavior?

6. After listening to the employee's version of the situation, and if censure of his actions is warranted, the supervisor should proceed with whatever criticism is justified. Emphasis should be placed on future improvement rather than exclusively on the employee's failure to measure up to expected standards of job conduct.

7. Fit the criticism to the individual. With one employee, a word of correction may be all that is required.

8. Attempt to distinguish between unintentional error and deliberate misbehavior. An error due to ignorance requires training and not censure.

9. Administer criticism in a controlled, even tone of voice, never in anger. Make it clear that you are acting as an agent of the department. In general, criticism should refer to the job or the employee's actions and not to the person. Criticism of the employee's work is not an attack on the individual.

10. Be sure the interview does not destroy the employee's self-confidence. Mention his good qualities and assure him that you feel confident that he can improve his performance.

11. Wherever possible, before the employee leaves the interview, satisfy him that the incident is closed, that nothing more will be said on the subject unless the offense is repeated.

———